STAR ACTING:
Gish, Garbo, Davis

CHARLES AFFRON was born in New York City in 1935. He received his B.A. in French from Brandeis University in 1957, and a Ph.D. in French from Yale University in 1963. He is the author of *Patterns of Failure in "La Comédie humaine"* (1966) and *A Stage for Poets: Studies in the Theatre of Hugo and Musset* (1971). Currently he is a professor in the Department of French and Italian at New York University.

STAR ACTING:
Gish, Garbo, Davis

CHARLES AFFRON

E. P. DUTTON ■ NEW YORK

10 9 8 7 6 5 4 3 2 1

Published simultaneously in Canada by Clarke, Irwin & Company Limited, Toronto and Vancouver.

Library of Congress Catalog Card Number: 76–8039

ISBN 0–525–0815–7 (Cloth)
Designed by The Etheredges

To the one
who fortuitously compelled
a frightened five year old
to see *A Woman's Face*,
and subsequent companions
in the dark.

Acknowledgments

The corporate complexities of making films are reflected in the difficulties of writing and organizing a book about films. I am particularly pleased now to be able to thank the people who eased my passage through those difficulties.

My first debt of gratitude is to those who so generously allowed me to reproduce the frame enlargements: Jack P. Foreman for Samuel Goldwyn Productions; Paul Killiam, of Killiam Shows, Inc., for the D. W. Griffith films, *The Greatest Question* and *Orphans of the Storm;* Herbert S. Nusbaum of Metro-Goldwyn-Mayer, and Allen J. Green (Wilmette, Ill.) and Seth Willenson (New York) of Films Inc., who afforded me access to MGM films; Jonas Rosenfield, Jr. of 20th Century-Fox; Herbert Schottenfeld, Robert Schwartz, and Bart Farber of United Artists Corporation; and Tino Balio, Director of The Wisconsin Center for Theatre Research for the use of Warner Brothers materials.

The curators and staffs of the various film collections have facilitated viewings and have been helpful in countless ways: Charles Silver, Mary Corliss, and Eileen Bowser at the Museum of Modern Art; James Card at The George Eastman House; Patrick Sheehan at the Motion Picture Section of The Library of Congress; Susan Dalton at the Wisconsin Center for Theatre Research. A special expression of gratitude is due William K. Everson for his unstinting generosity. I am only one of countless film scholars who have been able to rely upon his considerable resources.

The Arts and Sciences Research Fund of New York University supplied grants for travel to the various archives and for some of the photographic expenses.

Lillian Gish most graciously accorded me an extended interview at a time when she was particularly busy, thus putting me in her debt for her kindness, adding to the one I already owed her for the joy of studying her performances. I am, of course, beholden for similar joys to Greta Garbo and Bette Davis.

Friends and colleagues have offered me invaluable encouragement and editorial advice: Gloria Vilardell and Carol Jochnowitz invested their readings with a passion for the subject; William Rothman allayed doubts at a crucial time; Ted Perry gave good and practical counsel; Robert DiMilia offered excellent help in photographic matters; Richard Barsam's interest in the manuscript led me to Cyril Nelson at E. P. Dutton; E. Rubinstein provided the right critical challenges and waded through the text at its most unwieldy stages.

Special mention must be made of Tina Contini of Foto Excelsior, Molveno, Italy. Her artistry extracted beauty from images perhaps a trifle reluctant to be reborn as frame enlargements.

Contents

STAR ACTING:
Gish, Garbo, Davis

1.
Generous Stars

The women are goddesses, the men are matinee idols; they are all stars who command devotion and veneration. The reverential and celestial vocabulary has been consecrated by decades of usage and press agentry. The clichés' first connotations effectively separate public from performer by an expanse of astral geography. The gods reign on high, the stars blink in solar systems light-years away, and we mere mortals, worshiping at their shrines in blissful ignorance, celebrate the distance. We join cults, we become *fanatics*, we endow the star system with mythologies of nostalgia by collecting the stars' incarnations in roles X, Y, and Z and cherishing the relics of memorable and memorized bits. "Play it, Sam." We lose ourselves in reverie, in the comfortable group memory, the communal ecstasy of ritual, the shared sigh and laugh, the obscurity of spectatorship. Movies lap over us, gently rocking us in their flickering and moving images, and consistently remind us of our tiny dimensions as we contemplate gigantic faces, lips, eyes on the screen. Idols in size, they emit starlight to decorate the blackness; they furnish the only illumination in the space we occupy. Movie actors deserve their heavenly appellations.

The gloss and surface of movies, their hyperbole and commercialism help whole populations pass through depressions, wars, and political crises by lessening the pain of awareness and thwarting a measure of critical control. Friendship, love, life and death are trampled on the Road to Morocco, mindlessly soothed in the satin sheets of MGM's bedrooms, and lost in the studio jungles where the only good Jap is a dead Jap. The stars possess keys of entry to a nevernever land, a territory whose ambiguous shape allows us the luxury of patness and the most facile degree of wish fulfillment. Intellectually thumb-sucking our way through the intricacies of existence, we look up at Olympus, at the gods disporting themselves much as we do, but with style and class. That prompts us to endow them with superhuman powers, magical modes that liberate our everyday activities from the confusion of circumstance. Coated with layers of makeup that obliterate blemish and dissymmetry, modeled by a miraculous array of lights, located and relocated by the giddy succession of frames, the stars capriciously play with life and subject it to a range of fictions from preposterous to profound.

Film acting's pseudoreligious nature has been evoked with some degree of thoroughness in books such as Alexander Walker's *Stardom, The Hollywood Phenomenon* and Richard Griffith's *The Movie Stars*. Roland Barthes keenly appraises the phenomenon in *Mythologies:* "Garbo still belongs to that moment in cinema when capturing the human face still plunged audiences into the deepest ecstasy, when one literally lost oneself in a human image as one would in a philtre, when the face represented a kind of absolute state of the flesh, which could be neither reached nor renounced. . . . The name given to her, *the Divine*, probably aimed to convey less a superlative state of beauty than the essence of her corporeal person, descended from a heaven where all things are formed and perfected in the clearest light."[1] These discussions of the star phe-

---

[1] Roland Barthes, *Mythologies*, pp. 56–57. Full bibliographical citations for the footnotes can be found in the bibliography.

nomenon are undeniably accurate, but incomplete. The methods used in other studies of film acting betray the same incompleteness as they tirelessly accumulate the history of stardom (verifiable) and/or evoke in impressionistic language the effects of stardom on the public: the awe, ecstasy, adoration, and so forth. An almost total absence of analytical approaches to screen acting reflects the belief that screen acting is nothing more than the beautiful projection of a filmic self, an arrangement of features and body, the disposition of superficial elements. Garbo is Garbo is Garbo is Garbo. We mortals are left clutching our wonder, and victims of that very wonder, overwhelmed by our enthusiasm and blinded by the light of the star's emanation.

The prime function of certain stars is their incarnation of superficiality. They are totems whose mystery is either too impenetrable for interpretation or (more likely) simply absent. Valentino's bedroom eyes, Ruth Chatterton's chic (except when used ironically by William Wyler in *Dodsworth*) and June Allyson's pep are commodities whose symbolic powers are supremely manifest but completely without resonance. They are ciphers that have been emptied of substance by changing taste and are as essentially banal as moon/spoon/June. Filters of camp and nostalgia may briefly restore some luster to Norma Shearer's Juliet, but nothing can supply a dimension to her performance that goes beyond the particular railing or column on which she leaned. Screen acting is as catholic as the medium itself. It tolerates with varying degrees of good humor the staginess of George Arliss and the somnolence of George Brent, the vapidity of Alice Faye and the twitchings of Sandy Dennis. The stardom of Chatterton, Arliss, Dennis, and company is qualified by a law of ever-diminishing energy. The surface of an image can be beautiful, amusing, touching, diverting, but it must suggest sustaining depths. The symbols and processes of Dorothy Lamour and Loretta Young eventually trap us in the surface of their time and fashion, or in the exhaustion of their efforts to prove they are acting.

Yet screen acting need not be limited by the flatness of the screen image. So much in the film medium conspires to free the actor, to relieve him of the burdens of naturalistic portrayal, to grant him the metaphorical power of great painting and sculpture, to offer him the high style of classical theatre and opera. The masks, the megaphones, and the music of the more grandiose theatrical forms find their analogies in the dimensions of the screen, the close-up, and the vocabulary of transformation and movement supplied by montage, framing, panning, tilting, and dollying. The richness of decor and the limitless possibilities of ambience belong to the rhetoric of the plastic arts. The privilege of film acting is both dangerous and extraordinary. The challenge of its possibilities, the potential so manifest in the models of Greek tragedy, of lyric theatre, and figurative modes of representation, go beyond the canons of taste and the most easily satisfied dreams. Films are breathtakingly perched between the unequivocal reality of the photographic process and a style that is by definition magnifying, hyperbolic, and utterly frivolous in its relationship to everyday modes of perception. It is as if some great mannerist canvas were suddenly animated with breathing, moving, speaking creatures, as if its plays of perspective were limitlessly variable and the boundaries between configuration and existential realities were freed from the conceits of illusion.

Acting that responds to this set of tests truly does suggest the godlike. Benevolent, generous, it includes the viewer in its mystery and gives him powers of vision that go beyond contemplation to that of a double awareness—of self and the other. These acting gods bestow a boon of understanding; they welcome Prometheus; they reveal and open their beings to view. Courageously exposing secrets without betraying, they preserve the essence of ambiguity; they incarnate complexity in manners that guarantee our fullest apprehension of ambiguity and complexity. The forms they project prove the value of our looking and remind us that gods are made in the image of man. The quality of our perception is enhanced by Keaton's sitting on the drive shaft of "The General," Muni's manically spraying the screen with machine-gun bullets in *Scarface*, Ingrid Bergman's confusing espionage and sex over Cary Grant's shoulder in *Notorious*, Hepburn, K., turning "Charlie" into a love song and Hepburn, A., finding room in the breadth of her eyes and mouth for all the anguish of adolescent ecstasy. These examples are not distinct from their contexts. Hawks, Hitchcock, Huston, Wyler, and Keaton himself provided the contexts, and elicited responses that make us acutely conscious of our perception; we are in touch with phenomena rather than distant, and we are active in the assimilation of gesture, tone, expression, decor, and the general structure that contains the specific performance we witness.

The motor of this consciousness and the tone of our perception are set by screen acting's privilege of unaltered reiteration. Raptness is a state called forth by both stage and screen actors. Renewable scrutiny is not. Whether we were intended to pore over movies, to stop them in their tracks, to regroup them and abstract them, is a matter of conjecture not a matter of fact. The idolatrous fan who watches Garbo expire eighty-eight times in *Camille* and the critic who dissects the sequence on an editing table are merely responding to that option, and so much for the intentional fallacy. The permanent existence of an image, even a moving one, is sufficient cause for testing its durability and examining its components.

Olivier's Othello can be reseen only because it was committed to film. In the theatre, we may have seen him perform it every night of the run but can never have reseen it.[2] The nightly re-creation precludes the nightly re-seeing; the film is seen once and then, by definition, reseen. This differing performer/viewer relationship can be understood in terms of power. Olivier, on stage, always has the power to change his performance, its tempo and stresses, and thereby alter our perception of it. His stage re-creations make us nightly novices. At best, we imperfectly remember and compare variations of performance. Dominion lies in the will of the actor since the rule of the genre is the uniqueness of any given moment.

---

2 Leo Braudy, in *The World in a Frame*, distinguishes between stage and screen acting in terms of the ways through which they suggest character. He submits the whole phenomenon of screen acting to a provocative and illuminating examination in a psychohistorical and cultural context.

Screen acting, by its utter repeatability, transfers the power to us. What is viewed remains unchanged; the conditions of our viewing are variable. Like it or not, screen acting submits to an organization that is subsequent to its doing. The apparent fact of enactment on stages and in movie houses must not blind us to the essential disparity of the two perceptual events. Given the dissimilarity of the frames, acting appropriate to the narrative forms of both film and theatre must be dissimilar as well. Although stage and screen acting share the logic, the linearity, and the true-to-lifeness of the narrative, these common characteristics are appositely defined by the two distinctive contexts, by the angle and time of our perception, and by the degree of power we exert. In addition to the existential impossibility of exact reproduction on two successive nights in a theatre there are the questions of range, field, and dimension. Stage lighting may focus and mold (Luchino Visconti went so far as to simulate a "stage" close-up with the use of curtains in his Covent Garden mounting of *Der Rosenkavalier*), yet the actor's size is essentially controlled by the variant of distance between the stage and the viewer.

The processes of movies are not only spatially disengaged, they are also located in the past. Unlike existential processes, the movie's dynamics and movement are arrestable. A viewer's perception is faulty unless he accepts and then utilizes this fact. The link between past process and present perception expands the viewer's power. His viewing is capable of refinement, of reorganization. His relationship to the viewed and the completed is infinitely controllable. This affirmation of power is not open to theatre audiences, except if they turn off the spectacle by becoming inattentive, falling asleep, or walking out altogether. They have no other alternatives. Stage acting includes the viewer in the unique moment of its unfolding. The audience's activity echoes the performer's activity. When the stage actor speaks of losing an audience he means that the audience is no longer with him and has effectively wandered off into reverie or the lobby. How does a screen actor lose an audience that is *never* with him? He does it through a different category of exclusion. He disallows the specifically cinematic nature of the spectator's perception. The processes are ours when we watch a movie, and the thrill of watching is measured by the quality of activity in which we are engaged while doing it. The completed processes of screen acting invite our critical scrutiny and our re-creation of performance.

Garbo can die for me around the clock. I can stay her in that final moment of her life; I can turn off the sound and watch, turn off the picture and listen, work myriad transformations in speed and brilliance, and then restore the original without losing a particle of its integrity. The significance of this power exploits and transcends the mechanical. In its reproducibility the performance of a given work merges with the work itself. It can be submitted to the same attention we apply to any text. Olivier's performance of Othello on the screen is wedded to the text in a way it never can be on the stage. In its relationship to the viewer, the screen performance is indistinguishable from the text it is expressing. Having become the text, it can be read just as clearly as words, sentences, paragraphs.

Beyond the particularities of style already mentioned, screen acting, in its basic mode of perception, is closer to poems, novels, statues, portraits, and music than it is to stage acting. We are doomed if we gear our understanding of Hepburn in Cukor's *The Philadelphia Story* to a memory of her stage enactment of its Tracy Lord, or if we examine Bette Davis's Regina Giddens through the filter of Tallulah Bankhead's. The standards are inappropriate since the patterns are unparallel. The patterns of performance in the theatre are inextricably linked to those of life, and the stage rejoices in that linkage. The temporal and spatial patterns of film acting belong to the rhythm of the sonnet and the areas of canvas so demonstrably re-created and possessed by readers and viewers.

One of the most enticing paradoxes of film acting is the distance between the reality of the photographic process and what we are willing to accept as true to life on the screen; Lillian Gish in her twenties portraying a fifteen-year-old, Garbo as a ballerina, Bette Davis as an addlepated ante-bellum belle. These performances' success does not depend on our apprehension of verisimilitude. Star acting somehow transmutes the narrative into nonnarrative configurations. It stimulates our perception of the verifiable and repeatable. It acknowledges its own abstraction. All of us remember performances inapt for the screen because of the actors' excessive obedience to theatrical modes of impersonation, performances that brook no reiteration. Paul Muni, so attuned to quasi-abstract expressionism in *Scarface* and *I Am a Fugitive from a Chain Gang*, acts the shape out of *The Story of Louis Pasteur* and *The Life of Emile Zola* and splinters pattern with the fidgety gestures of his incessant part-playing. Gish's Lucy, Garbo's Grusinskaya, and Davis's Julie are only incidentally impersonations. They are patterns, and they relate to the patterns of their surrounding structures. Quite beyond the categories of psychological penetration, clarity of characterization, and force of personality that we respond to on the stage, the screen actor is a translation of flesh, a reflection of light, a version of life that through its genesis belongs to a style higher than that of the most precious theatrical modes. We respond to patterns of stage acting through our knowledge of theatrical convention and tradition, through a dynamic of type and expectability. We thrill to the simultaneous evolution of performance and play that is perhaps the mark of great stage acting. But neither dramaturgy nor stage machinery can release the actor from his poignant lockstep with us. The theatrical performance traps us in an inescapable and relentlessly in progress *now*, a present shaped exclusively through memory and prediction. Never with us in space and dimension, the screen actor only intermittently seems to be with us in time. Exempt from the laws of existence at its inception, screen acting need obey those laws only to the degree that they are obeyed in other art forms. If we have no difficulty in seeing the links between young ladies and roses in Renaissance love lyrics, we should not be confused by Lillian Gish's turning into a lotus blossom or Garbo's merging with a bedpost. When Davis's face almost fills the frame during Herbert Marshall's death scene in *The Little Foxes*, dramatic art is not mimicking life. It is forming patterns that invite our perceptions to play with its articulatable and verifiable processes.

Screen acting of this order enjoys its dissimilarity to existential modes of behavior. The betrayal of an exclusively human measure initiated in the projection and reflection of the screen image is compounded by the director's sense of form and the actor's response to form. We may think we are seeing characters up there on the silver screen, but we are really seeing stars.

Effective screen acting exploits this perceptual dynamics—it not only invites and withstands the activity of our scrutiny, it mirrors the activity. It sets a standard for variation, for composition and recomposition, for sets of processes that thrive on the potential of repeatability. As our ear is trained to distinguish musical themes, their variations, and permutations in the constantly shifting framework of a sonata or a symphony, as our eye is challenged by the tension of masses in sculptured marble or chiaroscuro on canvas, so the screen actor, by the richness of his being and manner, by his comfort in photographic contexts, sets us a challenge. Through the mixture of love and pity evoked by Marilyn's transparent vulnerability, Judy's upturned eyes and wide vibrato, by the ineffability of Tracy's virtuoso technique, the extravagances of Mae West's wisdom and torso, the hard-softness of Colbert's sophistication, Brando's peculiar doses of vanity and torment, or Dietrich's splendid aloofness and chin quiver, screen acting plays elaborate games with our perception, forcing it to behold complexities of space and attitude that take on resonance through recurrence. And if we do not see Brando's Stanley more than once, we see him again in his Terry Molloy, and even in his Fletcher Christian. Garland walks down the yellow-brick road and then back down it year after year, in Saint Louis, in the Easter Parade, and most unnervingly, in the Nuremberg courtroom. Lillian Gish and Lionel Barrymore are sweethearts in *Just Gold* (1913), a Griffith one-reeler; when they face each other thirty-four years later, in *Duel in the Sun,* the history of the movies reverberates behind them. The shape of an individual performance is a paradigm for the shape of a career; eternally young and aging, eternally bursting onto the screen and fading out in the final shot, the star acts us through the intricacies of altered time and space, refining our vision to follow the transformations.

These transformations are quite distinct from character impersonation and the acting out of plot information. They are also beyond the talents of those performers frozen into the woodenness of their masks—the Valentinos, the Alice Fayes. The benevolent processes are those that call us to participate, to savor the delight of their rhythms and rhymes, the flow of their contours. Inclusive and penetrable, they lead us through a calisthenics of art that trains us to keep up with the dexterity and grace of their activity.

I will examine the careers of three actresses, Lillian Gish, Greta Garbo, and Bette Davis. My purpose is to illustrate certain techniques for the analysis of star acting, and how we perceive star acting in context. Other actresses might arguably have been chosen but there are criteria for choice that go beyond the capriciousness of my taste.

In the case of Gish, one dictating factor is her long and fruitful association with D. W. Griffith. Consideration of her career establishes the pattern of relationship between star and auteur. The prestige, historical importance, and what I think is the enduring power of Griffith make his work accessible to modern audiences, and have, in fact, preserved his films—no small advantage when dealing with the silent era. During her years as leading lady in the Griffith company and as star at MGM, she was often called the Duse of the movies, and, happily, time has not made that bit of publicity absurd. Mary Pickford and Gloria Swanson may have the edge on Gish in terms of popularity during the teens and the twenties, and their accomplishments were considerable, but the vagaries of fashion and movie history have not allowed their talents to emerge from the period with the fullness of Gish's. One also suspects that the superhuman demands Gish made on herself were of an order different from those of "America's Sweetheart" and the Marquise de la Falaise de la Coudray. These demands are hard on an audience as well, forcing it to witness, almost to share a degree of suffering and an amplitude of feeling so graphic as to obliterate the distancing of conventions. Gish transcends expressionism in acting by developing a style for the projection of physicality that contains the quickness of sensation and the patterns of art. She is exemplary of the body as screen metaphor.

Garbo bridges the silent and sound eras of film. But more intriguing than that fact is the Garbo legend: the rather widespread opinion that she is not acting at all. Such is the nonsense of which legends are made. The mysteries and myths of ancient cultures are not impervious to analysis; Garbo releases various states of her being in configurations that are seizable. Her acting is of a complexity that makes it difficult to assess in the context of standard technique. Yet she herself supplies the clue in the model of concentration that we must emulate if we are to perceive her properly. Lodged within the triteness of most of her vehicles, the glamour of a pristine shell, and the authentic image of solitude she projects are areas of sentiment that are attainable if we are prepared to pitch our tension of awareness as high as that of the actress. Garbo sheds the seductive veils of the love goddess, but only for those who are willing to share her intricacies. Punished with the numbness of adoration if we are lax, we visit the depths of her being if we can withstand the painful intimacy of her method. Garbo often seems lost in the labyrinth of her own privacy. Analysis permits us to breach the privacy. Phaedra-like, she offers to lead Hippolytus through her personal maze. Unlike the reluctant Greek hero, we must answer her call.

Bette Davis uses neither the exertions, nor the athletic grace of Gish, nor the arcane suggestiveness of Garbo. With Davis all is clarity and strength, control over wide-ranging and often ungainly material, control over her own excesses of energy and vitality. All famous performers are ill served by their caricatures. The notion of a fragile, weepy-eyed Gish runs counter to her splendid toughness and resiliency. Garbo's wanting to be alone is really an urgent invitation to be alone with us. A swaggering and lurching Davis with body and arms stabbing their way through frames is supremely at odds with an actress who learned that every gesture counted, and whose sense of measure is transmitted to us as knowledge.

Leslie Crosbie in *The Letter,* is a character partially defined by self-possession, and is emblematic of Bette Davis, crisply disarranging the tranquillity of the night with her pistol, and then recounting her lie so well that she makes lucidity itself a truth. Just as Gish did, the actress responds to a major director. William Wyler's limpid images are animated by Davis, who helps us find out where everything is.

The three actresses chosen for this study make profound claims on us. They didn't earn attention, allegiance, devotion and love simply for a long-suffering body, a bewitching face, and a trunkful of imitable mannerisms. Gish, Garbo, and Davis, in the duration of individual shots and in the span of their respective careers, demonstrate the formal coherence of screen acting, but, above all, they relentlessly test themselves. The scope of these tests is the breadth of our awareness.

It would be absurd to derive a stylistics of screen acting from three stars, or from any number of stars for that matter. A theory of manner is disproved by the variety of our filmgoing experience. All the stars may glitter, but they do so in essential distinctness. A definition of great movie acting as the projection of inwardness is immediately countered by wonderful examples of extroversion. For each actor who seeks to bury his persona in character there is another who glories in displaying persona, above and beyond impersonation. I would be hard-pressed to establish similarities of technique between Gish's Lucy, Garbo's Marguerite Gautier, and Davis's Margo Channing, much less between Janet Gaynor in *Sunrise,* Anna Magnani in *Roma, città aperta,* Katharine Hepburn in *The African Queen,* Jeanne Moreau in *Jules et Jim,* and Vanessa Redgrave in *The Loves of Isadora.* Stanley Cavell eloquently defines the notion of individuality in star acting. "One recalls the list of stars of every magnitude who have provided the movie camera with human subjects—individuals capable of filling its need for individualities, whose individualities in turn, whose inflection of demeanor and disposition were given full play in its projection."[3]

Yet there is something in our mode of perception that contains the diverse individualities of great movie acting. The separate processes of Lillian Gish, Greta Garbo and Bette Davis are linked by the range of consciousness stimulated in the viewer. The quality of their activity resonates within us. They differ in type but not in the extent of their challenge to our spectatorship. As Margo Channing in *All About Eve* Bette Davis portrays acting. Reaching far beyond the "theatah" of the film, she summons her technique to show us the embarrassing and disquieting identities of art and life. In fact, the mannerism of *All About Eve* somehow explicates the talents of Gish, Garbo, and Davis, actress-goddesses who intercede for mortals, who, through the exigencies of style, force our vision to new heights.

Vision soars, and its soaring can be articulated with a precision beyond that of word portraits, or even the most eloquently *geistlich* evocations. When the

[3] Stanley Cavell, *The World Viewed, Reflections on the Ontology of Film,* p. 35.

fleeting images are stopped, the frames reveal that mood, spirit, presence, and all the incantatory properties of the star are indeed part of the tangible universe. The ways in which actresses are photographed, the decor that surrounds them, their transformations in a given shot, a given sequence, are verifiable. Although the abstraction of a frame enlargement betrays the transitory nature of film, it is no more of a betrayal than the analysis of any single element belonging to the dynamics of literary structure in a poem, a novel, or a play. The momentary arrest of the organism for examination need not denature it. The frame enlargements are final proof that the processes of film acting are constituted in a rhetoric whose parts thrive on our sustained critical attention, just as these actresses call forth the renewable raptness of their audiences. We do not only see stars—we see *with* them, and the longer we do so the more brightly they shine.

2.
The Actress as Metaphor: Gish in Broken Blossoms

Lillian Gish and D. W. Griffith spring from the turn-of-the-century theatrical milieu. The traces of theatre in *Hearts of the World* (1918), *Broken Blossoms* (1919), *Way Down East* (1920), and *Orphans of the Storm* (1922) are not disguised, and the last two are unabashedly drawn from popular melodramas of the period. Yet these creations also display a category of film rhetoric unrelated to naturalistic theatre and prose narrative. When Griffith "opens up" a play he does so by searching out the reverberations of the saga, the painting, the still photograph, the lyric.

The patterns of *Broken Blossoms* are primarily those of poetry; Lillian Gish's response to its demands reveals fundamental differences between acting as impersonation and acting governed by the fixed form of the movies. *Broken Blossoms* creates a tension between theatrical expectations for the stage and configurations pertinent only to the screen. It offers a field for understanding screen acting at its most specifically formal. The integrity of such acting to the cinematic text must be seen through the relationship between Gish and the film's general structure. In *Broken Blossoms* the unity of performer and pattern exemplifies the metaphoric factor of screen acting. It elicits our perception of acting's purely filmic quotient.

Actress and director fit the medium in no film more completely than perhaps in *Broken Blossoms*. Histories tend to illustrate Griffith's career with the epic and monumental; the battlefield and the ride of the Klansmen from *The Birth of a Nation* (1915), and the aerial shot of the Babylonian court in *Intolerance* (1916) are events of imagination and sweep quite characteristic of his style. The sense of spectacle in the obsessively intercut chase and/or rescue sequences and the fugal structure of *Intolerance* are grandiose gestures that literally stretch the theatre as far as the eye can see and brutally challenge the limits of our formal and temporal perceptions.

Broken Blossoms appears to be a return to the stage. Most of the action is confined to two interior sets, the rooms of Battling Burrows and the Yellow Man. Griffith does nothing to trick the audience into believing that the world of these characters is broader than the space of these rooms. Indeed, he does everything to emphasize the delimiting walls and the entrapment of the characters within. The far-ranging camera of *The Birth of a Nation* and *Intolerance* is most glaringly absent, and whereas the earlier films taught our eyes to stretch telescopically, *Broken Blossoms* focuses down to the smallest detail and the minutest gesture. These distinctions are somewhat misleading, for the memorable details of the epic films are as important as the concerted scenes. Lillian Gish and the admiring sentry in *The Birth of a Nation*, Mae Marsh's acting in both films, the homecoming of Henry Walthall, "The Little Colonel," and the wonderfully silly Babylonian lovebirds are only a few of the exquisite components we remember in Griffith's mammoth compositions. (Indeed, miscalculated details in *Way Down East* and, to a lesser extent, in *Orphans of the Storm* are more disturbing than general structural weaknesses.) Yet, despite treasurable moments of intimacy that refine our perception, the principal design of these films belongs to the fresco, insistently calling upon the alertness of a roving glance. *Broken Blossoms* makes no such demands. The quality of concentration it summons fits the tauter connections and narrower limits of its frame. If the exhilaration of *The Birth of a Nation* and *Intolerance* is sacrificed, consistency and density take its place and inexorably draw the viewer into the pattern to be trapped in the art as Lucy is trapped in her closet. Griffith deliberately restricts the scope of the camera and denies it its most obvious advantage over the proscenium, proving that movies needn't move over wide expanses to expose their nature. Without being unfaithful either to movies or to literature, the director adjusts the freedom of the camera to the audience's perception of the strictest of fixed forms—the poem.

Griffith is repeatedly attracted to allegorical configurations. In the broadest sense *Intolerance* is an allegory, its episodes designed to represent, to dramatize the concept of intolerance through the ages. The film's linking image of the hand rocking the cradle (Lillian Gish dimly lit) shows Griffith's facile use of symbolic conventions. He prefers to draw generalities from character rather than to leave that task to the viewer. In as tired a vehicle as *Way Down East* a title proclaims that the heroine's name is Anna, but she might just as well be called Woman. The grandiloquence is unsuited to a film flawed by dubious bits of crowd-pleasing "down-East" humor and melodramatic ploys that were worn out long before Griffith used them. Anna's interest as heroine is manifested only twice: the baptism of her dying baby and the snow storm/ice floe sequences. The rest of the film degrades a register of allegory worthy of Woman.

This is not the case in *Broken Blossoms*. Griffith envisions the film as a dynamics of idealism, innocence, and brutality. The three protagonists—the Yellow Man; Lucy, the girl; and Battling Burrows—consistently enact their ascribed characteristics, and every element of the film sustains the purity of the conceptual byplay. The names contain allegorical clues—man, girl, battling. The minor characters, Evil Eye, and Spying One, along with the title, complete the pattern. The credits reveal Griffith's risky intention. The risk is in the notion that the reality of filming can bear the strain of allegorical textures. If *Broken Blossoms* lacks obvious pictorial scope, its ambitions are great nonetheless. Much of its impetus seems unrelated to the particular strengths of the medium.

After a brief prologue in which the Yellow Man (Richard Barthelmess) is introduced previous to leaving China "to take the glorious message of peace to the barbarous Anglo-Saxons, sons of turmoil and strife," we see London's Limehouse, the principal exterior set of the film. With this set Griffith establishes the motif of enclosure. Even outside we are inside; the space is radically circumscribed by the opposing storefronts and the rear arches.

The Yellow Man's idealism has been deflated by the confines of this street, by the very bricks against which he huddles.

This shot is a melancholy, reflective emblem, the straight lines and angles of which are drawn into the curved body. This linear tension draws the viewer into the Yellow Man's reverie. The next is a closer shot, which lessens the distance and expressively uses the changed angle of the hero's head, the chin tucking in the shoulder, to increase proximity and intimacy.

Griffith's caricatural notions about Chinese posture perhaps have something to do with the hunched torso, but he uses it throughout the film when presenting Lillian Gish as well—pensive,

cowering before her father,

in a faint on the floor of the Yellow Man's shop,

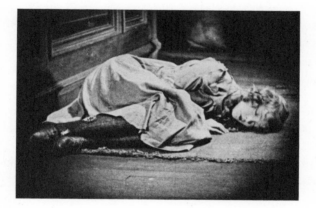

and, near the end of the film, crouching in terror beneath her father's blows.

Fear, thought, the frailty of the heroine and the habitual attitude of the hero are expressed in a single cast of body, a spatial indication of their nearness to an interior world—one they will briefly share. They both curl in on themselves, as they seek refuge from the hostile space around them, and direct our own feelings toward the small centers of these frames that are so often limited by the irising of Bitzer's lens.

The degree of introspection is then heightened; Barthelmess, leaning against the brick wall, is quite literally thinking about himself dreaming while smoking opium in a "scarlet house of sin."

Again, the linear strength of the composition draws us to the center—arm, pipe and torso form a triangle at the apex of which the drug-hooded eyes reflect inward.

The shots of Barthelmess leaning against the wall and smoking opium and of Gish seated on the wharf establish the film's landscape, a conceptual and emotional one contained in the minds of the protagonists. The limited dimensions of the spatial correlatives repeatedly bring us back to the inner worlds of Lucy and the Yellow Man where the force of imagination, through the processes of metaphor, transcends their everyday prisons. If Griffith means them to be allegorical characters, they, in a real sense, use allegory to exist. They escape their intolerable reality by substituting symbols for things.

Lucy is a fifteen-year-old (Gish had grave reservations about assuming the part because of her age) and her inner life is much simpler than the Yellow Man's, yet she accomplishes the film's most vivid gesture of poetic transformation. A desperate defense against her father's brutal domination, her finger-induced smile is a bit of "business" whose ambiguities of sentiment are extensions of its ambiguous position between the realm of representational acting and that realm of the film in which the actor becomes metaphor itself. It represents the way symbols are manipulated, the function of mask, the very root of artifice.

Lucy is in constant terror of her father. This is the prevailing attitude in which the physical changes are wrought; it is a limited field upon which the richness of Gish's invention is displayed. When Lucy sees Daddy the tiny twisted mouth echoes her hands twisting her shawl.

Battling commands her to put a smile on her face. The title reads: "Poor Lucy, never having cause to smile, uses this pitiful excuse instead." The fingers hesitantly come up to chin, then mouth,

and this is the result.

Gish plays a fifteen-year-old in mortal fear of her brutalizing father, and the actress never overreaches the character's age and experience. The restrictions of chronology control a degree of stylization appropriate to this extraordinary mixture of face and mask. The pained eyes burn through the pitiful, forced smile; the actress unites expression and emblem. She forces our attention to that line where art is hinged on its artificial conventions and its verisimilitude. The distance between mouth and eyes helps us apprehend the link between Lucy's specific plight and the universal burden Griffith has thrust upon her, the eternal victim.

The first encounter between Gish and Barthelmess sustains the pattern of contemplation initiated at the film's beginning, and, again, framing devices locate and organize our simultaneous perception of event and style. We see Gish while she is being seen by Barthelmess; the window separates, connects, and delimits, and provides a spatial referent for the process of observation.

Then the window itself becomes their common point of view. The close-up of Barthelmess recalls the shot in the opium den,

and what he sees is like a vision: "This child with tear-aged face. . . ."

The back-lit, soft-focus, Hendrick Sartov close-up of Gish, a lovely but facile device for idealizing the heroine, was to become a cliché. But it was in *Broken Blossoms* that it first achieved consistency as a significant element of the vocabulary used to photograph Gish. One of the film's tensions is in the duality of the presentation of the heroine—Lucy, as tangible victim of her father's whip and hammering fists, and as angelic vision in the eyes of the Yellow Man. The latter kind of shot disembodies her, deemphasizing her physicality by turning her into a chiaroscuro pattern, an abstraction that favors the film's allegorical penchant. Griffith opposes this to the stark, clear photography of the violent scenes Gish plays with Donald Crisp as Battling. The camera underlines the dialectic between phenomenon and ideal—the palpable and the transcendental—demonstrating its versatility as it shifts between the two modes, truly catching these actors as they pass from the realm of nature into that of allegory. Griffith abuses this technique in subsequent films with Gish, when the idealized heroine is denied the supporting apparatus of *Broken Blossoms'* style. Through the twenties to her last starring film at MGM, the vision retains its aura of beatitude and in *La Boheme* (1926) provides for some particularly cherishable shots, although it never again finds a context as congenial as *Broken Blossoms*.

The physical register is signaled when Lucy, returning to serve her father a meal, quickly fixes a "smile" on her face.

Then "the terrible accident": she spills something on Burrows's hand. Gish's performance, to this point based on pent-up terror and control, now bursts forth in a frenzy that is one of her specialties. Her loss of restraint and her willingness to decompose the harmony of her being set a standard for the portrayal of hysteria that only she herself will match. (Griffith gives her repeated opportunities to do so in *The Greatest Question*, 1919, *Way Down East*, and *Orphans of the Storm* where her tremblings are no less unsettling for their familiarity.)

Realizing the gravity of her error, Lucy hesitates to move, as though she might avoid the inevitable punishment by simply holding herself together.

As her fear mounts she tries to do literally that—hold herself together—but her face breaks out of its composure.

In desperation she looks down at her father's shoes. "Oh, look daddy, dust on yer boots!"

The various postures assumed throughout this sequence are all related to the closing in on oneself that is central to this film's plastique. Even the pathetic ploy to stay her father's blows gives Lucy the chance to huddle at his feet.

The room traps Lucy with her wild animal of a father. (Later on, close-ups emphasize Battling Burrows's bestial nature.) He grabs her, flings her to the other side of the room, and we are mercifully spared the close shots of the lash falling on her body.

The reiterated and almost unvaried master shot postulates the integrity of the space and the necessity of Lucy's suffering within it. The same is true of the master shot of the Yellow Man's room. What is, I expect, a shooting expedient conspires to the film's advantage by furnishing constants in the poetic pattern, akin to rhyme, meter, and recurrent imagery. Even the transitions recall the constancy of the setups. Lucy struggles to her feet, drags herself through the streets to the wharf (an often repeated locale), and finally she arrives at the Yellow Man's shop.

Here, the framing shafts of light provide a variation for our recognition of a set that belongs to the film's strong series of limitations.

The blossoms of the title, fragrant and so perishable, have a dual meaning. They refer to the name the Yellow Man bestows on Lucy, White Blossom, and they suggest the allegorical tradition of Renaissance love poetry that turns the beloved into a flower. They establish the stylistic linkage between the film's hero and heroine. Conventional role-playing is altered by the fact that Lillian Gish, in her twenties, is playing a fifteen-year-old, and Richard Barthelmess, an American-type to the point of caricature as later shown in *Way Down East* and *Tol'able David* (1921), has assumed the role of a Chinese. The Yellow Man creates the love poem by providing the regalia and the rhetoric, but he is also within the poem as object, rendered so by Barthelmess's version of lover. He is a blossom as well as Lucy. Actor and actress are profoundly alien to their roles; the characters are alien to their environments, and they create a space for themselves at the center of this film.

The meeting of Lucy and the Yellow Man evokes responses in Gish, Barthelmess, and Griffith that guarantee the blossoms' integrity. Nothing jars the internal structure of the poem. Lucy has fainted on the floor of the shop and the Yellow Man finally sees her.

His reaction is a reprise of the posture alteration he introduced at the film's beginning and maintains in every sequence. His ecstasy at what he interprets as a vision is expressed in the tilt of the head, the jutting jaw, the three-quarter profile, the severely outlined face.

Everyday existence, flesh and blood are abolished from this shot, a counterpart of the Gish, halo-lit close-ups. Barthelmess's mind and Griffith's direction place hero and heroine in the same realm.

When Lucy awakens, the miracle of the meeting of the two is seen in the delicate shifts of positions, eyes meeting and then afraid to sustain each other's glance.

Gish casts her eyes down and Barthelmess averts his face, both momentarily withdrawing into themselves before crossing the barrier to become intimate object and referent in a metaphoric relationship. Then their inwardness will be mutually inclusive.

The Yellow Man makes his room over into a temple for Lucy, and he garbs her as befits a goddess, adorning her hair with combs, offering her incense (which with childish finickiness she refuses). She admires her own transformation in a hand mirror—a reaction of superbly in-character, coquettish delight—and expresses gratitude for a small vase of flowers.

It had been her wish for a flower that brought them together on the street earlier in the film. Flowers are more apt for these characters than theatrics.

The film's motifs and attitudes prepare its most courageous scene, one in which actor and director fully meld the dictions of drama and lyric poetry. The intertitle proclaims the worst in Griffith's taste, his bent for overstatement, his belaboring the point the image so completely transmits without words: "There he brings rays stolen from the lyric moon, and places them on her hair; and all night long, he crouches, holding one grubby little hand." Barthelmess seems to be praying at Gish's bedside while she sleeps.

The moment is privileged, an epiphany linking the Yellow Man's religious ideals to his dream of love. What then occurs is a schema for the use of metaphor, its creation, and its power to fix the epiphany in time, to render it tangible through its correlatives. Barthelmess quite literally catches the moonlight in his hands, carries it across the room and showers it on Gish.

Griffith's prose is inadequate to the flow and grace of the shot, the quality of belief shaped by a flexible actor and sustained by a patient camera. A pattern of circular arm movements that involve the whole room is followed by a third frame enlargement of Barthelmess's hands close to his face in an ambiguous reminder of the prayer stance. Then, even at that instant when the light is released, a slight hunch of his shoulders preserves some aspect of character during his most total transport. Kneeling by the bed at the foot of his shrine, he once again projects qualities of religious and sexual ecstasy, sublimely confusing the two just as lyric poets did from the early Italian Renaissance to the English pre-Raphaelite period.

The transition from the first frame to the second, from contemplation to prayer culminates in touch, the contact of face and hands. The whole sequence is a rapid shift of emphasis—from his hands circling to hers, and from her face bathed in the light he bestows to his own beatified by her hand. The light, which is the linking factor of these exchanges, is explicitly part of the scene's theatrical content, and its value accrues through scarcity. Light alone, the light of a very special and personal moon cornered by the Yellow Man, breathes life into these characters. Metaphor is their only means of sustenance.

Yet if *Broken Blossoms* has the cast of lyric poetry, it is lyric poetry drama-tized by the intrusion of other modes. Griffith creates a tension of manner that constantly places the idyll in jeopardy, forcing a confrontation between the interior, private world and the harshness of the exterior, physical one. His obsessive opposition of idealism and necessity appears in contexts ranging from the plight of his virginal heroines in Biograph one-reelers to Belshazzar's flamboyant paradise destroyed by the barbarous Persians in *Intolerance*. The configurations of *Broken Blossoms* are particularly successful in animating conflict with paradox.

The Yellow Man gives Lucy the doll she admired in his shopwindow.

Gish is at her prettiest here. She passes from childish delight to maternal tranquillity, expressing love for the doll surrogate that cannot be directed to the Yellow Man. The gesture with the doll's hand on her cheek is a structural link between this scene and the finger-smile sequences. Instead of a tortured smile, the doll's hand induces a rapture that extends the characterization. In this shot Gish combines emblems of little-girlhood and womanhood to sustain the allegorical pattern of the film. We and the Yellow Man perceive an essence of femininity, granted shape and scope by the stylization of a woman playing a fifteen-year-old who plays at being a woman.

If in the moon sequence Barthelmess enacts the proximity of spiritual and physical love, it is now reiterated in a different, more strident key. He corrupts Gish's child/woman portrait with a terrifying close-up of menacing lust.

She recoils at his approach (the ever-present crouch still serves well),

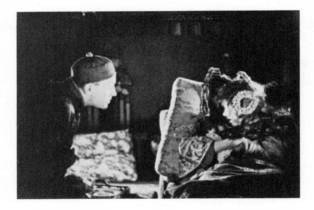

and passion is modulated into reverence when he kisses the hem of her sleeve.

The poles of the film are disturbingly close in this sequence, providing an ambiguous current for Griffith's abstractive characters. One of the triumphs of Gish and Barthelmess is the pulse they make throb beneath the conceptual surface Griffith imposes on Lucy and The Yellow Man. *Broken Blossoms* is most emphatically an *acted* poetic allegory.

The sexual ambiguity of the Yellow Man's gestures toward Lucy is further complicated when Battling Burrows discovers his daughter at the shop. Griffith uses precisely the same kind of terrifying close-up to express the father's rage.

By treating lust and fury similarly, Griffith throws awry the pat polarization of characters and concepts: Yellow Man/peace and Battling Burrows/war. The disorientation of these values will be finally accomplished when Barthelmess—who was to bring Buddha's message to the West; who enshrined poor Lillian Gish in his personal temple—standing next to an illustration of prizefighters, faces down and shoots Donald Crisp.

The hunched stance is apt for expression of both irony and menace.

Up to the film's last minutes, Griffith generates a crescendo of terror, pain, and violence following Burrows's entrance into the love nest. The precious enclosure and the hermetic lovers are rent asunder; the words of the lyric poem are disarranged and strewn across the now familiar areas of the film. If the audience feels panic during the dénouement of *Broken Blossoms,* it is because the elegiac rhythm and the idealized surface have been so radically altered. The stillness of epiphany is shattered by extremes of theatricality, modes borrowed from melodrama that test the integrity of the poem with the purity of their excess. *Broken Blossoms* is as much a clash of literary styles and shapes as a clash of ideologies.

At this point in the film the particular strengths of Lillian Gish are given their greatest and most fulfilling challenge. Torn from her bed and thrown to the floor,

she witnesses her father's destruction of the room with only a hint of the expression of fear that she will eventually summon.

Still clutching the doll, she is dragged down those familiar streets, home through the fog. Then Griffith cuts back to Barthelmess and his discovery of the wreckage and her absence.

Barthelmess's despair and anguish, his self-abandonment, prepare for Gish's great scene. All of their acting in miniature, in repose—acting that aimed toward the private center of their poetic existence—is now reversed, and the walls no longer seem adequate to contain their performances. As the world breaks in upon them, each responds with frantic extensions of their beings into the physical universe. Barthelmess's hysteria is stylized Chinese; Gish's version goes beyond recognizable style.

A particularly inspired invention locates her explosion of hysteria in a closet, the film's smallest space. The general pattern of containment is both respected and supremely violated. This most circumscribed area, suited to the interiority of the lyric poem, provides a frame for the screen's rawest manifestation of unchecked emotion and frenzy. Gish presses herself to the closet wall.

This shot is intercut with Crisp's mask of rage and a scene of Barthelmess thrashing on the floor of his room clutching Lucy's torn robe.

The spatial boundaries of the film gain emotional coherence through Griffith's obsessive intercutting. (A directorial trademark, it governed the entire structure of *Intolerance* and was later brought to a thrilling if dangerously close to a parodic level in the finale of *Orphans of the Storm*. See pp. 55–58, Gish on the guillotine and Danton racing to her rescue.)

Griffith now cuts back to Lucy locked in the closet with only her doll: Gish cries out, "Don't daddy, don't! They'll hang yer."

Then begins a confrontation between actress and closet, and an assault on our collective claustrophobia that set a standard for any subsequent scene of enclosure. The space is delimited by body, hands, eyes, and face.[1] (In *The American*

---

[1] Alexander Walker in *Stardom, The Hollywood Phenomenon*, p. 74, finds an analogy useful in describing the effect Gish produces here. "When she shuts herself in a closet she creates great eddies of claustrophobic panic not by pounding on the wall, but by the more disturbing means of whirling round and round. Just as a body immersed in water displaces its own volume of liquid, Gish uses space to displace her hysteria."

Cinema, p. 50, Andrew Sarris notes Griffith's influence on Hitchcock, who makes considerable use of confinement in films throughout his career, abetting his shower-phone-booth-trapped ladies with, in the first case, a particularly active knife and in the second, an army of birds.)

Gish's gaze is both a measure and a mirror of anguish. The relationship between prison and prisoner is established, and the close-up unflinchingly captures the various stages of development of terror from her mute, little-girl confusion to her full-throated scream.

A sense of duration unfortunately is not conveyed by the frame enlargements. The camera relentlessly records Gish, and she spares the audience nothing, forcing it to share the plenitude of her suffering. The sequence is finally modulated; Gish reassumes the crouching position, drawing herself into a corner, while Crisp hacks at the door.[2]

When he reaches through the opening he has made, the conflict between their worlds is conveyed in purely spatial terms.

All the confines are breached as Lucy is pulled through that same opening, her spirit raped as she passes from one realm into another.

Griffith is fiendishly inventive in scenes of menace, as *Broken Blossoms* demonstrates. The final beating features a tapping motion with the phallic whip handle, a disquieting prelude to the fatal strokes that we do not see.

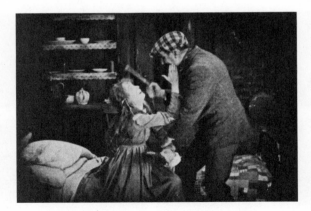

[2] The breadth of art can even accommodate a comic variant of this horror—Marie Dressler and Wallace Beery in *Min* and *Bill* (1930).

Lucy is left alone to die. Isolated now by her pillow, she still clutches the doll that links her to the Yellow Man, but also very much her father's daughter, she composes her final "smile."

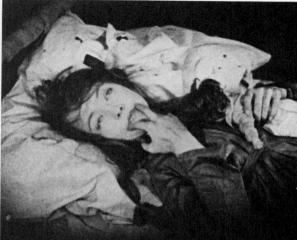

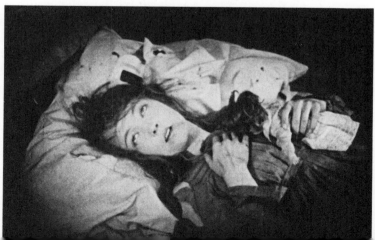

In a shot that seems to be held forever, her death connects the various attitudes and spaces of *Broken Blossoms:* the peace of the Yellow Man's room, the agonizing smile-poem, and the bruises inflicted by Battling Burrows.

The stillness is interrupted by the confrontation of the Yellow Man with Burrows, but it is resumed in the final sequence by an ineffable cadence of echoes of posture and placement. Lucy is returned to her altar to be venerated along with the other icons, and her death is consecrated through the joy and passion of Barthelmess's suicide.

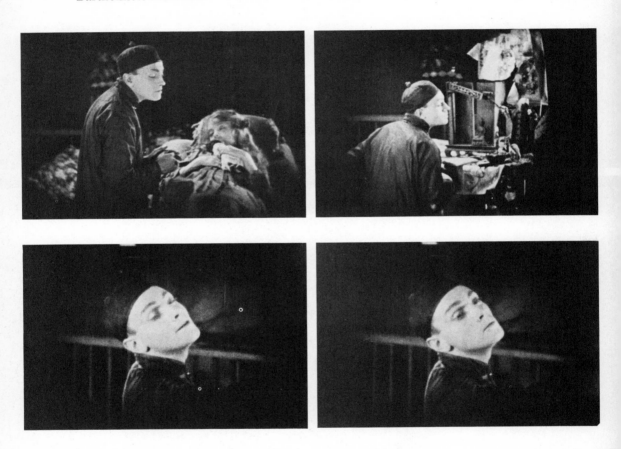

Peace is restored and the pattern is completed by the sublime tilt of the head, which forms the proper closure of the poem that was begun when the Yellow Man first leaned against the brick wall. Between these wedded images Lillian Gish and Richard Barthelmess act out the impossible, escaping from themselves through a refinement of gesture and stance to incarnate a totality of being that ranges from the most exquisite presence of flesh and pain to the airy reaches of aureoles and karma. That is the scope of *Broken Blossoms.*

3·
Actress and Auteur:
Gish and Griffith

The shape of Lillian Gish's career with Griffith is paralleled by the Marlene Dietrich–Josef von Sternberg canon. Actress and director throve, through a series of films that responded to mutual needs and possibilities, until the pattern, thus firmly established, prohibited further development. The harmonies of *Broken Blossoms* (1919) and *Shanghai Express* (1932) are lost to the excesses of *Orphans of the Storm* (1922) and *The Devil Is a Woman* (1935). Gish's departure from the Griffith stock company is traditionally explained in financial terms—she had become too important a star for the director's troubled bankroll (and perhaps for his ego as well). Whatever the reasons for it, the break was essential to Gish as actress. Griffith had repeatedly exploited a particular register of Gish, and *Orphans of the Storm* is quite literally the last step. The director's obsession with the image of the heroine in peril passed through exquisite permutations in *Broken Blossoms*. But stylistic confinement and limits are not necessarily positive. The primordial Griffith situation tests several facets of Gish's behavior but does not permit her to display others. After *The Blue Angel* (1930), Dietrich was Sternberg's exotic flower, delicately ironized, she was the center of a constantly varied set of compositions of light and texture. Gish was always Griffith's little girl/very young lady. Her vulnerability to menace was sublimely appropriate to the complex of reverence and sadism that qualified Woman in his imagination.

A RUSH TO FEELING

The design was fixed for Gish in *Hearts of the World* (1918), produced just a year before *Broken Blossoms*. The pre-war section of the film suffers from the least durable element of Griffith's style, an idealization of characters who are deprived of the contextual nuance that is the mark of *Broken Blossoms*. Yet *Hearts of the World*, at its considerable best, is an elaborate and gripping example of the peril-rescue film that Griffith perfected in his earliest Biograph days.

Gish can abandon her simpering poses at the outbreak of hostilities. She submits to an extended range of agonies in the remainder of the film: she goes from hysteria to near-madness during an air raid

(a harrowing sequence that includes the disquieting face of a chemise-clad neighbor), or, on discovering her dead mother, she shapes the anguish with tenderness, a cry of grief, numbness, and then full-fledged dementia.

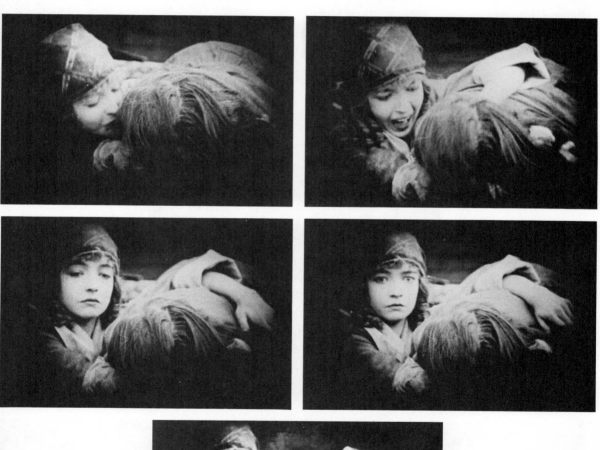

Extracting the last frame in this series from context does Gish some injustice for it isolates the bug-eyes and the set of the chin. They are not in the least caricatural in the development of the shot.

She flees into madness, wandering through the ruined town and battleground carrying the wedding dress she has yet to wear.

In a wedding night worthy of her romantic predecessors, Scott's deranged bride of Lammermoor and Doña Sol of Hugo's *Hernani*, Gish joins her wounded and presumed dead hero.

But Griffith has infinitely more in reserve for his victim: a beating at the hands of the horrible Hun (Gish wrote of her mother's fright at discovering welts on her back after the day's shooting.[1]),

[1] In *The Movies, Mr. Griffith and Me,* p. 201.

and a particularly perverse version of the entrapment motif, when she is wedged between the legs of this lustful enemy.

(Griffith, the Southern gentleman, is caught with his demeanor down by the attempted rapes from *The Birth of a Nation* through *Orphans of the Storm*. Both Mae Marsh and Lillian Gish preserve virginity and innocence, but the nick of time is sorely tried.) Just before the final rescue—accomplished by sister Dorothy, "The Little Disturber," who throws a grenade after great procrastination and much cross-cutting—Gish is further jeopardized: she is pursued by the *Boches*, kills one and implores hero Bobby Harron to shoot her rather than to leave her to a fate worse than death.

Gish's role in *Hearts of the World* is strenuous, and her stamina and dexterity are necessary elements of silent-screen acting. Athleticism and sheer physicality bridge one kind of gap between the serious and comic modes, locating Keaton, Chaplin, and Gish in a single tradition. Yet at one point in the film, the demands made on her are of a scope that hints of things to come, of the depth she will bring to her Lucy in *Broken Blossoms*.

Another Griffith specialty is the scene of reunion and recognition. The homecoming of the Little Colonel in *The Birth of a Nation* with its balance of varying rhythms in the hectic preparations of Mae Marsh opposed to the measured gait of Henry Walthall, their hesitant meeting on the front porch, and the mother's arms seen reaching through the door indicate Griffith's sympathy for this type of theatrical dynamics. The analogous scene in *Hearts of the World,* excessive by comparison, is not suffused with the same tenderness, but it offers Lillian Gish a chance to be something other than sweet or frightened out of her wits. After months of separation from fiancé Bobby Harron (she has recovered her reason in the interim), she comes upon him disguised as a German. In one very lengthy shot she passes from murderous anger to wonder, joy, and the fullness of tears.

Gish's reactions are of a rapidity and promptness ideally suited to emotional scenes in what are essentially action films. The emotions are not shallow, yet their expression is always lurking within an episode. Her body rhythm conforms. She is ready to sacrifice grace to pertinence, and if her acting often seems hectic it is true to the frenzied pace set by Griffith. Gish rushes us through an emotional gamut in the same way Griffith rushes us from place to place, as we breathlessly follow the predicaments of his protagonists. *Broken Blossoms* is, of course, the exception, and its brevity is also a marvel of expansion and repose. Griffith's other major films tend to pursue Gish, the actress, as they pursue the heroines she portrays, and her breakneck responses are proof of her understanding of the medium.

SHARP AS A HATPIN

The Greatest Question (1919) is a peculiarly mixed bag of Griffith's moralizing, cruelty, action, melodrama, and spiritualism. Gish, in the film's major role, is quite unrelated to its central thesis; "the greatest question" concerns the links between the dead and the living. The plot is of Byzantine complication, replete with flashbacks that progressively reveal a murder she witnessed as a child. Yet despite the deficiencies of Griffith's scenario, the film is enormously exciting. Its nonsense (an offensively conceived and portrayed family retainer, Zeke, represents no progress over the rendition of blacks in *The Birth of a Nation*) is effectively engulfed by Griffith's major tic: destroy the leading lady.

A bare moment after Gish appears on screen, her mother dies—an old refrain by now.

She is taken in by Mother Hilton (Eugenie Besserer). This actress (whose place in movie history is unworthily assured by her "mammy" to Jolson's "Jazz Singer") matches the emotional level of Gish in their few scenes together, and she eventually demonstrates an affirmative answer to "the greatest question."

Gish's childlike, idyllic romance with Bobby Harron in this film sets a mode that becomes dominant in *True Heart Susie* and *A Romance of Happy Valley* (both released also in 1919), but here it is merely relief for a set of perils and adversities that only Griffith's morbid invention can exceed. To help the "good" family, she hires herself out to the "evil" family (unbeknownst to her they are the man and woman who committed the murder she saw as a child). Her mistress, jealous of the attentions paid her by the master, mistreats poor Lillian; she beats her for breaking a dish and almost murders her in her sleep.

In the film's climax the heroine is pursued through several floors of the house to the attic where she is finally trapped by the lecher.

They are surprised by the suspicious wife. Gish then realizes the couple is guilty of the old murder, and the chase resumes down the stairs until she is cornered.

The hatpin is one of Griffith's happiest illuminations. Not even the guillotine makes us suffer for Lillian Gish in quite the same way as that slim needle. All this is loads of fun, and puts the leading lady through her olympic paces. She can give no more than she does, and the excesses of physical anguish she manages to register are quite simply unsurpassable. Yet one aches to see her do something else, to escape the most deadly type-casting a director ever conceived. A talent has been honed, it makes us feel knifelike pain, yet it is deprived of work in those areas of feeling that give pain a dimension and a location beyond wound and scream.

Gish's virtuoso technique, radically sensational here, is insufficient to grant spatial dynamics to the accidental agonies contrived by Griffith. Buster Keaton, for example, teeters on a ladder, and the laughter he provokes is balanced over the geography of his peril, sounding the grace of his encounter with gravity. Gish races to an encounter with a hatpin whose sole resonance is the harum-scarum. *The Greatest Question* and other examples of this manner in Griffith detach Gish from the sustaining web of gesture and metaphor that transforms her *Broken Blossoms* screams into melismatic arias. Gish's acting is more than adequate to any situation; not every situation is adequate to an actress who relates the breadth of gesture to the reach of poetry.

ADORABLE IN BUCOLICA

True Heart Susie (1919) and *A Romance of Happy Valley* (1919) are very personal films for Griffith, and in their way are as original as *The Birth of a Nation, Intolerance,* and *Broken Blossoms.* More overtly allegorical than *Broken Blossoms* (locales and characters such as The Land of Make Believe, The Pike that Never Was, Old Lady Smiles, Sporty, etc.) and absolutely faithful to their pastoral intentions, they exhibit a style that commands respect and even affection, although they are alien to modern taste. Our delight in these films comes from their total lack of condescension, and the belief of director and actors that sophistication can be abandoned, that life can be rendered in simplistic and reductionist modes. The freshness of these dreamy evocations of rural America is preserved by the splendid photography and the equilibrium of style. Gish is never asked to be more than cutesy-pie, and she is precisely that, avoiding all hints of glamour or depth. She is a paragon of homely virtues, caring for cows and people,

wearing her funny little hat and crying a bit,

playing innocent love scenes with Bobby Harron (whose film trademark is three inches of bare leg peeking out below his trouser bottoms).

She invests these conceits with treasurable grace and humor, yet she is just as shackled by uninflected sweetness as she was by uninflected terror. The rightness of Gish's Susie makes us despair that she will ever be able to rid herself of a too true heart.

STURM UND STURM

The last two films Gish made with Griffith, *Way Down East* (1920) and *Orphans of the Storm* (1922), are a return to the principal manner and place her in situations of ever-increasing emotional and physical intensity.

In the first scenes of *Way Down East,* with the gentle humor of her Susie, she plays the country cousin imitating her snobbish relatives and finally getting the chance to look elegant herself.

Her success is short-lived, for she is abandoned by a scoundrel after a phony marriage (her wonderful laugh-cry).

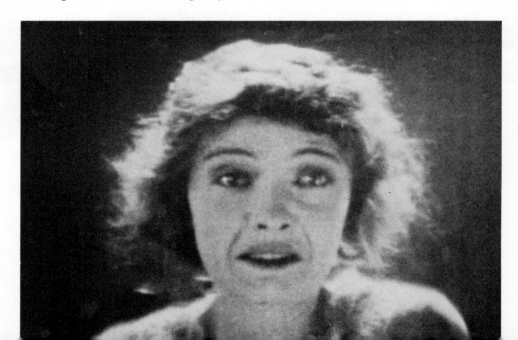

Then, in the full flower of *pathétique*, she baptizes her dying baby and wails over her loss with a boundless grief. (This situation is prefigured in *The Mothering Heart*, 1913, a Biograph two-reeler.)

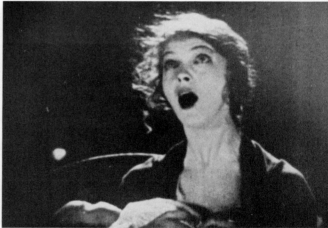

In transitions from sadness to dumbness to openmouthed total despair nothing is held in reserve. Gish gives the impression she is playing her final scene, the final one of her entire life. She spares neither herself nor her audience, avoiding any suggestion of prettiness. Griffith relishes such scenes, and their power is unrestrained. Melodrama is by definition excessive. Gish nourishes it with something that approaches religious fervor, and an ability to arrange her features in configurations so extreme, so lucid, so open that authenticity is extracted from the patently bathetic. The mask of eternal victim is not so rigid as to preclude its occasional displacement and the subsequent release of Gish's special persona. One of the strengths of her work with Griffith is precisely the distance between mask and personality. As she travels between cliché and self, from a stock situation to the uniqueness of context in a moment like the baptism, she demonstrates a dynamics basic to great screen acting.

Nothing else in *Way Down East* is worthy of the Gish treatment, the generosity of spirit that we measured in *Broken Blossoms*. The innocent love scenes with Richard Barthelmess are photographed with such a delicate balance of light and texture that the stars seem almost cloyingly attractive.

It was the final sequence with the heroine forced out into a raging blizzard,

fainting on an ice floe, and rescued just before going over a waterfall that caught Griffith's imagination and upon which he lavished his art. (In his very first film at Biograph, *The Adventures of Dollie*, 1908, a child sealed in a barrel went over a waterfall.) These scenes are undeniably effective and put Gish in a series of extraordinary compositions: her cape buffeted by the wind, her face covered with snow,

lying on the ice with her hand achingly trailing in the water.

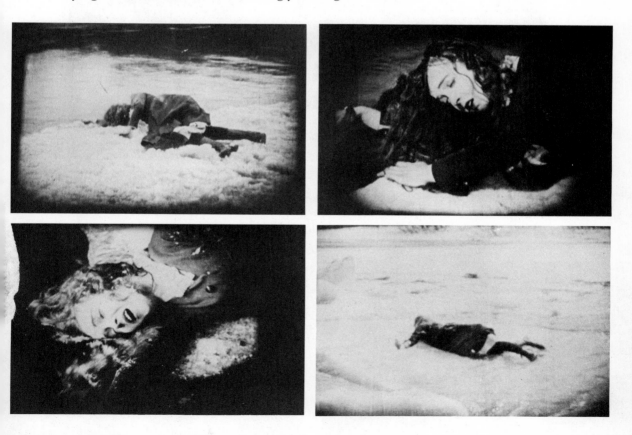

The story of the shooting has been told and retold, most eloquently in Gish's *The Movies, Mr. Griffith and Me*. The courage of Gish and Barthelmess gives startling results, and the sequence never fails to elicit the expected *frisson*. But acting? Griffith has constructed a symbol of fragility and he delights in putting it in the direst jeopardy, fairly tantalizing the audience, capitalizing on the lurid fascination with peril. One of Gish's major accomplishments is the amount of personality and individuality she brings to the caricature, along with that frightening dedication.

Orphans of the Storm is the final step, where the pattern is pushed to its limit. Gish is introduced as the familiar wide-eyed ingenue.

She has been separated from her blind sister (Dorothy Gish), and Griffith fabricates for her the recognition/reunion scene par excellence. Hearing the voice of a street singer, she gradually realizes it belongs to her sister.

She rushes to the balcony to call out in joy and extends that small body of hers, coming through the window, and finally right out of the frame into the spectator's lap.

Again we are stunned by the fullness of Gish's response, her physical stretch as a precise analogy to the emotional one. Griffith unabashedly milks the episode, interrupting the reunion with arresting soldiers. A furious struggle is followed by variants of the first balcony shots, this time turning the joy of reunion into the frustration of a new separation.

Gish continues to reveal a ferocity rare in her previous films though hinted at in *Hearts of the World*. She follows the Griffith pattern of intensification and crescendo as her strength is further tested in a struggle with her sister's captor, and later, when she is dragged away from the revolutionary tribunal.

Gish, that symbol of feminine daintiness, fills the massive sets, projecting herself to the extremities of the spaces she inhabits. This is a change of scale for her. The confinement motif is present in *Orphans of the Storm*, but it is principally reserved for Dorothy Gish as a prisoner of blindness in a cellar. Lillian rips through Paris, invades the aristocrats' soirées, roams the streets, measures herself against the crowds. It is the most grandiose, free-wheeling role for her in the Griffith years. Even the inevitable and treasurable, tender moment is played before a crowd. She discovers her sister again, this time during her own trial.

In the apparent loss of control, the scream, the smile belying the fingers that caution Dorothy to be silent, we see a precious characteristic of Gish's style. Something of an anomaly, it seems to be a very conscious decision to let loose and abandon control. She quite literally plans to open the floodgates and sweeps everything aside—absurdities of plot, simplicity of conception, our diffidence, and the taste for "cool" acting. Lillian Gish brooks no half measures, and her yielding of self earns our awe, fear, and love.

This abundance of feeling for the heroine is drawn out by Griffith in what must be his *summa:* Gish's ride to the scaffold and last minute rescue by Danton. Christ-like, reviled by the crowd,

she is strapped to the guillotine.

Bewilderment is followed by hysteria, then resignation.

Griffith spares no detail; photographing her in all possible positions, he fairly chortles over the scope of this final predicament.

The logical conclusion of Gish's career with Griffith is the image of her head jutting out of that brace.

This is the ideal frame, replacing the aureole, the soft-focus nimbus, the pretty-girl pose. He has brought his leading lady to that ultimate meeting with the lens—her head in splendid isolation, she is offered up, as it were, to camera and posterity. If the blade doesn't drop in *Orphans of the Storm*, it does in the Griffith-Gish collaboration. There is little more to ask of an actress, but one shudders with apprehension over the outcome if it had. "Yes, Mr. Griffith, whatever you say."

In their first film, *An Unseen Enemy* (1912), Lillian and Dorothy were locked in a room and menaced by a gun that appeared through a hole in the wall.

The dangers became more sophisticated and elaborate in the intervening eleven years, and they were punctuated with scenes of tenderness and reflection. Yet Lillian Gish had to leave Griffith to get out of that locked room, to get her neck out of the guillotine. She had to grow up. Her subsequent films in the twenties prove that a fascinating and challenging woman was lurking all the time in those pinafores and beneath those funny hats. The dedication, force, sense of the camera, and above all, the belief in form developed with Griffith were to be channeled by Gish into some of the most remarkable films of the late silent era. No other actress ever passed through a more grueling initiation to earn her stardom.

4.
Before Glamour
at MGM:
Gish, Vidor, and
Seastrom

A KISS OF LIFE

The White Sister (1923), Lillian Gish's first vehicle after leaving the Griffith troupe, exploits the actress's star quality without completely betraying her dedication and seriousness of the previous years. An expensive showcase, Italian location sets, quality photography—the luxury of the whole enterprise as opposed to the ensemble context of a Griffith film—put "beautiful" Gish squarely in the center. Early on she is shown prophetically admiring her own portrait (as "The White Sister") and, although the portrait motif will be taken up again in the film's most extraordinary scene, here it establishes prettiness, per se, a concept basic to filmmaking but often unemphasized by Griffith.

The White Sister is a new direction for Gish because it is emphatically picturesque rather than filmic. It is almost as if a still camera were photographing all those real Neapolitan palaces and landscapes, and the handsome features of the protagonists, Lillian Gish and Ronald Colman.

The director, Henry King, had already proven himself somewhat in the Griffith manner with the bucolic *Tol'able David* (1921) starring Richard Barthelmess. But it's a long way from rural America to location Italy, and although *The White Sister* has its merits, it is predominantly a lifeless series of illustrations.

Some of the known Gish ingredients are present. There is the great scene of hysteria when she learns that Colman has been killed during an African expedition (he really isn't dead, but it takes her several years to find that out, and in the meantime she has become a nun).

The disasters include a scene of entrapment during an eruption of Vesuvius, when Colman pleads with her to give up the veil and almost rapes her, then a windstorm that does lovely things with her nun's habit, and a flood. But all of this is curiously unexciting, and the decisive encounter with Colman is ineptly staged. Griffith's hand is woefully absent.

Yet several moments in the film liberate Gish, allowing her full range and the chance to respond as a mature actress with a face and a character that correspond to her true age. The first occurs just before she receives the false news of Colman's death. While looking out the window at street singers she fondles his letter, initially in quite a conventional way.

The standard pose and situation are then altered, her gaze is directed through the singers toward the reaches of her imagination, her hands establish an unsettlingly intimate relationship to the letter. She creates a shape for closeness and projects it far off at the same time.

She almost never had the chance to use props in this way under Griffith's direction. The doll in *Broken Blossoms* and the wedding dress in *Hearts of the World* were subsumed in the first by the weight of impersonation of a twelve-year-old, and in the second by the horrors-of-war plot. In *The White Sister*, the conventionality of the image is in inverse proportion to Gish's very individual powers of invention. While continuing to possess the universe in her body, in the configurations of her limbs and features, she will appropriate exterior reality with ever greater frequency.

This way of dealing with objects is at the core of the film's most fully realized scene, indeed one of the most memorable in Gish's career. After her hysterical crisis she goes into a coma and, some time later, wakes from it in a hospital room. Her fiancé's portrait has been placed there and for a while she believes it to be truly he. Rising from her bed, she beckons to her picture-lover, kisses him, and only then realizes that reality has betrayed her.

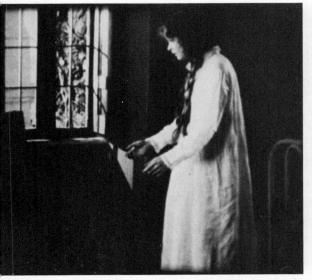

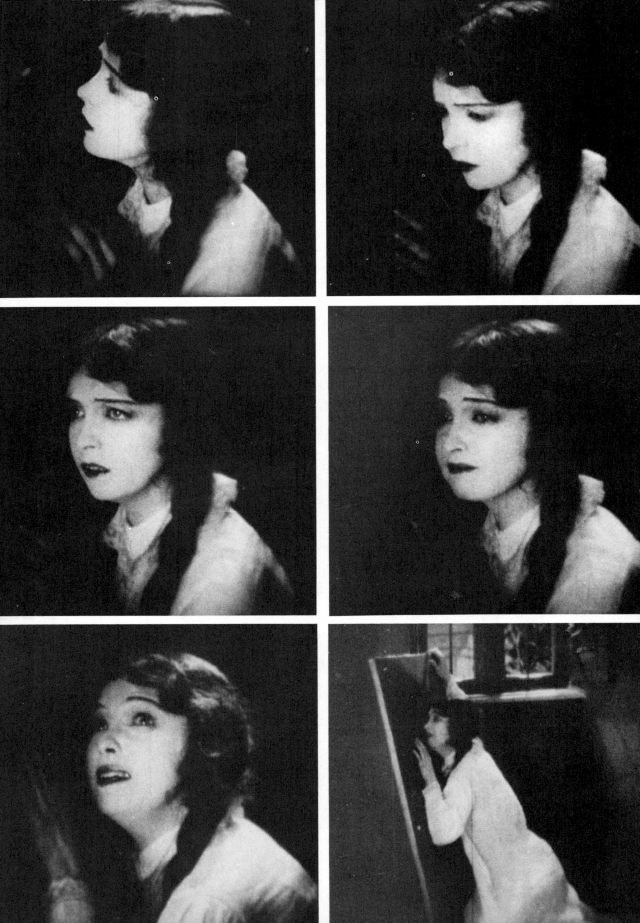

Henry King matches the patience of Lillian Gish, permitting the situation its full expansion, coming as close as the actress allows and for a duration that admits the rustle of feeling. In the final three frame enlargements Gish bridges logic and love—the knowledge that Colman is paint and canvas and the fullness of her belief in his presence—in the kiss she bestows, in the embrace she is loath to relinquish. The high metaphorical style of *Broken Blossoms* is gone but Gish supplies a new one; the touch and spirit that emanate from her inhabit the frame, calling all it contains to her being, the richness of her conviction, and her devotion to the medium. She has the gift of transformation. In her hands a letter and a portrait take on the texture, the complexity, the life of her will. The physical is charged with the actress's very breath. Otherwise, only Garbo will possess quite this degree of metaphoric power.

The White Sister never again exploits Gish's genius. It settles for the tableau-like formations of ceremony and iconography—her assumption of nun's habit with an uncomfortably realistic shearing of her tresses,

a *pietà* with a sick child (a pale reminiscence of *Way Down East* and a prefiguration of Henry King's *Romola,* 1924).

Her first reunion with Colman has some shock value. For a moment she forgets she is a nun, but quickly recovers, and the scene is resolved in the expected hysteria and lots of running around.

The White Sister is ambiguous in its treatment of Gish, succumbing to certain clichés of her previous films—her beauty and that of Italy itself—yet intermittently coming alive with the actress's vitality. The nun's cowl has replaced the soft-focus aureole, and Lillian Gish is impatient for contexts that call for extremes of invention and rendition. The style of her Lucy and its transcendence of naturalism are occasionally recalled in *The White Sister,* despite the general awkwardness of the direction and the film's shapelessness. Henry King's career was long and varied to the point of facelessness. He is adequate to the needs of Alice Faye, Jeanne Crain, and Jennifer Jones, but he fails at the challenge of Gish. He is unable to sustain her tension, unable to meld actress, sentiment, and decor with anything approaching the consistency of Griffith even at his most self-imitative. *The White Sister* is the kind of film that allows the star only fleeting minutes of acting pertinence. Such movies (Garbo's career is littered with them) are unwieldy containers that work best when transparent. The star then shines through. Gish, even when ill served by the limits of Griffith's imagination, is never left to her own devices. These devices, although considerable, give only intermittent life to *The White Sister.*

TO CALVARY WITH LOVE

After her two independently produced films, *The White Sister* and *Romola,* and the painful litigation with her partner/unwelcome suitor, William Duell, Lillian Gish returned to a studio context. She yielded to the blandishments of Irving Thalberg and signed a contract with MGM. Their faith in their new star is proved by the big budgets, the already recognizable MGM production values, and the prestigious directors, King Vidor and Victor Seastrom, for three of the five films she made for them: *La Bohème* (1926), *The Scarlet Letter* (1926), and *The Wind* (1928). Gish, impressed with Vidor's *The Big Parade* (1925) and its star John Gilbert, requested and obtained both the director and the leading man for her first effort, *La Bohème*.

La Bohème is all too rarely seen, and Vidor is unduly modest about his contribution to it. The film fairly relishes the richness of its cinematography and its technical assurance. It displays the high standards of the studio product, a corporate effort in which the individual talents of the contributors are enhanced rather than homogenized. MGM cannot match Griffith for vision and the stamp of the director/*auteur*, but it does foster the collaboration of directors, actors, cameramen, and set designers on a work distinguished by expert craftmanship and, in the case of *La Bohème*, by breathtaking vitality. Lillian Gish has recounted (in *The Movies, Mr. Griffith and Me*) her unfamiliarity with the new studio context, with the lack of rehearsal and the impersonality of the working conditions, yet despite this, and for quite different qualities, she gave the kind of performance that, along with *Broken Blossoms*, proves her supremacy over other silent film actresses.

Again, Gish's whole body renders the essence of a particular gesture or situation, whether it be the silly flightiness of the beginning, or the grueling *Via Crucis* of her return to John Gilbert at the end. Her physique is tuned to the clarity of a given metaphor, and she is thoroughly consistent to and totally expressive of the context. It is, in fact, an extension of expressionism in acting, and one would have to turn to Emil Jannings in F. W. Murnau's *The Last Laugh* (1924), or to the great comedians, to find such a complete manifestation of the connections among situation, mood, and posture. When Gish warms herself near Gilbert's stove it is not just her hands or her nose, but the whole of herself, turning around, exploiting the opportunity with a commitment that never suggests telegraphy or semaphor. The sign is clear, yet with nuance and timing it is broken up and reconstituted—the hands, the nose, and the body ceaselessly redefine the space and the object—stove.

The first extended love scene demonstrates the actress/director relationship. The teasing standoffishness of Mimi is Gish's invention, as documented in both her own and King Vidor's autobiographies (see bibliography). The sequence's energy and movement, that headlong quality, are characteristic of the director who, from *The Big Parade* to *Duel in the Sun* (1947), and *Ruby Gentry* (1952) keeps his lovers on the go. The combination is irresistible, and John Gilbert's participation is far from negligible. The sequence begins with an ingenuous and fresh (and clothed) *déjeuner sur l'herbe.* Hollywood discovered painting long before *La Bohème,* but the exploitation is admissible only when applied with Vidor's gusto and lack of reverence.

Gish's Mimi animates the scene, clapping her hands, darting about in a variation on her Griffith little-girl joy served up here with maturer ecstasy. Until this point in the film she has avoided the physical advances of Gilbert; her Mimi is a cloying and almost unbearable tease. (One wonders how the film would have turned out if, as intended, she had never kissed Gilbert.) The silliness and unpleasantness of this attitude has a purpose. She dances off into the woods, pursued by Gilbert. Averted kiss becomes yet another dance.

The chase resumes, she hides behind a tree, and Gilbert loses her only to find her seated by a pool.

Movement has finally subsided and the stasis of reflection liberates her. Having expressed her love through the dance in the forest, through the pastoral conceit of the sylvan chase (a motif reiterated in *The Scarlet Letter*), the wood sprite casts aside high style, changes register completely, and rather than yield to her lover, she emphatically declares her love. It is she who bestows the first kiss.

Her timid afterthought is followed by a full-fledged embrace,

one that has been amply supported by the freedom of Vidor's direction, the superb chiaroscuro lighting, and the strategy and rhythm of Gish's performance. Love *is* best expressed through distance—through the correlatives of the dance, the chase, the forest. And the final yielding of self is magnified through the filters of style that have preceded it.

More than half the film is keyed to light comedy and youthful romance, with Gilbert leaping over the rooftops to cling to Gish's window and Gish doing a version of her lover's historical play for the Vicomte (delightfully played by Roy d'Arcy).

This paragon of fragile femininity runs the gamut of cloak and dagger conventions, assuming the roles of hero, heroine, and villain, and the sequence provides a reversal of the official Gish persona.

The audience is waiting to suffer with Mimi and Rodolphe, and it will not be cheated. The attitudes of Gish the victim, so painfully elaborated in her Griffith days, are summoned also in *La Bohème*. It is melodramatic perhaps, but the accouterments of guillotine, snowstorm, hatpin, whip, and so forth are gone. The little-girl allegory is gone, the moral burden she so courageously bore is gone. Gish's Mimi is defined by situation, character, and form rather than ideology. The variety of manner she brought to the film's preceding episodes now sustains her. The suffering and the emotions are qualified by the richness of the initial contexts and Gish's playing in them. The physical universe is given shape by Mimi's presence. This is to some degree the same pattern that will emerge in Garbo's films, where the actress supplies all the clues for our interpretation of phenomena. But Garbo will draw phenomena within her. Gish, so able to extend her being to the furthest reaches of a given context, transmits that extension to the film as a whole. She darts through the film, weaving it with her various strands of mood and plasticity. Garbo often envelops the frame to hide its poverty. Because of Vidor, the frame is worthy of Gish's pattern, which is to answer energy with energy.

Rodolphe believes himself betrayed.

Mimi convinces him of the contrary with a white lie, whose untruth he subsequently discovers.

When Gish's hair comes down we know we are in for something. Pleading with Gilbert,

hanging on to his neck and thus being dragged all over the floor,

she is finally thrown down. The sight of Gish, lying like a rag doll, is too much for Gilbert and for us.

She finds blood on her lips, and reacts to it with panic.

All the violence and pain are then translated into these loving close-ups.

Calm, pardon, and infinite tenderness emanate from the face, newly framed by the camera and the hair that now functions as the limiting context rather than as a signal for violence. Gish, the actress of extreme situations, unites the opposing reaches of her range in this brief sequence. It is all there—composure and dis-composure, the pristine image and its shocking blemish, the abandon lavished upon both the athletic and contemplative moments. She is nobly aided by the tension-filled set, its bareness providing a dynamic playing space of disconnected planes. The final close-up reestablishes for us the poignant whiteness of her face, the near-translucence of her skin. And John Gilbert's hysterical loss of control, so inept and graceless in his films with Garbo, complements Gish's giving all. He exteriorizes without her sense of shape, but the manner is similar. His exuberance fits the role with this leading lady as it never will with his introspective Swedish co-star.

La Bohème's final sequences rank with the most harrowing in Gish's career, and are perhaps the most affecting since the menace comes from within. Lillian Gish's Mimi, in the final stage of tuberculosis, struggling through the streets of Paris to be with her lover, and dying on camera, is heaven-sent to King Vidor. The actress's body assumes countless configurations: she turns the wheel of a textile press;

she stretches herself to pull the giant lever;

she lifts off the heavy bolt;

she staggers under the load; and she is helped by co-workers after collapsing.

The last frame is a variation on the rag doll metaphor in her quarrel with Gilbert, and it does little to soften the blow that is about to fall on the audience. In this close-up she hears the doctor announce her imminent death.

There is barely a rustle of life left in her eyes. Her pallor has become pain, the face is elongated, narrow, instead of the pert valentine to which we are accustomed. The rhythm of these final minutes has been posited by the alternation of enormous exertion and utter lack of vitality. Gish pursues this strength/weakness pattern to the end. Seeming to have no bones in her body, no tension in her muscles, she struggles to her feet and somehow tumbles out to the sidewalk.

Then she begins an aching journey through Paris to be with Gilbert. Long shots stress the shape of her body outlined against stone walls (the second frame enlargement is particularly reminiscent of the UFA expressionistic style of lighting and design) and are intercut with close-ups of the agony-filled face and medium shots of her efforts to catch on to a cart and a carriage.

One of Vidor's key obsessions—the heroine dragged or crawling—finds perhaps its most apt exponent in Lillian Gish, hanging onto the back of a cart and, in an unfaked shot, being pulled over the cobblestones.

Renée Adorée in *The Big Parade,* Jennifer Jones in *Duel in the Sun* and *Ruby Gentry,* and Bette Davis in *Beyond the Forest* all grovel and stretch, but their sufferings are incidental to their careers; Gish was bred to the manner of pain.

Aided by compassionate strangers, she breaks away in another spurt of strength, and falls in the Bohemians' doorway.

The deathbed sequence has been amply described by both Gish and Vidor: the actress's Lon Chaney–like efforts to simulate the clinical reality of a consumptive's expiration, the fears of crew and actors upon seeing her in such a state. The story's faintly legendary quality (she went for three days without liquids and stuffed her cheeks with cotton to remove all the moisture from her mouth) is always dispelled by the film itself, by the anxiety it instills in the audience through its version of dying and death that transcends makeup. Gish hovers between lifelessness and joy as she is reunited with Gilbert.

Her frailty is contrasted to Renée Adorée's refulgent beauty and health.

Then, thinking herself dead, she does it: she dies on camera—no twisting, no eye-rolling, but rather an absence of life.

Sartov lights her to emphasize the whiteness of her skin. Her face is turned into a death mask, her vitality is trapped in a stasis that recalls *Broken Blossoms*. This is the ultimate contemplation of the actress—a composition that locates a *motion* picture in a memorable pose—a portrait, seemingly at odds with the movement of the film medium, but actually enhancing that very movement through its stillness—the resumé of all the previous gestures and expressions in one key image. That particular image in *La Bohème* is a disturbing reminder that Lillian Gish is an actress who gives her all. She seems to have literally done just that.

THE PRIVACY OF A SCAFFOLD: *THE SCARLET LETTER*

Gish's next film at MGM, *The Scarlet Letter* (1926), was made with a director, Victor Seastrom, and a co-star, Lars Hanson, for whom she has particularly fond memories. And both hearkened back to the Griffith manner and contexts that Gish had found congenial to her art. Despite the stamp of big studio lavishness and care in production, there is a non-MGM quality about *The Scarlet Letter*, as well as the last Gish–Hanson–Seastrom collaboration, *The Wind* (1928). Both films are deadly serious; neither is designed to appeal to the Saturday-night movie audience out for a thrill or a laugh or a cry.

Seastrom is the moving force, and these are director's films in the best sense of the term. *The Scarlet Letter* excels in mass effects, the great public scenes of conflict between Hester Prynne and the Puritan community. Seastrom redefines the space of the town square, making it an area successively filled and emptied, now a formal pattern with paths cleared, then with serried ranks of extras. The church, the town hall, and the scaffold are the other spatial elements that constitute the dynamics of the public drama.

Lillian Gish is familiar with this sort of expanse. She was not an "orphan of the storm" for nothing (Gish in the stocks is an unintentionally comic variant of Gish on the guillotine),

and the two great concerted scenes elicit responses that delineate the social and personal resonances of Hester's predicament. In the first she refuses Dimmesdale's exhortation to reveal the name of her "fellow sinner" (himself) with an almost completely unvaried set of chin, eyes, and shoulders in a shot repeated eleven times.

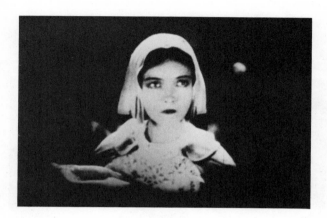

The fullness of gaze, establishing a secret language between Hester and Dimmesdale, is an extended prefiguration of the extraordinary deathbed encounter of Bette Davis and Charles Boyer in *All This and Heaven Too* (1940) (see p. 274).

Again in the finale, Gish's lack of self-consciousness and embarrassment, in a film about the repression of the self, qualifies Hanson's public confession and death with the same tender privacy she bestowed on the doll in *Broken Blossoms* and the letter in *The White Sister*.

There is a calm about Gish in these moments that bespeaks her understanding of dramatic potential of situations in which the dynamics of mass pivots around the actress. The hysteria of Griffith's crowd scenes took on contour in the reach of her body, which she stretched beyond possibility. The hush of *The Scarlet Letter's* Puritanism is drawn inside the actress's eyes and enfolding arms.

Other aspects of Hester Prynne suit Lillian Gish's more familiar expressionism. In projecting the role's sexuality she is abetted by Seastrom's invention and fervor. After the avowal of her previous marriage, Seastrom sends her out into the snow hysterical,

and then caps the sequence with a strategically projected shadow on her apron.[1]

[1] This film's symbolic sexuality is evoked (with some errors of detail) by Raymond Durgnat in *Eros in the Cinema,* pp. 34–35. "Every evening she sits, very much alone, in her cottage, spinning, the starched white collar of her Puritan dress covers her breasts and the fire flings the whirling shadows of her spinning wheel across her apron. The contrast between her rich femininity and her loneliness; between the stiff dress and the tremulous delicacy of Lillian Gish; her placidity and industriousness; has the superb erotic solidity of which the Swedes seem to possess the secret."

She proved her aptness for love's ecstasies in *La Bohème,* and yields to passion here with her arms flung wide and hair flowing.

A different brand of Gish passion is exhibited when she defies the elders who want to take away her child.

Later, distraught by the illness of her child and the unexpected return of her husband, Henry Walthall (an echo from the world of Griffith), Gish transforms her face into a succession of symbols for despair.

Such gestures as hands freely mingling with and blocking out areas of face are exemplary of Gish's ability and willingness to translate expression into disharmonious physical states. This is not overacting, but acting that is more figurative than purely lifelike. Gish balances these two extremes of representation, a manner she perfected in *Broken Blossoms*.

The success of *The Scarlet Letter* is, however, guaranteed by Seastrom, by the integrity of his vision and the full use of decor, lighting, camera placement, and his sensitivity to landscape and texture. This "Scarlet Letter" may not be pure Hawthorne, but it emerges with a stylistic unity that sustains the conflict between desire and society, and the congruence of character and place that will be plumbed in Gish's next film with her Swedish director—*The Wind*.

FREEDOM AND THE FINAL STORM: *THE WIND*

If *The Scarlet Letter* is grim by MGM standards, *The Wind* (1928) is a complete aberration. Uncompromising (except in the tacked-on happy ending), relentless in its depiction of the links between psyche and nature, sparing no detail that conveys the harshness of life, it is a hallmark of the art to which Lillian Gish dedicated herself. And for that very reason it hastened the end of her reign as star at MGM. As she battles the storms of her mind and the inexorable wind blowing over the prairie, she fulfills a career that offers her up as a sacrifice to the exquisite pain of the moment. Her being is engulfed by elements and situations, and she, in turn, suffuses them with a personal substance that unequivocally translates them for the spectators. Gish was lost and found in Lucy's closet, in Mimi's agony, and, again, in Letty's battle with the wind. Griffith, Vidor, and Seastrom all provided her with the means to strip away the barriers, and commingle the depths of her feeling and the shape of her face and body. In *Broken Blossoms* and *La Bohème*, the harrowing truths accompanied by the relief of a good cry are audience-tested. Seastrom and Gish deny us this balm in *The Wind* where Letty's agony is managed without a hint of the pathetic. Gish's suffering has gone beyond that, into a realm of art that brooks no pity.

The film is constructed as a single crescendo, the tension mounting from Gish's first appearance and first encounter with the wind. There are few scenes from which the wind is absent. If it is not qualifying her appearance, buffeting her hair and clothes, she hears it, senses its omnipresence. Seastrom is as relentless as his subject; singlemindedly he pursues the theme, relating the violent life on the plains and the violent conflict between genteel heroine and rustic ways to the passion of the elements. The climactic sequences show to what high degree Gish and Seastrom complement each other.

Alone in the cabin during a particularly severe windstorm, she first displays her mounting frenzy as numbness with an unnatural stillness of her body.

Then frightened, she runs into the storm after her departing husband, but she is thrust back indoors by the force of the wind.

Confined and alone, her madness mounts. As she looks dumbly at a swinging lamp that charges the frame with its own dynamism, her shoulder blocks out her mouth.

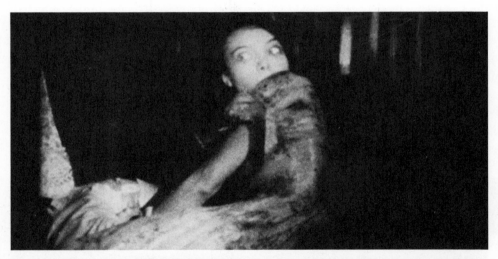

The selective use of facial features was already illustrated in *The Scarlet Letter*. In this film it becomes a dominant motif, lodging the quality of the character's mind in clearly defined areas, which function as a series of masks that sum up a state of being in one feature, then another.

The menace of the wind is augmented by Montagu Love, the traveling man who has been trying to seduce Gish throughout the film. Again she runs outside only to be pushed back.

Her body is immeasurably extended as she attempts to resist the insuperable force of the wind and the excruciating tension under which she is placed. The situation of stress may remind us of other Gish films, but her physical reaction is of a new order.

After being raped by the villain she somehow finds the strength to shoot him.

That odd little glance down at the gun is suggestive of her madness. (Gish, Garbo, and Davis all do very well at shooting men—Garbo in *The Mysterious Lady, The Kiss,* and *Mata Hari,* Davis in *The Letter* and *Deception.* Gish gives a veritable lesson in rifle deportment in *The Night of the Hunter*.) With mounting hysteria, she buries the body, and then gives what must be the champion version of craziness as she stares out the window and sees the body being uncovered by the wind.

The pathology of mind is conveyed in the pathological photography of an incomplete face, a further embellishment on the mask motif. This time Gish centers everything in the eyes and is able to unleash their force because her mouth is withheld. Seastrom permits her this extreme stylization, a mouthless face, and she carries it through to the limits of expressiveness. She is relieved of the burden of realism and sings her mad scene in pitches higher than those of any coloratura soprano.

Her hair is streaming down her back. She turns her face, believing the dead man has come back to haunt her, and discovers her husband (Lars Hanson).

The wind provides the shape and feel for the happy ending, as the couple embrace in the doorway.

This ending, forced on director and cast after the film had been completed, to some degree denatures the cumulative force of what precedes it. Yet I find it a treasurable moment: a last vision of Lillian Gish, triumphantly facing the wind, holding her small body in linear opposition to it, stretching to the confines of the frame, then sharing a reverse embrace with Hanson. The image possesses the most stunning aspects of her acting, her strength and her abandon. With power and generosity she enhances the medium, responding to its most stringent demands, both moral and physical. Tempered by her various ordeals, she emerges victorious in that doorway.

The Wind, a proper measure for the range of Gish, closes the circle and returns her to that ideal world of *Broken Blossoms,* to the simplicity and richness of allegory, to the pain of Lucy's closet. Seastrom and Griffith, Hanson and Barthelmess provided Lillian Gish with a pure context that released her power to carry us beyond reality in the wonder of her little-girl eyes and the expanse of her embrace.

5.
From Orchids to Roses:
Garbo's Silent Films

Silent films demonstrate with particular force the process of exteriorization in art, the rendering of existence through symbolic referents ranging from a word, a cliché, a convention to the most hermetic verbal and visual configurations. As soon as mind, sentiment, and situation are expressed, they must come to the surface; they must emerge in the form of perceptible elements. Depths of feeling are suggested by their referents; a referent can only lead back to the depth, it cannot *be* depth. The secret is essentially betrayed by its outward manifestation. This exterior manifestation succeeds when its dynamics reflect the shape of inner qualities, most specifically through the processes of metaphor, paradox, irony, perhaps even ambiguity. The movement on the surface of the page or canvas or screen and the contexts and structures of words, shapes, and images relate to the core of the experience. They remain outside, they are tangible, but their palpability need not denature the unsayable (what defies articulation). Great art lets us know that the depths exist. It testifies to the importance of the secrets.

In the preceding chapters I have related silent films to the same category of style as pantomime, ballet, and opera. They all radically alter the modes of human discourse. Silent films are theatrical since they operate with a semblance of verisimilitudinous human encounter. Yet their filmic stylization is intensified by the absence of voice. The face and body take on the added work of the voice, and hopefully, expressivity does not turn them into semaphors. The best silent films are not superficial, but they do pay homage to the fact that we perceive surface, not depth. A surface projected on a screen is a surface of infinite nuance that, in the manner of some verbal structures, has intimations of great areas beneath it. The degree of emotional exteriorization and the plastique verging on the acrobatic that mark the style of Lillian Gish show the variety and depth that silent screen acting achieves through the full acceptance by actress and director of what can be indicated on the surface.

Garbo's surface was, logically, that aspect of her being that was most successfully exploited during her silent years. The Garbo cinematograph is quite distant from Gish's back-lit, haloed, soft-focus emblem of long-suffering female. Whether as Lucy with her head on the Yellow Man's pillow (*Broken Blossoms*), or the becowled nun in *The White Sister,* or Mimi in love and dying (*La Bohème*), Lillian Gish, in stasis, has a moral quality, a burden of sincerity and thought, a meaning, and a sense of character that can be articulated and translated. She *is* virtue, she *is* sacrifice, she *is* love in these cameolike close-ups. The shots of her in movement are related to the situations on both a literal and metaphorical level. Gish is always acting something, even at her most abstract and beautiful.

Garbo has few opportunities to "act something" in her silent films. (Many would argue that this is also true of her talkies, but the words impose their leaden reality and create an illusion of subject matter. Audiences believe words more than images.) She *is,* but *is* more frequently in relation to photographic contexts than to recognized or felt states of being. Her better roles in talkies will lead the public toward the recesses of her imagination. With a few notable exceptions to be discussed later on, the silent films exploit her spatial possibilities, the ways she inhabits environments and invests them with her presence; she requalifies herself in the process, and, most important, makes us blissfully aware that we are observing. Garbo tunes our eyes to perceive her as a filmed object.

FIRST IMPRESSIONS

Even the many senseless Garbo silents find ways to promote and enhance our contemplation of the actress. The plots are without pretense of nuance and sophistication, the situations are dictated by the tritest set of conventions. *The Torrent* (1926) and *The Temptress* (1926) share their *T*s, a flood, and in each a hero vainly attempts to resist Garbo's charms. These films differ in many details and exhibit quite singular delights, but I suspect that the MGM story department had little to do with the variations. Yet Garbo does not simply play the vamp in these silent films; they do offer her some opportunities to extend her range as actress. Their greatest value lies, however, in their ability to show her off, as if they were constantly varying lenses and points of view, endowing her with a priority of visual essence, and to which she responds with increasing freedom and pertinence.

Usually in a film's first shot of the heroine, there is a measure of standard star treatment in the effort to give visual impact to the leading lady's screen "entrance." But in Garbo's case often the mechanism is intricate and extends well into the body of the film.

The opening sequence in *The Temptress* is among the more elaborate. It was shot by her mentor, Mauritz Stiller, and the attention he lavishes on her is certainly one of the causes for his dismissal from the film. But he leaves us no doubt about the magic of the star and the eventfulness of her apparition, which were only intermittent qualities in her principal European films, *The Saga of Gösta Berling* (1924) and *Die freudlose Gasse* (1925). Even her first American film, *The Torrent*, hardly establishes the Garbo presence at first glance. The demure Spanish girl is undoubtedly attractive as she sings with the birds in her garden.

But we need bistros, opera stage, moonlit nights, and a flood before we can have the emergence of a face that has acquired an intrinsic value; we see it outlined by darkness and an enormous fur collar in the film's final shot.

In *The Temptress* she is both offered and withheld. Stiller tantalizes us as he leads Garbo through a series of configurations that are designed to endow her with visual importance. He forces the viewer to want to see her—to make seeing a process that requires active and creative participation. She is like some beautiful animal dimly perceived in the forest, she is pursued and finally captured. Garbo is the boon.

She first appears in silhouette, standing in a box overlooking an elaborately staged masked ball.

Stiller dwells on the revelers for their picturesque qualities. (Orgies were quite the thing in 1926.) And the confusion provides a richly textured context for Garbo as she flees from the box and her lover, only to find herself caught in the swirl of dancers.

Grabbed by a masked devil, she breaks away again. The framing pillars single her out in the foreground, extracting her from the general pattern of massed dancers in the background.

She is caught and released again and again; she eludes our grasp as well. Surrounded by other merrymakers on the lawn, she is then rescued by the hero, Antonio Moreno, and when they are alone, he contemplates the masked lady. As he comes close to her we see that her mask is the laciest, skimpiest one imaginable, so singularly flimsy as to call attention to the very concept of mask.

The frenetic activity is now arrested and concentrated in the triple observation, that is, Garbo seen through the multiple optic of Moreno, the camera lens, and our eyes. She is thus magnified, and the revelation is worthy of the effort to perceive it. At the hero's insistence she removes the mask.

A shot of Moreno's reaction extends the tease. The unmasking is prolonged until she finally raises her eyelids.

The phases are many: the silhouette, the ball, the devil, the lawn dancers, the distant masked figure, and finally the mask itself. They lead us to a secret. The surface of the image is not betrayed by making it profound nor by providing conceptual space below it. It is rendered essential by the space above it—a space to be traversed through our active, heightened awareness of objects.

None of Garbo's subsequent screen entrances aspires to the complexity of that in *The Temptress,* but even her most pedestrian directors find some gimmick to give her a special character signaling the audience that it is about to witness something splendid. Fred Niblo, who took over direction of *The Temptress* from Stiller, even fabricates a second entrance for her when she arrives in South America to further "tempt" the hero—her carriage door opens, a foot and ankle appear, etc. This tired commonplace works marvelously for Joan Crawford in *Rain* (1932) because it is done with a panache that belies its age. Here, it is justified only by the vamp aspect of Garbo's temptress, and is much less interesting than the ploys of the film's first sequences.

The brief establishing shots in Garbo's next two films will exploit the most important elements of *The Temptress*. In *Flesh and the Devil* (1927), alighting from a train, she materializes before the hero's eyes

(so nicely reprised in 1935 in *Anna Karenina*),

and in *Love* (1927), she is veiled in a snow-storm, and then unveils at the inn where she has taken refuge with Vronsky.

Shots of her racing her car in *A Woman of Affairs* (1929), or laughing in a cab in *Wild Orchids* (1929), or sitting in a museum with Conrad Nagel in *The Kiss* (1929) scarcely measure up as engrossing perceptual events. It was Fred Niblo's *The Mysterious Lady* (1928) that most remarkably granted to Garbo's first appearance the qualities of wonder, discovery, and raptness that seem to be the best justification for stardom.

The sequence owes some debt to Mauritz Stiller's setups in *The Temptress.* The opera/theatre box will often be a frame for Garbo, with its dual point of view—seeing and being seen. (Important situations in the talkies, *Anna Karenina* and *Camille,* 1937, also use this device.) In *The Mysterious Lady,* Garbo is not simply observed by an adoring pair of men's eyes (Conrad Nagel's), but she increases the powers of eyes as she intently focuses her own on a performance of Puccini's opera, *Tosca.*

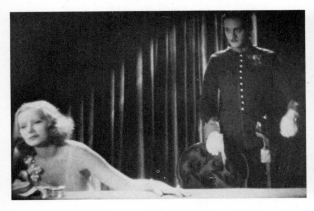 

The shifting point of view in these shots is manneristic, forcefully making us conscious of observing first Nagel looking at Garbo looking at the stage, then of our looking over their shoulders. *Tosca* is a pretext, and although we may be thankful for MGM's largesse in providing shots of the stage, the true spectacle is Garbo, the spectator in the box. The profile shot leaves no doubt about that.

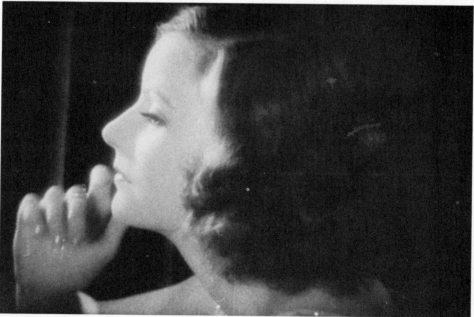

Her eyes are mirrors, reflecting back to our own, but taking their source of primal intensity from those of the object itself. This sequence restates the subject-object relationship by concentrating both factors in Garbo's gaze. There is no clearer reminder in any of her films that observation is our first duty. The observation per se is elicited by the beauty at the frame's center; our conscious manipulation of the observation, as we sort out the various mirrors, fixes the beauty as part of a process that is ceaselessly alive in the multiple reflections. No other Garbo film so quickly and profoundly sums up the value of her screen presence in an opening sequence. She will make striking entrances but, never again, find a device to equal the pose and glance of her own looking.

THE TIME OF SIGHT

The Mysterious Lady pursues the qualities so remarkably worked out in its opening. It is the type of vehicle that persistently draws our attention to the actress as image rather than enactor. The absurdity of its plot is no hindrance to the film's value, since the value is in Garbo seen in movement. She appropriately supplies a particular brand of screen acting, even if those aspects of acting we normally recognize—registering of emotion, trueness to life—are largely absent. She responds to the flatness of this vehicle, whereas her characteristic style in other films would unbalance the grossly synthetic situations of *The Mysterious Lady*. These situations are merely contexts for her visual presence; they provide a duration for the perusal of that presence. The film sustains the Garbo surface through constant reorganization of its elements in a kind of prismatic effect that Josef von Sternberg also understood so well and used in his films with Marlene Dietrich. The plot similarities between Dietrich's *Dishonored* (1931) and *The Mysterious Lady* are obvious, yet they are less significant than the formal relationship between this particular Garbo film and the Dietrich vehicles from *Morocco* (1930) through *The Devil Is a Woman* (1935). Fred Niblo's invention and eye did not begin to match Sternberg's, but the veils, candles and various other devices that will be used to qualify the Dietrich image are amply present first in *The Mysterious Lady*.

The sequence following the opera encounter reinforces the manner of Garbo's exposure. Nagel accompanies her to her door, she enters and flips the light switch.

Clearly, she is not alone. A bust in the doorway shares the shaft of light, and this is the first of the Garbo/statue combinations, which will be capped in *Inspiration* (1931), *Mata Hari* (1932), and *The Painted Veil* (1934). (See pp. 134, 174–175.) Here, the space delimited by the radical framing light exhibits two art objects. One happens to be a live movie star. The bust is on its pedestal; Garbo's opera box is still a vivid memory for the viewer.

Nagel is then invited in, and the inevitable seduction recalls the opera performance. He just happens to play a sexy Puccini, and Garbo's silent vocal cords, so expertly tested in *The Torrent*, again come to her aid. These devices have some bearing on what passes for plot development in *The Mysterious Lady*, but they also put Garbo in another kind of spotlight, in a private *Tosca* so to speak.

The performance is interrupted when the lights begin to go on and off, and eventually stay off. Again, a peculiar lighting effect freshly defines the familiar object. In the climax of this sequence, Garbo lights a candelabrum. She now furnishes her own illumination, just as, in the opera box, her eyes supplied the key to vision. Slowly lighting the candles, she figuratively sets her face ablaze in the final close-up and draws us back to her eyes.

This is all supposed to be a plot to lure Conrad Nagel, an army officer, into her clutches. He is undone, but the allurement extends to the spectator, who is trapped by those craftily lit mirrors and led to savor the satisfactions of this object, at once whole and fleeting, that carries with it frames and lights and challenges our ability to preserve in our consciousness its perpetual reconstitution.

The remainder of the film relies on extravagant hairdos, costumes, and situations to sustain the image. Garbo sings to Nagel's accompaniment twice more, and one rendition employs the fillip of his desire to strangle her (no, not because of her rotten singing but because of her theft of his military secrets) superimposed on her confident chirping.

The *Tosca* situation is drawn into the film's dénouement even though, during Garbo's second recital, she "mysteriously" sings "Ocha Chornya." She kills her Scarpia to save her Mario, but one-ups Tosca in melodrama. To allay suspicion, she sits on the edge of the dead man's chair and drapes his arm on hers.

The opera stage of the film's opening sequence is transformed into the villain's study, the open door is Garbo's proscenium. That extraordinary dress, its schizoid shape in lace and fabric hiding and revealing at the same time, is her costume; the "frizzies" are her counterpart of stage makeup, and the involuntary necrophilia is a sublime bit of play acting. The film's sense is realized as Garbo passes from witnessing a stage *Tosca* to amorously disporting herself with a dead man.

Sidney Franklin's *Wild Orchids* (1929) affords Garbo her most interesting series of visual contexts. Its order of invention is such that the film becomes a set of variations on a theme in an exotic mode, the theme being Garbo. I have scrupulously avoided discussing the intentions of her directors, for they were probably quite distinct from what we now perceive on the screen. Yet in the case of *Wild Orchids*, a film in which only three actors are credited, and two are clearly supportive of the leading lady, the purpose is clear. The vehicle is hers. As such, it makes small demands on her capacity to suggest interior states, or to make her feelings apparent. Yet it celebrates, with particular fascination, her objectness, and her capacity to render that aspect of being.

The first important sequence uses the telescopic space of an ocean liner's corridor. Garbo, striding down straight to the camera, is interrupted by a Javanese prince whipping his servant.

The corridor and the whipping are peculiar enough to command our attention and prepare us for the close-up of Garbo's reaction, which is a mixture of curiosity and revulsion that adds an unfamiliar version of her extraordinary features to our collection.

The frame-filling fur collar and the diagonal set of her cloche thrust the face upon us. Garbo clearly knows the degree of expression that will convey the situation without seriously jeopardizing the arrangement of her face, which we always perceive in its formal repeatability. The scene's sadism is intensified by the all-conquering close-up of the leading man, Nils Asther.

The sexuality is less simple-minded than that of this often-reproduced scene from *The Temptress*, and considerably more integral to the structure of the film.

In the final episode the romantic triangle is subsumed in a tiger hunt. The triangle is a lopsided one. Nils Asther and Lewis Stone are among Garbo's most challenging co-stars, yet they never divert the film's attention away from the leading lady. For instance, the shot of her falling asleep and the ensuing sequence illustrate the director's singlemindedness. The frame is again rich in nuance; the sharply modified light gives full prominence to the actress's face as thoughts of the prince cross her mind. And again, Garbo's performance is governed by a sense of the measure that guarantees the integrity of her face as image.

The superimposition of Asther's face on her pillows is a bit of a shock, but it is not nearly so surprising as her awakening and her scream of fright.

There is but one other example of this amount of facial contortion in Garbo's career, and that is in *A Woman of Affairs* when she witnesses the suicide leap of her husband (John Mack Brown).

Garbo's two screen screams are silent ones, and the sudden loss of control they signal is uncharacteristic of her temperament and acting style. She was, in spite of the various approaches used to present her, an actress of reflection, of long durations, and one whose talent enabled her to sustain a legato line with a fineness and clarity that belied its length. The extended concentration on the actress prior to her scream in the pillow sequence is a prime instance of precisely that kind of span. The burst of violence is significant as a reminder of that which Garbo does *not* ordinarily do. Her personal style is alien to screams and other gestures of verisimilitudinous acting. The scream and the accident that prompts it are discordant to the sense of Garbo's screen personality. This sense belongs to processes of elucidation and synthesis, whether they are in the exotica of *Wild Orchids* or the sentiment of *Camille*. As even her poorest films and most unrewarding roles require from her little in the way of "plot" acting, so the scream of *Wild Orchids* is finally modulated in this typically Garboesque sequence: she goes to the bed of her husband (Lewis Stone) and seeks comfort in his arms and on his pillow.

This pre-Production-Code shot of connubiality restores repose, and, in a matter-of-fact way, restates the pillow motif with the variants of the husband and the age contrast. Garbo has been photographed supine in erotic scenes with all her leading men. It is something of a trademark. This shot is tender rather than erotic, and reveals the increasing awareness of her director and/or studio that their leading femme fatale can look ravishing, even when devampified in the arms of white-haired, blind husband. The next sequence, on a train bearing Garbo, Stone, and Asther to the prince's palace, completes the pillow motif. During Stone's absence, Garbo has fainted, and Asther raises her head, with the pillow behind it, to his.

Would-be lover has replaced blind husband; the face and its framing pillow are constant. The rather schematic relationships of the fiction are thus referenced in purely spatial terms.

Intimacy is but a prelude to the panache of Garbo's extension into the succeeding exotic boxlike frames. One rapidly follows another, fairly challenging our ability to redefine her in the shifting contexts: for instance, an interminable, servant-lined stairway leading to the palace,

and at the foot of an amusingly long (and tracked) banquet table (a commonplace in silent films, marvelously used in *The Temptress* where above-table formality and below-table shenanigans were juxtaposed),

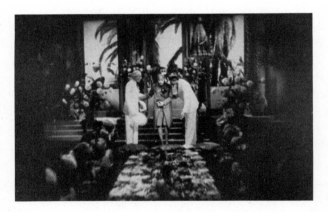

then in front of the primitive artificial downpour-air-conditioning system,

and, in one of the most inspired groupings in all of Garbo's films, where her particular movie-star pose is subtly ironized by the tiny handmaidens.

The mixture of symmetrically formal, exotic, and comic elements is pursued. The evening's entertainment is inevitably Javanese dancing, and Garbo, seated between two framing pillars as well as between Asther and Stone, is photographed from behind the native dancers. The final shot of the solo dancer's sinuosity opposing Garbo's own body diagonal and draped arm prepares for the film's most interestingly developed sequence.

Logically, the next step is the star's assumption of Eastern costume, merging two forms of exotica, Javanese and Garboese. The prince makes a gift of the dancer's costume she has just admired (instantly lengthened and enlarged by the four tiny maids, we must assume), and she dons it with great delight and much preening.

Even the dullest viewer must find this a peculiar sight. She has worn strange costumes before—those required by the operatic roles in *The Torrent* qualify as honest-to-goodness dressing-up, and her gowns in *The Mysterious Lady* are outlandish enough to belong in an opera. Yet the situation in *Wild Orchids* is more significant; it is the draping of the Garbo image. It supplies her with a willful transformation that goes beyond conventionalized costume wearing. It is as if Garbo has accepted a star's clothes-horse duty and integrated it into her stylistic uniqueness. Her "deep" acting metaphorizes emotional states; here, body is imagistic metaphor, and the process of the change can be witnessed through the filter of the actress's own awareness—her delight at being at the center of the process and her promptness in executing its intricacies.

From the brightness and the two mirrors in her dressing room, she passes to the darkness of her husband's room. The light comes up again, and the curtains of his bed become a proscenium for her preposterous native impersonation.

Stone's reaction is utterly appropriate, both to what he sees and to the unfolding of the sequence. "What in heaven's name have you got on? You look silly. Take off that stuff and go to bed." What in heaven's name *has* she got on? She does look silly in the dumb show between the bed curtains. Irony is the technique here for increasing our awareness of her superficiality. This is not simply a movie star in costume, but one who seems absurd in a costume. And then in an inspired transition, the camera pulls away and Garbo again takes to the shadows. First she is outlined in the doorway, then against the stones of the terrace.

Irony gives way to wonder, in fact it promotes wonder that something so exquisite could follow something so ludicrous. How right it all seems! The costume is made her own by the quietness with which it is now worn in the depth of the shadows. Then, when she reaches the area of the terrace directly opposite the prince's room, the plot, the decor, the costume, and the actress suddenly make perfect sense.

This time the prince is preceded by his long shadow instead of a cowering slave. Asther and the camera close in from different angles on that glistening object that is desired and fondled by all sets of eyes. Mirrors, curtains, portal, terrace, and shadow have provided the dynamics of focus that now gives Garbo the right to the costume, and us the power to seize her image in it as a paradigm for her essential presence. The exotic has lost its coefficient of distance and is integrated into the way we *must* perceive the actress.

This film is tireless in searching out revelatory contexts for Garbo, such as her stocking being removed while she, wrapped in a native shawl, is seated;

then, saronged, she is frozen backwards in a doorway;

then she is part of a shadow in a window, restoring sight to her blind husband.

She is seen in a pukka, by campfire light, in a tent, half out of a tent in the arms of Nils Asther, running through the jungle, and, finally, restored to her original self, declaring love for her husband after all, but wearing a hat whose ebb and flow prove that Garbo fits in the center of any frame.

The very subject of *Wild Orchids* is an extension of the visuality imposed on the viewer through these insistent framings and placements. Its plot can finally be expressed in terms of vision and acuity: the husband is unable to *see* his wife until she acquires individuality, until she escapes from her conventional, wifely identity; the prince, whose riveting glance is a correlative for sexual aggression, seeks to destroy the woman with his eyes. It is significant that the husband begins to see his wife when she appears to him as an image, silhouetted in a window. His eyes can finally apprehend the fullness and complexity of her visual self when, in the final shots, she is framed by that particularly dynamic hat, an image that completes the series of configurations that account for the interest of *Wild Orchids*.

Garbo's final silent film, Jacques Feyder's interesting, perhaps overrated, *The Kiss* (1929), never seeks resonance beneath the actress/object. The twice-enacted murder sequence, photographed from a radically different angle in each case, is the raison d'être of the film, and it constitutes a cinematization of creative perception.

Garbo, however, is fully exploited in only a few scenes: in an Art Deco study,

in a witness box, where she is sporting widow's weeds and a tricorne,

in certainly the best final clinch of all her films, her face is severely outlined by Conrad Nagel's shoulder and head.

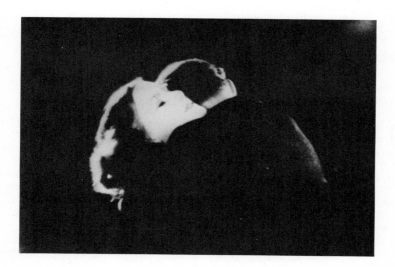

(*As You Desire Me,* 1937, is so shabbily made that it commits the cardinal sin of thrusting Melvyn Douglas in front of her during their last embrace.)

Yet Feyder, despite his smartness in rendering the film's ambiguities, neglects his star's most arcane plasticity.

Feyder and Clarence Brown were reputedly Garbo's favorites, but only Fred Niblo in *The Mysterious Lady* and Sidney Franklin in *Wild Orchids* fully extended her exteriority in silent films. Perhaps it was because they understood that merely to watch Garbo on the screen is a film event, per se.[1]

THE OBJECT TRANSCENDED

Garbo's silent film acting is not confined to her breathtaking plastique. The introspection, patience, and reflectiveness that characterize her style were already developed before 1930, even though these facets of her art were rarely required. Paradoxically, it is these several opportunities in her first films, without the heavenly distraction of her voice, that afford us the clearest perusal of her technique. The inflections of her body sustain a degree of scrutiny that leads us to the discovery of mechanics of silent screen acting reminiscent of Lillian Gish's most exalted moments.

Edmund Goulding, so attuned to this actress's possibilities in *Grand Hotel* (1932), guided her through her first full-fledged Garbo performance in *Love* (1927). Flashes of insight in the earlier films are embryonic: laughter and tears, on learning that her lover will not follow her to America in *The Torrent,*

[1] Otis Ferguson, particularly inspired by Garbo's performance in *Camille,* describes this very quality in *The Film Criticism of Otis Ferguson,* p. 171: "But the gauge of Miss Garbo as this or any other figure may be taken from her command of the screen in her first tranquility, before an explicit relation with the audience has been built up or the action has provided for revelation by word or gesture. It is more than the distant shimmer of beauty, or a resonant husky voice, or a personal dignity wide enough for the demands of both humility and arrogance. It is more than can be measured in any of the dimensions through which we receive it, because sound waves and planes of light are only a medium of reflection for the regions of the spirit concerned here. Greta Garbo has the power of projecting not only the acting moods of a play but the complete image of her own person; and seeing her here, one realizes that this is more than there are words for, that it is simply the most absolutely beautiful thing of a generation."

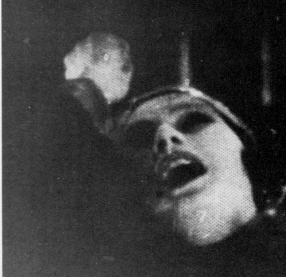

tough cynicism at an unwelcome invitation to desist from tempting in *The Temptress*.

But her most famous silent vehicle, *Flesh and the Devil* (1927), shows off bad acting that must be blamed on the poor direction of Clarence Brown. The love scenes smolder; the shared cigarette and communion cup still preserve their erotic flavor;

yet there is no excuse for the unrelieved caricatural vamping.

Her husband confronts her and her lover (John Gilbert) *in flagrante* and the best response she can manage is to bite her lips.

An outburst of hysteria results in an embarrassing case of the shakes.

Her performance is stereotypical, and the visual appeal is lessened by unflattering camera angles.

Goulding's *Love* (1927), a version of Tolstoy's novel *Anna Karenina,* released the same year as *Flesh and the Devil,* is definitely the product of a different mind. The material is congenial to Garbo. (She is ill at ease in roles that call for evil ways. All her roles are sympathetic from *Love* through the end of her career. Her monumental perfidy in *Mata Hari,* 1932, which forced Ramon Novarro to blaspheme, is amply redeemed by the final hospital and prison scenes.) Her opportunities in *Love* are varied, and if they sometimes lack her later restraint, freshness is a good swap for super-cool.

Anna Karenina's reaction to Vronsky's racing accident permits us to compare early and mature Garbo. In the silent version she is extroverted, revealing her anguish to the other spectators.

A trifle overdone? The same situation in Clarence Brown's 1935 talkie version of *Anna Karenina* is certainly understated, but to a degree that leads us to wonder whether the actress was suffering from a mild case of indigestion instead of concern for her fallen lover.

The situations in Goulding's *Love* expand, finding a breadth appropriate to Garbo's power to sustain our concentration. The film is wildly unfaithful to the Tolstoy original, changing the period and whitewashing the hero. Vronsky never falls out of love with Anna; she sends him off to his regiment and then commits a sacrificial suicide. (The most widely known print of the film even has a happy ending—Anna and Vronsky are reunited after Karenin's death.)

In 1935 Clarence Brown will give us views of Kitty, Levin, Dolly, and the end of love, but he truncates all of it, and especially Garbo's ability to respond. There are practically no love scenes in the talkie, and the best elements of *Anna Karenina* run a poor second to their counterparts in *Love*. For instance, while riding in a gondola with her Vronsky, Fredric March, Garbo sees some Italian children and becomes a bit disconsolate; instantly the lovers decide to return to Russia and Sergei, Anna's son.

But in *Love,* as she picnics with John Gilbert, Italian children pass by, and what a look she gives!

Eyes are extended into gesture when she stops one of the children and caresses his face in a prefiguration of the scene she will play with Sergei upon her return to Russia.

Her eyes are re-creating the child's face, making it that of her own son. After the child's departure, we see Garbo's dejection, and the first full-blown instance of the mask that became her hallmark.

In *Love*, the presence of a camera and the duration of a shot provide texture and time for thinking. Garbo withdraws into herself but truly shows more of that self than when going through the obvious motions of acting. She makes films a contemplative art. (How appropriate she would have been to the shot durations of Ingmar Bergman's *Persona* or Michelangelo Antonioni's *L'Avventura*.) Her contemplation is integrated into the love scene,

and only then do Anna and Vronsky decide to leave Italy.

In both versions Garbo's most torrid lovemaking is directed toward her child. In the talkie it is virtually her only lovemaking. And both directors relish the pathetic situation of a mother's return to the son she so reluctantly abandoned. In fact, in Clarence Brown's rendering of the novel, it is the only scene that offers Garbo the kind of exposure upon which she thrives. These scenes follow the same pattern in both films, and it would be unkind to cavil at the deficiencies of the talkie. Yet the comparison elucidates the fullness of Garbo's style in 1927.

Goulding captures her anxiety with a composition that thrusts her eyes into sharp relief as she enters the room.

He gives her still more time as she sets up toy trains for the sleeping child. Then Sergei (Philippe de Lacy) sees her before she realizes it—before her love is transferred from the toy to the child.

In Brown's later version, the hysteria prior to the meeting is undeniably effective—the servants are perturbed, Garbo strides nervously to the child's room. The physical embraces are similar, yet the mother-son embrace in *Love* benefits from the interruption with the toy, which concentrates the tension to allow it to mount even higher.

The erotic element is stronger in *Love;* Philippe de Lacy takes Garbo's face in his hands as a lover might, and she answers with abandon. Freddy Bartholomew, in the later version, merely pats Mommy's face.

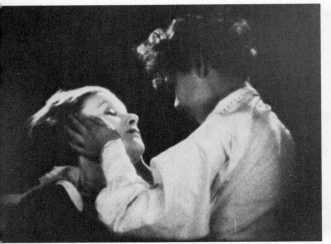 

In *Love*, the Goulding version, when Garbo is banished from the child's room, she confronts her husband with an expression of sadness, deprivation, and helplessness that avoids the chill of the analogue in *Anna Karenina*.

Clarence Brown resolves the sequence with some amount of class, as Garbo ignores the berating Basil Rathbone (one of his most felicitous performances—he avoids the trap of making Karenin wholly loathsome). The camera, in one shot, follows Garbo down the stairs and out of the house, with husband always clearly delineated in the background. That purposeful walk is acting of a high order.

Goulding's overt approach, with its greater emotional demands on Garbo, tests us as well. Garbo's face is the vehicle of feeling. The more her features are observed, the more eloquent they become. The image acquires depth through the profundity of sentiment and the ability of the actress and the director to locate those beautiful features in configurations that are the external sum of life and the most faithful reflection of its dimensions.

The strangest paradox of Garbo's silent career is A *Woman of Affairs* (1929), a film that is botched in almost all of its details by the ubiquitous Clarence Brown. Still, it contains the sequence that, prior to *Grand Hotel* (1932), most eloquently showcases the actress and arguably ranks among the finest moments of her entire canon. There is no distinction to be made between the style she uses in this sequence and her later work in talkies. All of it was there in 1929 and it blossoms despite the inexpert hand of her director, whose contribution is well characterized by the blankness of John Gilbert, the mugging of Douglas Fairbanks, Jr., and the deadly dollying to symbolic objects that come from the "show and tell" school of direction for stagy compositions.

Garbo's performance, emerging whole from the dead weight of context, is perhaps the most compelling proof we have of her creativity, and the triumph of star over matter that carries her through the talkies.

Prior to THE sequence, there are several others of unusual interest, such as, the playful put-down of her hysterical brother (Douglas Fairbanks, Jr.),

her resignation, unblemished by self-pity, in the scene in which she feigns loose morals to hide her suicide husband's embezzlement,

or, contemplating the photograph of her former lover's wife without the slightest hint of jealousy, she includes in that glance self-awareness and areas of feeling that she has habitually reserved for her relationship to objects.

An object elicits the most significant span of her silent film acting:[2] lying ill in a Parisian clinic, she fondles a bouquet sent by ex-lover John Gilbert, simultaneously conveying possession and loss. The flowers are hers—her composure grants them presence and remembrance as the perfect surrogate, possessing intrinsic value as well as metaphoric transference back through the actress's eyes.

When she dozes, the bouquet is removed and placed in the anteroom, where, in the meantime, John Gilbert and his wife have arrived. Clarence Brown mercifully concentrates on Garbo in the ensuing scene, keeping the reaction shots of the other characters to a minimum. He provides her ample space to occupy. The framing elements and time span of the shots contain the actress rather than distracting from her with his usual cramping and chopped-up effects.

Garbo emerges from her room in despair over the disappearance of her flowers. The master shot has spatially rearranged the heroine and the bouquet of the previous sickroom scene, establishing a distance to be traversed and a chance for the link to be renewed, indeed redefined.

[2] Details of this, and many other crucial scenes in Garbo's films are evoked in Richard Corliss's excellent book, *Greta Garbo*.

The medium close-ups show a mixture of delirium and conscious anguish that are related to the sequence's immediate development and to the essential metaphoric process. Garbo is aware that the flowers are gone; Garbo in a fevered state grants belief to their real power.

Love and roses are identical for Garbo as they are for Herrick and Ronsard. The actress's apparent loss of control is a signal so rare in her acting that it carries an extra measure of conviction, conferring on the flowers their privileged status. They belong to an existence in which they are not ornamental but are necessary to the very continuance of that existence. This is the function of the deconventionalized metaphor, and just as Renaissance poets managed to keep their roses fresh, Garbo invests hers with a life as vibrant as her own.

Brown's shots of the actress's field of vision and the superimposition of the magnified vase are gratuitous.

The situation and the intensity of Garbo's glance make abundantly clear what she
is looking at, and the above shot only interrupts the crescendo as she reassumes
the metaphor.

The world is bounded by actress and object, and their conjunction is emblematic of vitality, life, breath itself. As Garbo approaches, she invests the
flowers with all the energy lodged in her eyes, abolishing spatial distance, and
more significantly, the distance between people and things.

Yes, the bouquet is a particularly delicious frame for the actress's face, but the depth of that face is plumbed. The intentness of Garbo's progress and the completeness of her embrace establish a new entity, a union of depth and surface so thorough that distinctions between the two are impossible. The frame we see, suffused with actress and flowers and lit by a conviction at the base of Garbo's imagination, is unalterable. There is room for nothing more. The actress has created the matrix.

The series of expressions that follow, ranging from utter relief at having regained her life to panic at the thought of losing the flowers again, and to two kinds of hysteria, give the sequence a fluidity and pulse that are particularly fitting to the medium. The transitions, the organic and spontaneous nature of this epiphany, are only imperfectly captured in the frame enlargements.

The eloquence of her face diverts attention from details such as the position of her body, and most particularly her left hand, which is constantly modulating the reaction, and in the third of the series, demonstrating quite palpably how to hold on to life.

When Garbo abandons the flowers for John Gilbert, she miraculously finds yet new ways of looking, of focusing her gaze. The man and the metaphor awaken different realms of her being and her face is radically altered.

The line of her mouth is another key to her transformation. She exhibits a sentimental response pertinent to her feelings for Gilbert, to his social presence.

She gracefully executes the remainder of the sequence—the embrace, her joy, her realization that Gilbert's wife is watching, and gallant acceptance of her situation—and brings us down from the peak without a jolt.

A dramatic order of plot and recognizable theatricality has been reestablished. The poetic order, a fusion of actress and flowers—by definition a thing of heady tension—had to give way. For John Gilbert, Garbo merely wears the face of an extravagantly beautiful woman in love. In the business with the flowers nothing so specific as love animates her, but a power welling from the source of life. That face is reserved for the flowers alone. It is relieved of sex, men, actors, directors. Garbo proves that objects know more than people, that they can accept depths of meaning intolerable to the order of sociality imposed by the presence of others. Garbo's career—her playing to things—is a reflection of this understanding. The logical outcome is her response to the object most constant in her world and most essential to her being—the camera lens. For it she reserves the truth.

6.
Grusinskaya's Room: Drawing In

Garbo as ballerina seems as appropriate as Garbo as opera singer (*Romance,* 1930), carnival kootch girl (*Susan Lenox,* 1931), Balinese dancer (*Mata Hari,* 1932), and night club chanteuse (*As You Desire Me,* 1932). Five (including *Grand Hotel,* 1932) of la Garbo's first seven talkies display her as a performer. No less was expected of Continental leading ladies. Dietrich rarely emerges from the cabaret, and Anna Sten made her debut in *Nana* (1934)—Goldwynized—leaning against a lamppost, pitifully trying to light that familiar torch. (Anna Sten's voice would seem to bode a triumphant career in the world's music halls when measured against the grace of Garbo's terpsichorean exercises.) In *Grand Hotel* Garbo is exposed as never before. Her other lady-of-the-stage portrayals do not call for a stance, and a sense of body so wholly discordant to her esoteric self. Their theatrical activities are quickly established, and the main business is then pursued without digression. The embarrassing passes at Siva's statue during the first sequences of *Mata Hari* are not alluded to in the rest of the film.

Her deep knee bends are particularly unforgettable (choreographed by Louis B. Mayer himself, no doubt), but they do not impede her more characteristic march through bedrooms toward the firing squad at a pace suited to her body. As the opera singer she is at first heard (dubbed) but not seen, and then during a staging of *Martha* near the film's end, she is replaced by a stand-in. The substitution is supremely obvious, and it is a shameful loss if we remember Garbo's Carmen and Mélisande in *The Torrent* (see pp. 91–92) and her repeated silent singing of *Tosca* in *The Mysterious Lady* (see pp. 99–101). During the single café sequence in *As You Desire Me,* the audience within the film observes an act that we cannot see. The spatial limits in *Grand Hotel* spare us Grusinskaya's on-stage Odette-Odile, but even Garbo, usually so disdainful of the banalities of verisimilitude, accepts a degree of ballerina impersonation—we see the tension of her arms, wrists, and back; she turns around her room to express joy; she rises en pointe to reveal her utter lassitude.

A dancer's body is always with her, and Garbo's efforts toward consistently altering her posture are justified. But they are not correct. She cannot impersonate away her physical bigness that verges on gawkiness, and the curve of her back and shoulder, the caved-in look. For that intimate relationship to the ground she treads, so dominant in her style, she would have been banished from the barre. Garbo as a dancer is something of a joke, one of the few that was appreciated by the creators of *Two-Faced Woman* (1941). She *can* manage the "Chica-Choca." (Her grace in the ballroom sequence of *Anna Karenina* is, however, less of a surprise than the remarkable verve of the sequence itself in a film characterized by somnambulism.)

Garbo in a relatively brief role in an all-star omnibus is even more disconcerting than is her ballerina manquée. After *Anna Christie* (1930) her early talkies obsessively concentrate on her face and body, almost to the exclusion of production values and/or leading men. She carries lopsided burdens on those wide, sloping shoulders—for instance, the absurdly miscast Gavin Gordon starring in a film for the first and last time in his career,

and a particularly tacky series of sets and costumes in *Romance*, or a visibly uncomfortable Clark Gable, and the murkiest of scripts in *Susan Lenox*, or another poor script and a fading Ramon Novarro in *Mata Hari*. *As You Desire Me* was released in the same year as *Grand Hotel* and reverted to the MGM pattern for Garbo—one or two carefully shot scenes and an insecure leading man— Melvyn Douglas unintentionally comic having a go at the grand romantic manner.

Even Erich von Stroheim seems out of sorts, his accent on again, off again in the most unpredictable way. The Italian villa in which they disport themselves is unattractive, shabby, and clearly more appropriate to Hedda Hopper's acting in the film than to Greta Garbo's.

Garbo's salary obviously devoured most of these productions' budgets. Miraculously, she manages to salvage minutes, even whole sequences, despite the unflattering contexts, and to develop a manner born of desperation.

Grand Hotel represents MGM's attempt to repackage their product. If one star pulls in ten customers, five stars ought to attract fifty. The formula will be repeated almost without variation in *Dinner at Eight* (1933). (To appreciate the importance of Goulding to *Grand Hotel* one must compare him with George Cukor, who in *Dinner at Eight* had not yet developed all the gifts of visual grace that were eventually to make him a superb director of stars in general and Garbo in particular.) In *Dinner at Eight* the male stars, John Barrymore, Lionel Barrymore, and Wallace Beery, remain constant, and the substitution of Jean Harlow for Joan Crawford in the plebeian role is no surprise. Marie Dressler for Greta Garbo now seems supremely appropriate, given the sympathy of their performances together in *Anna Christie*.

This new context would appear to function contrary to the special qualities of Garbo's talent. From the inflection of her voice to the odd way her neck, arms, and legs are connected to her torso, she scarcely merges into a preconceived design. Indeed, in most of her films, the design is exclusively hers; Gavin Gordon and the others make feeble or frantic attempts to find their places.

Their lack of success destroys these films' integrity, but Garbo's contribution is not completely jeopardized. Ultimately her partner was William Daniels who was responsible for the photography in all but five of her American pictures. Although his support in the duet sometimes faltered, the camera at least shows her off to best advantage, right at the center of her self-generated pattern.[1]

Grusinskaya in *Grand Hotel* is only one of five principal roles, and it is the shortest in duration. The problem of fitting Garbo into the ensemble is averted since the only other star she is seen with is John Barrymore. Furthermore, the mechanics of character introductions establishes Garbo's singularity—the three male stars appear in the opening scene, calling from identical telephone booths, their conversations intercut at decreasing intervals; Joan Crawford's entrance is the culmination of the film's most complicated shot, which includes the largest number of characters and announces her relationship to John and Lionel Barrymore and, less directly, to Wallace Beery. Garbo, however, is first seen alone, her face practically buried in bedclothes. The film does pretend to have a life of its own, distinct from Garbo's. She may hide in her bedclothes; but as Lewis Stone ironically says, "Grand Hotel—people coming, going. Nothing ever happens." Crawford dances with Lionel Barrymore. Beery shoots John Barrymore. And Garbo? How will this ill-proportioned ballerina survive the weight of those minutes during which she has been absent, not even hovering at the edge of the frame about to make an entrance? A role so suited to her temperament is completely alien to her physique, and its structure differs from those she is used to portraying. Yet these alien qualities draw from her a performance that guarantees the film's survival.

Grand Hotel's opening scenes posit the formal elements pertinent to its locale and its star. The film resists the temptation to "open up" and relishes its fixed form. The enclosure of space is essential to Garbo's Grusinskaya, the character most circumscribed by her room, wanting so often to be alone in it. Her final exit from the lobby to greet the sun is a stunning gesture of liberation from the room, the hotel. In *Grand Hotel*, Garbo renders the drawing in and the emerging, embodying an identity of performance and space.

In the specific setting of the Grand Hotel the telephone is the most characteristic means of communication.

[1] Daniels himself makes some not very enlightening remarks about photographing Garbo in Charles Higham, *Hollywood Cameramen: Sources of Light*, pp. 67–72.

(A phone is ultimately used as the murder weapon.) No one uses the phone more often or more effectively than Garbo. The phone abolishes the interlocutor—the camera is relieved of the burdensome action-reaction shots as it frames the solo performer. Actresses such as Luise Rainer (*The Great Ziegfeld,* 1936), Geraldine Page (*Sweet Bird of Youth,* 1962), and Liza Minnelli (*The Sterile Cuckoo,* 1969) glory in the convention's egotism. With shots of operators and phone booths, the telephone mode, so appropriate to Grusinskaya's moral and physical aloneness and to Garbo's technique as an actress, is given priority among the various styles of the film.

Hotel atmosphere is exploited in the initial lobby sequences. The area of public encounter tunes our perception of faces. The complexities of a lengthy lobby shot accumulate the actors; the camera sweeps back and forth, locating them in shifting positions. Lewis Stone is the key—the cynical doctor whose face is horribly scarred, the permanent resident of the Grand Hotel who opens and closes the film. His self-consciousness about disfigurement underscores the Barrymores' first exchanges.

The camera then thrusts to a revolving door, where Joan Crawford's face shocks us—all smooth skin, razor-thin eyebrows (à la Garbo)—each feature has an identity of its own, so sharp is the delineation.

The white furbelow on her black dress and her black cloche provide clear boundaries, but it is the time of the whole shot, the activity and the quality of the components that give Crawford's face its power, or rather, give us the power to grasp it. The attention elicited will be useful in Grusinskaya's room, for if the exercises necessary to see Crawford are eye opening, those that Garbo commands are gauged by her own finesse. Scrutiny is imperative in both cases. Whatever one's opinion about their acting abilities, there is no doubt that the five movie stars in this film are equipped with starry faces.

The comings and goings, the quickness and brightness of it all, and then the drawing in to the faces culminate in the actress in Grusinskaya's darkened room that both the camera and we must seek out. In contrast to Crawford, who bursts into a lobby filled with movement, Garbo lifts her face from a satin sheet to catch the only light in the frame.

If *Grand Hotel*'s melodrama creaks, nevertheless its space is invested with the integrity of these actresses, and our apprehension of their faces is, by turns, promoted and increasingly refined.

The maid snaps on the light and Garbo is fully revealed—almost frighteningly —her hair pulled back severely from her forehead, her eyebrows stretched high leaving enormous space for the deeply creased lids.

"I've never been so tired in my life." The corners of her mouth are drawn down, but not quite to the tragic-mask depths Garbo reserves for utmost despair. The audience begins to suspect it is watching a Garbo mimic. The years of legend, the husky voice, and the broadness of gesture in this first sequence conspire to turn Garbo into what we feared—a being so conventionally an actress that there is room for no degree of invention. Getting out of bed, she arches her back and assumes poses that immediately show the incompetence of her ballerina impersonation. What remains is a generalization of her peculiarity: her body first buried in an enormous bed, then assuming extravagant postures.

She turns her upper torso into the next close-up, hugging herself and muttering in a most eccentric accent lines that never fail to provoke merriment: "So threadbare—the Russians—St. Petersburg—the Imperial Court—the Grand Duke Sergei." She looks up, her eyes widen:

"Sergei—dead." Her eyes close, her head droops: "Grusinskaya . . . All gone."

It would be hard for any actress to survive the weight of this opening scene with its numbing clichés, and an actress as personal and quirky as Garbo is particularly undermined. The exteriorization of the character practically excludes the Garbo version. She thrives on silence, the unsaid, the paradoxical, the ambiguous, but we are deafened by the Imperial Court and the Grand Duke who are, unfortunately, not "all gone."

Succumbing to someone's notion of a ballerina's sufferings, she voices an amateurish inflection on "I was frantic."

To describe the audience's reaction to her previous performance her hand supplies the commas for "I finished, I waited, I listened," and then flops down at her side on "but the applause didn't come." Garbo's imagination is absent from this hollow and stifling situation. The depressed ballerina makes ridiculous demands on her talent for understatement. While attempting to be true to the character, she is unfaithful to the core of her art.

An aspect of that art is revealed a moment later. The impressario, in an attempt to lure her to the theatre, lies to her, saying that all the tickets have been sold. She is a bit reassured; there are slight movements of the pupils of eyes, her eyebrows, her lips, and a flicker of thought on her face. This is the way she signals transition. The expression is not precise in indicating mood A or B. It exhibits movement per se, an almost imperceptible flutter that will eventually compose itself, but for the moment is all potential.

The landmarks of her face suddenly become vulnerable to change. Our familiarity with these landmarks is exploited, forcing a raptness consistent with her own.

The body, so weighted and fatigued, springs taut, and the contrast is sufficient to pardon any inauthenticity in the pseudodancer's posture. She is responding to a new body rhythm, now crisp and concentrated, as she nervously yet surely unfastens her robe.

Her height no longer seems a liability; her superiority of stature is one of her credentials as artist. The inwardness of depression has been transformed into the concentration of the ballerina who is already creating her performance before she leaves the hotel for the theatre. This is sustained as she strides down the hall.

Four elements are merged in this shot: (1) Garbo's stride is forceful but mechanical and unrelated to (2) her expression of concentration that is not interrupted (3) by her acknowledgments to admirers who line the corridor, nor (4) by her putting on her gloves. The continuity is broken by the obligatory Garbo/old lady/dog/child scene. (In at least half of her American films there are important episodes showing Garbo's tenderness to the aged, animals, or the young.)

After the performance, her initial depression is reprised. In her tutu, framed
by the doorway, she utters the now caricatural "I want to be alone," but with a
simplicity that challenges the clichés of temperament and deep despair.

In profile, in her unlikely swan queen outfit, she gently repeats the line, working
against the obvious elements of the situation and the kind of rhetoric that elicited
such a graceless "I was frantic" in her first scene.

In the cause of artiness she is seated on the floor to undo her ballet slippers.
She is the only lighted object in the frame, and the pretty pathos, as she caresses
and kisses each slipper, is trite.

Goulding does not linger on the effect. More disconcerting is the first shot of Garbo in her dressing gown; as she crosses the room to get a syringe, she shows much more leg than is wanted for suicide preparations.

Most of the subsequent shots are close enough to eliminate the bare knees, a singularly inappropriate bit of cheesecake.

Then follows the first of her telephone encounters, all of which are different and interesting. The telephone cuts off her space. It is a constant played against the variable of Garbo's face and body, and is finally transformed by her presence. Here, the camera tilts up to her, creating effective intermediate space for the phone.

"They didn't miss me at all." For a fraction of a second the phone is no longer a phone but is something upon which to cradle a face. "Goodnight, Pimenoff." Her eyes toward the ceiling, the phone is down in her hand. "They didn't even miss me." She has not hung up but uses the instrument to extend conversation into reverie, only to pick it up again and tell the operator that she has finished. An abrupt gesture will not do; the reverie continues as she twists the phone several times before putting it down.

The camera comes closer, the shadows on her face deepen, the framing hair is thrust into greater prominence to soften the sides of her brow. Ruminating on her future after she will leave the stage, she raises her face to receive all the light, saying, "What would she do—grow orchilds?—raise peacocks? . . . die." Her eyelids and the corners of her mouth sag.

The meeting with John Barrymore signals the disappearance of the ballerina pretext. She is relieved of that category of impersonation to concentrate on emotional states, their essential mechanics, their formal rendering in a physical context. Prey to anxiety, surprised at finding a man in her room, and interrupted in her suicide attempt, she looks at him as if to penetrate his face, but her body barely betrays her agitation. She makes a gesture for the phone, a requirement of probability in the script, but she does it so uncommittedly that the theatrics do not intrude on the personality of her playing. Her restraint and urbanity defy the conventions of this film, its style, and its epoch. She laughs nervously, cries a bit, pulls away from Barrymore, comes around the chaise longue, and sits down with her back to the camera. From a different angle a closer shot of her back, shoulders, and head also includes Barrymore, who asks "What on earth have they been doing to you?" She abruptly turns her profile into view facing his: "You must forgive me."

Gaining control of her body, she accepts her situation with infinite politeness and the least amount of fuss: "I have had a very trying evening. I was so alone. Suddenly you were there."

The context has been transcended by her ability to accept fully and to integrate any circumstance into her being—meeting an old lady as she is getting into an elevator, or seeing a strange man in her boudoir as she is contemplating suicide. Garbo's gift is not naturalness, but rather the power to make a whole range of events, from the utterly common to the utterly preposterous, extensions of her self.

The mysterious man in her room becomes something necessary, indeed, expected. The suddenness of his profession of love is no surprise to an audience attuned to the commonplaces of the genre. It is Garbo's reaction that transforms a stock situation, supplying it with a complexity, a richness, and a duration to which it has no birthright. Barrymore has refused to leave her room, and she seems strangely resigned, confused, but drained of nervousness and energy. To his "Oh, please let me stay" she reiterates, "I want to be alone," with that same gentleness and politeness of a moment before. During his pleadings, she turns her face three-quarters to the camera, and then the metamorphosis begins. It is not a set of grimaces, cliché masks that pass for expressions in acting, but the clearest graphics for ambiguity and change. The actress succeeds in summoning deepness to the surface of her face without betraying depth and without simply being murky. She finds a style pertinent to the wordless situation. Now, the face questions, presents a blank to be filled in and a receptivity to the voice that professes love.

Garbo's eyes widen, reaching up, searching for the alertness required by Barrymore's presence; the outline of the mouth becomes fuller and sharpens.

If an answer is not immediately to be found, she begins to entertain the possibility of its existence.

This face, unrelated to anything previous in her Grusinskaya, is exempt from script, and, I suspect, from direction. In the shortest interval of time, without a trace of discomposure, Garbo registers varying degrees of self-consciousness through the alteration of the relationships between her features. This is a truism, for, in fact, it defines facial expression. Yet in Garbo's face, the alterations are visual events controlled by the star mask that she carries through all of her films.

The mask is both cherished and jeopardized, and the rhythm and degree of alteration constitute her screen personality. The alterations in the preceding four frames seem enormous, but they are actually very slight—shifts of chin, mouth, and eyes that, because of our familiarity with her face, cannot fail to be noticed. The rapidity of the transformation heightens our awareness. Each time I see this shot I experience the same nervousness as when I hear a great singer about to negotiate a very difficult passage—will she get all the notes in on time? will she do it beautifully? will the fixed shape of the phrase contain the vitality of the performer? With Garbo, we see the notes, and their articulation in no way destroys the pattern and integrity of the sequence.

She then yields a bit.

The turning in toward Barrymore is accompanied by a tilt of the head, a reservation only partially belied by the half-smile on her lips. This initiation of a profile creates an ambiguous movement by directing that expanse of face away from us toward her costar and withholding the plenitude of her expression, and she offers him something even less penetrable than we have seen. The play of profile/full-face is an essential element in this film; the dynamics of encounter is often outlined in its terms. (The meeting of Barrymore and Crawford on the landing is a breathtaking succession of facial planes.)

The full profile is achieved, replete with smile and a sense of relief and the trust that would logically precede a clinch, or, as this scene has it, a kissed hand and an even franker smile.

Yet as soon as Barrymore's eyes no longer meet hers she withdraws into confusion and perplexity, the same as in the beginning of the shot, with the smile melting into an expression of wonder.

This effect is pursued to the last instant; her head actually comes closer to Barrymore's but her features remain as distant as they were at the outset.

It is both puerile and unnecessary to ascribe precise thoughts to Garbo during the various stages of this shot—as if she were plucking at an imaginary he-loves-me/he-loves-me-not daisy. This is a dangerous temptation when studying the separate frames. The shot's duration and the rapidity of the alterations must be reconstituted. Then, the mechanics of change are once again subsumed into those features, the entity imposes itself on the components, and both are fully perceived. Garbo preserves both, retaining her facial personality while adventuring into such subtle transformations. The extent of her achievement can best be grasped by considering some of the alternatives: the masklike impersonations by Paul Muni, the exertions of Luise Rainer, the affectations of other MGM lovelies: Norma Shearer and the later Joan Crawford. Garbo rarely plays at being someone else, nor does she use her face like a semaphor. Her face is like a fabric—so rich that its texture is interesting in itself, so flexible that it retains its design in all degrees of tension. In this shot, the banality of Grusinskaya's mind is transcended by the mobility of the face expressing it, as in those moments in Viennese operetta or musical comedy when the conventions of kitsch somehow lead to strength, grace, and integrity.

In Garbo's next scene with Barrymore, the situation is essentially the same, and it calls for an even more profound transformation. The morning after, she is lying on the chaise (Adrian, the costume designer, has, of course, supplied her with a "morning" negligee) reminiscing about her youth in ballet school. Her animation is excessive, her arms uncharacteristically flung wide. This is more ballerina impersonation and it is particularly useful since its abrupt disappearance furnishes a sharp threshold into the category of being that permits Garbo to reveal rather than impersonate. But the ballerina does not completely eradicate the creature of the previous love scene. Those barely parted, trusting lips accompany the intentness in her eyes as she looks at Barrymore. They are now thoroughly suffused with a smile. She learns his nickname, "Flix," distorting it as if to make it synonymous with "love." She laughs for the first time in the film.

When Barrymore admits to being a thief, Garbo again startles us with the peculiar rhythm of her response: "What is it, Flix?" She runs her hand up and down his lapel.

This gesture, both erotic and comforting, is broken off as he drops the pearls into her hand.

Her disbelief and confusion over their evening encounter instantly return.

In a close-up over Barrymore's shoulder, we see her darting eyes trying to comprehend—to focus on something. She succeeds in sharpening her gaze, first on Barrymore, then down at the pearls. "Oh, no." With her face slightly tilted, vulnerable, her voice still so trustful and loving, she asks, "Did you come here just for this?"

She flings away the pearls, and Barrymore explains why, when, and how he came to rob her, inviting the cruelest perusal of his acting style as his hand relentlessly describes the why, when, and how of his confession. Then he tells her how much he truly loves her.

In the next two shots Garbo demonstrates the difference between sign language and effective screen acting.

"Don't you understand? Don't you?" The sense of her understanding is perhaps the key to her range. No comic-strip-light-blub understanding, its intensity pierces all surfaces and suffuses the frame. Her understanding leaves nothing out. In its first stage she raises her eyelids a bit.

Then a new shot (and a marvelous match in a film not always distinguished by the smoothness of its editing) brings her into close-up, and her eyes begin to yield although her face is still withheld.

Finally the distance is bridged and her understanding is signaled as she offers her face—lips parting, eyes softening.

Her caressing hand accompanies the reiterated "Flix," and her lips make visible a kiss on the word, much sweeter than the one she will implant on Barrymore.

Her total acceptance recalls the scene with the flowers at the end of *A Woman of Affairs* (see pp. 126–130). This is Garbo's sexuality, an appropriation in both the physical and metaphorical senses.

Barrymore is then put to perhaps his best use in the film. She kisses him, pulling his head down and across her face,

blanking out her expression before its recomposition to the right of center in the frame.

Then her mouth gains a fullness she has reserved for the fullness of this particular moment, yet the scheme is not complete. She transfers her joy to Barrymore at the end of the shot. Looking down at the back of his neck, almost imperceptibly blowing on it, she gently kisses it.

No lover ever sees Garbo's beauty as the camera does. Finally, she nestles into his neck, turning his head so that it sharply frames the right side of her face.

Yes, she has understood, and in doing so has made us glimpse the progress of an encounter from distance and doubt through stages of trust to an unparalleled degree of intimacy. A bit of space between faces, a changing mouth contour, an unpredictable pattern of eyelids, and a meeting of cheek and hairline destroy the myth of the inscrutable Garbo. An actress can scarcely let us see more. She registers this plenitude in successive spatial patterns; Garbo understands so that we may understand. She draws us within by discovering herself.

The fineness of Garbo in these shots emphasizes the gaucheries of the scene's finale. After some rapid neck nibbling and pecking she resumes the ecstatic ballerina postures—exteriorizing, playing the role. The broader the gesture, the more she hides. In some perverse way, the wrongness of her Grusinskaya, so out of proportion to what she does well, serves as standard. It affords yet another transition—from Garbo the actress, desperately trying to ape an alien style to Garbo the artist, whose technique, at once unique and pervasive, establishes all the rules for our perception. In *Grand Hotel*, the extremes are side by side. *Two-Faced Woman* contains an even more inconsistent performance, but, whereas in the later film impersonation almost smothers those fleeting instances of personality, in *Grand Hotel* it functions as a threshold, allowing us access to Garbo.

It would be churlish to criticize her playfulness in the rest of this sequence—darting about in the frame, almost breaking out of it, gesticulating with arms fully extended, dancing, planting Pimenoff's hat on Suzette, and adding a flower to the surprised maid's coiffure.

Yet we are relieved to see her kneel by the telephone table and cherish and cradle the phone with tenderness as in the scene with Barrymore. In the final close-up she settles in with the receiver, holding it as no one ever held a phone before. She has called Barrymore, "just to tell you that . . . I'm happy!"

A trite sentiment, baldly stated, but it is infused with a deep and trusting voice and a smile whose significance was fully established when it was framed by the back of her lover's head.

Garbo appears four more times in the film, in sequences ranging from brief to very brief: her departure for the performance and her meeting with Barrymore in the lobby; her triumphant return, laden with flowers; back in the room with Suzette and the telephone; her leave-taking. The first two are charming examples of the Garbo tease—she is in and out of doors before the audience has a chance to grasp her. While the episodes involving Crawford and the male stars are becoming more intense and protracted, Garbo tantalizes with sudden appearances and lengthy absences.

The final telephone sequence is a set of variations on the previous one. Barrymore doesn't answer, and Garbo transforms the phone three times from surrogate lover to frustrating instrument: longing for him,

imploring the operator,

invoking him,

and despairing at his absence. Garbo relates most interestingly to Barrymore when he cannot see her face.

Garbo's last sequence is the only one in which she merges her public and private worlds. She strides nervously on the landing, anxious to know if Barrymore will indeed meet her on the train. A drunk collapses after she enters the elevator, a gag that doesn't break her pace through the corridor and lobby. The measure of her gait, her detachment from the urgings of Pimenoff, her utter concentration—all are capped when she asks the porter, "Have you seen Baron von . . . Gaigern?"

The pause is not related to normal discourse, but to her personal rhythm. It is a sign of language's inadequacy to her feelings rather than mere nervousness.

In her final apparition she emerges from the revolving doors. Garbo, so comfortable with metaphors—flowers and phones—extends her presence into a cosmic one like the sun: her face isolated by the enormous fur collar, bright in the center of the frame.

"The sun . . . It'll be sunny in Tremezzo. We'll have a guest, Suzette." Suggesting three directions at once with an arm extended toward Suzette, her body pulling toward the car, and her face stretching to the sun, she possesses the whole space.

For verbal counterpoint, she looks at her maid, Suzette, on the word "guest,"

and at the sun when she says her maid's name. The complexity is maintained until the last instant, for she manages to slide into the car while seeming to pull away from it.

This final gesture is exemplary of the Garbo paradox and the varieties of its expression throughout the film—the withholding and yielding, the hiding and revealing, with a simultaneity that forces our eyes to move with these moving pictures.

The other stars' contributions to *Grand Hotel* are not negligible. Playing against type, with a very professional consistency of characterization, Wallace Beery is the only one of the principals to affect a German accent. Beery manages to sustain his impersonation throughout the film, and this is remarkable considering the weight of personality he brings to all of his roles. John Barrymore contributes a stagy elegance: a glossy surface at once pertinent to the character he is portraying and useful as a contrast to Garbo's depth. Lionel Barrymore carries into all of his performances something like a whole foreign language, but his Lionelese is a constant, whether he is crotchety German, crotchety French, or crotchety American. Here he and Garbo never play a scene together, but his orneriness and collection of facial and vocal tics ultimately prove to be quite moving. (Lionel will prove to clash noisily with Garbo in *Camille*. He also appears with her in *The Temptress* and *Mata Hari*, but he falls well behind Lewis Stone's seven appearances in the "Films with Garbo Sweepstakes.") Joan Crawford's Flaemmchen is one of her best remembered performances. The later developments of her career —the hardening of her lines, her posture, and her voice—radically depart from the warmth and vulnerability she displays here. (But they do work splendidly well for her in Cukor's *The Women*, 1939.) Pragmatic about sex, she maintains an unexpected air of friendliness, a kind of amiable voluptuousness. A glimpse of what her physical freedom might have been if her career had followed less stereotypical patterns is seen in the imaginatively staged scene in which she discovers Barrymore's murder.

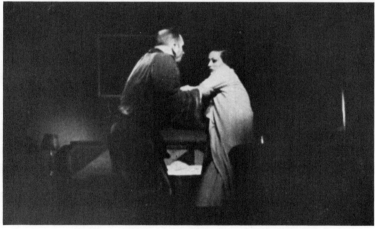

Crawford mixes a variety of tempos: slowly approaching the corpse; breaking loose from Beery's grasp and rushing to the door; crossing behind Beery again toward her own room; and she punctuates this with mounting anxiety—a whimper finally turning into a full-throated scream. So many other nice details would seem to add up to good screen acting. Yet it becomes progressively clear that the positive elements are ultimately sacrificed to veneer, and to the voice and drama coach. Our memory of Garbo sabotages Crawford's performance, for Garbo's ballerina allows her to sink deeper into herself while Crawford gradually convinces us that the depths do not exist.

Yet even if their talents are unequal, these stars command our attention. The film does not die during Garbo's absences. In fact, her absence enhances her presence—it is absence that establishes the space of the hotel. This space offers Garbo her most appropriate playing area. Near the beginning of the film, a shot posits the circles, balconies, and the checkered floor pattern over which everyone must tread to enter or leave.

The formal elements, circles and checkerboard, are designs not essentially apt to hotels, but to art. The intensity of style defined by a hotel per se is increased by the abstracted spatial arrangements. A place of circles and squares is suited to the esoteric actress, Garbo. The abstractions of a hotel and a woman like no others cling to each other's designs.

While relishing the brevity of her role in *Grand Hotel* and its place in the film's structure, I do not mean to suggest that Garbo is unable to sustain an extended performance. Her whole career bears testimony to the contrary. *Queen Christina* (1933) and *Camille* are perhaps the best examples of the obsessively Garboesque vehicle—the camera and our eyes are unable to detach themselves from her. But *Grand Hotel*, with its elaborate frames and its weaving of melodramatic ploys, guarantees her exclusive and unrelieved intensity. It is as if she had to be kept bottled up like a fragrance so heady that one must be chary of its use. Garbo is contained in the pattern and the depths of the Grand Hotel. We penetrate her room—interlopers, like John Barrymore—and share her secrets, but with an intermittence that insures the retention of their potency. The film's structure grants her centrality; and as we are led—on those several occasions—to her revelations, we are given proof of the strength of our perception. An actress can give us no more.

7:
A Career for Camille

Without words Garbo animated objects, men, and places with her glance, her smile, the enigma of her body and "soul." "Garbo Talks" is not simply an ad man's invention. It suggests her momentous entrance into the new era, a nostalgia for her appropriateness to silent films, and a fear that her Swedish accent would prove impenetrable. The fear disappeared with the wonder of her sound. She is exempt from accepted patterns by dint of her accent; her personal inflection thrusts her beyond necessity and grants to her posture and face the resonance of uniqueness. Hollywood was not exactly unfamiliar with foreign actresses and foreign accents in the thirties. Dietrich's vocal/visual entity was probably as responsible for her success as were Sternberg's gauzes, angles, and sets. Luise Rainer parlayed *Gemütlichkeit* and a telephone into an Oscar. The Dietrich defective *r* sings the actress's presence; Rainer's voice throbs with "foreign" sensitivity. Garbo's tone and verbal inflections do so as well, but, finally, they liberate her from geography and from language itself. Just as her plastique subsumes role-playing and episode, leading her into areas of expression beyond character and plot, so her voice, while clearly enunciating words according to the dictates of conventional syntax and conventional emoting, reveals the inadequacy of normal discourse. The platitudes, banalities, and graceless constructions of MGM dialogue provide a context for sonority and harmony that disorient the connotative power of language. Garbo doesn't need words to express meaning. (The triteness of the words she must use occasionally impedes meaning.) Her being is meaning. Verbalism is merely the medium for her utterance, for an aural phenomenon that is engulfed in the wholeness of her presence.

Yet Garbo talks with the talkies, and if her words sound like no one else's, words they are nonetheless. Although those realms of acting that belong to impersonation, role-playing, "business," and the transmission of information are minimal in Garbo's career, she is occasionally forced to inhabit them. Their frontiers provide a framework for that area of self that is free of conventional style. One of the many Garbo myths is that her acting is pure instinct, which goes beyond technique or which isn't technique at all. Perhaps there is some truth to this allegation. Her greatest moments are those nonverbal and nonverbalizable ones, when she somehow seizes the most transitory states and is able to pass them on to us in their purity, avoiding the words, gestures, and expressions of explicit translation. The end of the love scene with Barrymore in *Grand Hotel* can only be described as what it is. It does not stand for; it does not denote. Garbo by-passes her own capacity to conceptualize in the shot and relies on something secret that, for want of a better term, may be called *instinct*. Yet the privileged moments that form the core of the Garbo canon are contained in a larger context that is loaded with episode, dialogue, and decor—the elements of a dramatic structure rooted in a verbal theatrical tradition. Garbo's career in talkies is, to some degree, qualified by the relative success of these surrounding contexts.

PLACES FOR A STAR

Sound does not inhibit the camera's fondling of the star, as in the clumsy yet fervent adoration in the early talkies. The patterns of Garbo's silent films persist relentlessly in the quest for the ultimate framing, the shot that will reveal her more fully than any previous one. First, the meaningful "entrance." In the English- and German-language versions of *Anna Christie* (1930), the star is withheld for about fifteen minutes and then appears in a fog-shrouded doorway. (The more explicitly tartish costume and makeup of the German version are its only distinctive features.)

"Dancing" and "singing" in *Mata Hari* (1932) and *As You Desire Me* (1932) (see p. 134), she is less striking than on a staircase, "the toast of Paris," in *Inspiration* (1931).

We too raise a glass to this lady, so happily related to the double banister and her admirers' upstretched arms.

Whether striding through a crowd with her back to the camera in *Queen Christina* (1933), or alighting at the far end of a railroad platform in *Ninotchka* (1939), her arrival is an authentic event. The excitement on seeing Garbo for the first time in any given film depends on an accumulative process, our formal sense of theme and variation. How will she seem this time around?

Another conceit of the silent era (see discussion of *The Mysterious Lady*, pp. 96–101) is the signal that elicits the audience's awareness that it is watching. Ramon Novarro's blindness in *Mata Hari* increases our perception of Garbo's visual presence. What is withheld from the hero becomes doubly important for us. The plot of *As You Desire Me* is hinged on the contemplation of Garbo. Everyone examines her intently in order to establish her identity, to verify her resemblance to the portrait of a woman presumedly dead. (Of the many grave errors in this film one is the quality of the portrait, another is the banal, ingenue type to which Garbo must attempt to conform.)

When not performing before the public as singer or dancer, she undergoes another kind of collective scrutiny: as monarch in *Queen Christina*, she faces down a crowd.

She publicly abdicates.

In *Anna Karenina* (1935) she suffers the contemptuous attention of an opera audience for flaunting her adultery.

The Painted Veil (1934) avoids the more obvious kind of perusal of Garbo and relies exclusively on decor, photography, costumes, and lighting to enhance our alertness. Here, adultery is not defined in a public context, but rather by a rare and touching domestication of the star. Her scenes with Herbert Marshall are kitchen confessions, linked by the image of a coffeepot.

Yet *The Painted Veil* would not be a Garbo film if it did not take advantage of her essential distance from coffeepots and kitchens: while drinking a cup of coffee, she decides to investigate the Chinese festival she sees through a window containing her own reflection.

We are then treated to a precious glimpse of Garbo's self-transformation, an alteration of conventional womanliness akin to her Javanese bedecking in *Wild Orchids*. Here, nothing so specific is needed—only Adrian's white turban wrapped around her hair, completely remolding the contour of her head right before our eyes.

This prefigures the cowl she wears in the film's final sequence.

(The helmeted Garbo, finally helmeted by her own hair, appeared in *Mata Hari* as a constant motif.)

In *The Painted Veil*, the transformation signals entry into the exotica of MGM chinoiserie, an ambiance whose artificiality reaches a dizzying degree of high style through Garbo. Only a collaboration such as that of Fred Astaire and Vincente Minnelli in the "Limehouse Blues" number of *Ziegfeld Follies* (1946) can rival Garbo's *orientale*. (Without derogating Barbara Stanwyck's considerable contribution to *The Bitter Tea of General Yen*, 1933, imagine Garbo in the final sequences of that film with Nils Asther. That is a seductive might-have-been, renewing the excitement of the *Wild Orchids* match, this time with their glorious voices, Frank Capra's ripest direction, and a situation worthy of the most decadent imagination.) Suitably garbed, Garbo strides through the set, with its absurd rendition of Chinese architecture, as if to the manor born.

Yes, it is decor appropriate to musical comedy, operetta, or opera. "It doesn't seem possible, it's so strange"—yet Garbo exhibits this very possibility while stating the contrary. The strange is possible, indeed necessary, when Garbo is juxtaposed with a giant Buddha.

This pattern is reinforced when she arrives at a city whose gate is guarded by an enormous, frowning statue. Once there she complains to Marshall, her vindictive husband, "You've been as silent as a stone god." Her caressing of Siva in *Mata Hari* thoroughly established all her expertise in statuary, and previous to that, in *Inspiration,* she herself posed for a Minerva-like figure.

The super-Sternbergian photography of *The Painted Veil,* with its mosquito netting, latticework, moonlight, and flickering torches, qualifies Garbo in a way reminiscent of Dietrich.[1]

[1] The film's director Richard Boleslawski, quoted in John Bainbridge, *Garbo,* p. 213, seems to have been acutely attuned to Garbo's photogenicity: "She was so completely thorough in her art that one found her almost as marvelous as the camera itself."

Garbo is carefully photographed, but without the elaborate set of filters that Sternberg draws from natural and some unnatural phenomena. Dietrich is the center of a weblike design of light and texture; Garbo usually constitutes the whole design. Her first scene with Erich von Stroheim in *As You Desire Me* is an exception. Peculiar angles and highly contrastive lighting produce one of the most wildly erotic moments in any of her films.

Yet Garbo needs little other than herself to vitalize a frame. A tasteless room in this film takes on grace when she stands on its threshold.

The weight of her career and the multiple being that projects its shape on a particular role, prismatically modifying situations, tend to compensate for the generally uninspired architecture of her talkies. An interesting set is a bit of a shock, an accident that gives added edge to her presence, such as the long stairway curving up to Robert Montgomery's apartment in *Inspiration* (Wyler and Welles had not yet invented their dynamics of elevation),

another staircase and entrance hall in *Anna Karenina* (see p. 123). The virtue of most of the art direction and furnishings in Garbo films lies in their blandness.

They are acceptable when they don't get in the way. Inversely, *Conquest* almost smothers Garbo in a welter of elaborate sets, areas, and planes that do not relate to her acting or to her way of integrating the physical world with her personality.

Notable exceptions to the lackluster and the inappropriate settings are Rouben Mamoulian's *Queen Christina* and George Cukor's *Camille* (1937). Christina and Marguerite Gautier are her most demanding roles, and the carefully wrought physical contexts contribute to her success in both cases. The art direction in *Queen Christina* belongs to the usual MGM paint-and-gloss school, but Mamoulian's patience matches Garbo's. He allows her to inhabit the film: to stand in window frames, to touch tables, to sit on a throne, and to make her sitting there seem essential to the character as well as to the rank of queen.

Striding with breathless rapidity through the throne room after the abdication, she is as apt for state occasions and massed effects as for the languorous intimacies of a boudoir.

But it is her register of intimacy that most fully releases her being on places and objects. In the inn sequence, Garbo progresses through various stages of sexual ambiguity and leads an audience to a new level of perception; she startles us with our own prowess for understanding. Until this point in the film, the fun and high spirits of Garbo's androgynous tomboy radically tamper with her glamour-girl image.

Putting on boots, kissing her favorite lady-in-waiting, and more or less rollicking with the soldiers, she plays an identity game fully as delicious as Dietrich's "drag" in *Morocco* (1930) and *Blonde Venus* (1932) and Hepburn's midsummer masquerade in Cukor's *Sylvia Scarlett* (1935). Forced to share her room with John Gilbert, she passes from *slight* embarrassment and curiosity to delight over her predicament. After she removes her jacket, the barest alteration of posture is only one step removed from the previous ambiguity, and is not at all conventionally feminine.

Our knowledge that she is indeed a woman dressed in a man's clothing and disporting herself like a man is now challenged by a deeper confusion that abolishes sexual typing. The actress hovers in that area between male and female, leaning into her identity as woman, to be sure, but not abandoning the richness of her compound being. Garbo's rare quality of womanliness forces an audience to reexamine what it already knows—that she is a woman. A white blouse and a bent knee thrust the complexities of her nature beyond travesty and role-playing.

The processes of reappraisal and reinterpretation of sexual identity elicited by Garbo are then extended into a broader physical context. Her eyes, hands, and body seem to fondle a room and its objects, creating a version of a love nest for remembrance. The sense of place emanates from her oblique absorption in self. Her own image is reflected in this rustic mirror while she searches for Gilbert's.

A peculiarly mixed effect of sensuality and absence of the love object idealizes sexual satisfaction with the cherishing wrappings of premature nostalgia. The geometry of the spinning wheel sets the actress in a formal context.

Wool reintroduces texture; its softness establishes the motif for Garbo's imprint upon yielding surfaces.

She slithers across the bed with an unnatural turn of the body.

This turn leads into the increased focus of face upon pillow as her love for a man is evoked in the solitary contact with an object; it recalls the effect this pattern produced in the flower sequence of *A Woman of Affairs* (see pp. 126–129).

Garbo's sight is unhindered by closed lids. In this extreme close-up, vision and visionary are identical.

After sinking into the softness of her pillow, Garbo touches a religious picture and then consecrates the wooden bedpost with pillowlike tenderness and holy devotion.

A treacly score, characteristic of MGM's efforts in the thirties, does not weaken Mamoulian's pattern of transformation. The actress is impressed into surfaces whose receptivity ranges from the hard depth of the mirror to the yielding of wool and pillow, and there is a fusion of hard and soft when she applies the poles of her touch and being to the wooden bedpost. The abstracting quality of the spinning wheel helps organize the sequence, isolating Garbo with only the shape of an object. Garbo bestows her unaffected commitment upon things, forming the connections in the viewer's perception through the stillness of her presence and glance.[2] Her technique, if that is indeed the word to describe it, often lies in her patience and trust that our powers of concentration are equal to her own. The harmony of her face with the grace of her body and the quite unnatural slowness of her pace focus our gaze, drawing us within the actress's persona and the world it animates.[3]

Near the beginning of *Queen Christina,* Mamoulian posits Garbo's face as the field of most significant activity.

[2] In Tom Milne, *Rouben Mamoulian,* p. 74, Mamoulian describes his conception of the scene: "To my mind it's a sonnet. It was done to a metronome. I explained to her: 'This has to be sheer poetry and feeling. The movement must be like a dance. Treat it the way you would do it to music.' "

[3] Kenneth Tynan's "Garbo" (*Sight and Sound,* p. 187) is one of the most famous pieces on the star. The critic's general appreciation is especially applicable to the inn scene in *Queen Christina:* "Tranced by the ecstasy of existing, she gives to each onlooker what he needs: her largesse is intarissable. Most actresses in action live only to look at men, but Garbo looks at flowers, clouds and furniture with the same admiring compassion, like Eve on the morning of creation. . . ."

At its climax, the path is retraced from the star's mind, through her eyes to our own, as we sum things up in a face that is all. Tears and grief at her lover's death, and her search of the universe that complements her earlier search of the room at the inn, are finally resolved in the famous "think-of-nothing" close-up, which is held for a span that belongs to her face alone, its evenness and our memories lodged within it. We observe the perfect image as it plays with past and present, the shape of films, of *Queen Christina,* and of Garbo herself. Its span calls on us to prolong, to repeat, to inhabit the instant with actress and camera. Our mutual dexterity and perception of form bridge the varieties of time and space.

A STAR AND OTHERS

Garbo's decor is often more cooperative than her costars and scripts. Watch John Gilbert's bug-eyed double take after her *Queen Christina* travesty.

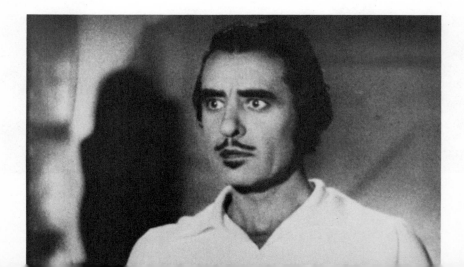

Most of her leading men mug and overplay. Robert Montgomery, in *Inspiration,* survives it simply because he seems intelligent. Herbert Marshall comes closest to matching Garbo. The Garbo–Marshall duets in *The Painted Veil,* gussied up by Richard Boleslawski's fancy staging, their hush, their similar harmonics, and their timidity are unlike the Garbo-Asther-Javanese fireworks in *Wild Orchids,* but they do show that this actress can be answered, and not necessarily in Swedish. In this respect, *Conquest* is her most frustrating film since Charles Boyer's style and allure are consonant with Garbo's. Napoleon and Marie Walewska must struggle against destiny, Clarence Brown's uneven direction, an excess of pseudohistoricity, an episodic structure, confusions of tone, and a script enfeebled by censorship. The success of the stars' partnership is fully demonstrated by candlelight, when Boyer, from the depths of his eyes, summons Garbo from the depths of hers, or on a wintry terrace when she unaffectedly walks into his arms. Yet *Conquest* is finally a measure of what they might have achieved together, of other films they might have made.

Garbo's career in talkies is full of mixed opportunities and compromises—bits of films and even whole sequences that emerge from the poverty of the studio imagination. Gish flourished to some degree in the consistency of Griffith's auteurship; Davis was polished by her years of apprenticeship at Warner Brothers and the firm hand of William Wyler. Garbo, symbolically absent from MGM's super-star-studded *Hollywood Review of 1929* (featuring Gilbert as Romeo to Norma Shearer's Juliet in the balcony scene!), and isolated from the ensemble in *Grand Hotel,* is only intermittently sustained by the elaborate machinery of the studio that boasted of "more stars than in heaven." The accidents are sweet. A sublime encounter with Marie Dressler in *Anna Christie* must be weighed against the scenes in her films with Gavin Gordon, John Gilbert, and others, in those two shots where, for all aesthetic purposes, she is alone.

For *The Painted Veil* there is *Susan Lenox: Her Fall and Rise*. The treasurable *Ninotchka* (1939) is countered by a graceless, interminable film that fully deserves its terrible reputation, *Two-Faced Woman* (1941), which is yet another of Garbo's struggles with the impossible. Having proved in *Ninotchka* that being a comedienne means primarily being an actress, she prevails over the farceurs in *Two-Faced Woman* to build something that resembles a performance, when Ruth Gordon, Melvyn Douglas, and Constance Bennett have run out of gags.

ACTING AS FOCUS: *CAMILLE*

Miracles are singular by definition. In *Camille* (1937), actress, role, director, and context constitute a film rather than a performance. *Camille* has the stamp of the best (and worst) that MGM had to offer—luxury—in a product that sustains luxurious weight. George Cukor's sophisticated sense of detail and period thrives in *Camille* but is wasted in the hodgepodge of *Two-Faced Woman*. The actress's age and experience and the subtilization of her art are appropriate to Marguerite Gautier's sentimentality dosed with irony and self-awareness. As proved by *A Woman of Affairs*, *Queen Christina*, and *Grand Hotel*, the challenge of love is Garbo's standard for the perusal of self. Simultaneously extending outward in caritas and benevolence, she deepens the penetration of her own identity, until that identity is finally extended outward as well.

The Ninotchka/Garbo light touch should have come as no surprise to the audience of Camille. (It had been perhaps forgotten during the leaden, interminable *Conquest*.) Her bemused smile, her candor, and humor are consistently applied to *Camille*, relieving its dated theatricality, refashioning the material of situations and character with a measure and a tone we recognize as creative acting. Garbo always acted against the grain, supplying less and more than expected, offering personal versions of the deadeningly familiar clichés. The roles of her career constitute a worn-out grammar of melodramatic types, a rhetoric frozen by its conventions. Garbo reorganizes these types with a being that functions as style itself. She tests the emptiness of the adventuress and the world-weary, lovelorn beauty; she refuses to accept their banality. Roles are pretexts for pushing the self yet further. Quickening her pace when languor dogs her heels, she somehow gives more attention to the *ands* and *buts* than the *I-love-you-trulys*.

Camille's general excellence—its costumes and decor and the level of its playing—is a field upon which Garbo imposes her design. The difference between *Camille* and most of her other talkies is the degree to which the shape of her performance takes on relief from the sustaining texture rather than in spite of it. None of her films is without memorable moments. In *Camille* they are not memorable simply because we force ourselves to forget those endless stretches of Garbo-less territory. The concision of her performance in *Grand Hotel* showed off acting as response to form rather than incident. That response is not diluted by her role as Marguerite Gautier, which keeps her on screen for most of the film's duration. Grusinskaya was a set of variations on ambiguity, a flux of gestures and expressions representing the mechanics of change and the mobility of sentiment. In *Camille* Garbo's generous ambiguity is the only possible answer to questions of moral judgment and value. In fact, value itself is equivalent to the extent of revelation as her being is unveiled by varying degrees of mask and sincerity. She does this without the firefly nervousness so appropriate to the hysterical Grusinskaya, or the baroque identity games of her Christina. Her reliance on the most subtle shifts in weight and tone exploits our perception of focus in acting. She controls our vision by constantly refining and then blurring the clarity of her own image. Before, Garbo led us to contemplate the plenitude of her feeling through the winding passages of disguise, androgyny, hyperbole, and metaphor; she now keeps us hovering above her feeling, constantly alert to the barest changes of intensity that signal its revelation. We stare at the pattern of Garbo, and the motion of her picture is governed by the clarity of focus she commands at any particular moment. During the film's first sequences, she tells Robert Taylor, "I'm not always sincere." It is this consciousness of sincerity and of degrees of authenticity that shapes her performance and our alertness.

The light manner is established throughout the first, long sequences at the theatre. Cukor keeps his crowds and characters moving at a clip.[4] The broad comedy of Laura Hope Crews and Lenore Ulric, the dancers' activity, the roving eyes of Henry Daniell and Robert Taylor are related to Garbo's rapid progress through the milling spectators, the security of her public gaiety, genuinely vivacious and yet not nervous.

[4] Cukor gives an interesting account of Garbo's rhythm and inventiveness in Gavin Lambert, *On Cukor*, p. 112.

No giggles for Garbo, but a promptness of life, an amused detachment devoid of real cynicism. She hears protestations of love from a handsome young man, first with delight and then with the barest suggestion that what he says is more than amusing.

Later, when she realizes that Armand Duval is not the Baron de Varville, her regret over his embarrassment is followed by a touching smile that does not betray the sociality of the situation.

Her insincerity is lightly worn, and this very lightness augurs the possibility of its disappearance.

The froth of her badinage with Henry Daniell in the next scene draws a complaint that she is not sorry enough about his departure for Russia. "Oh, but I am sorry." The words, affected by a transparent and acceptable hypocrisy, are also accented by her fingering the string of his monocle.

Then, fondling the chain around her own neck, she accepts his money with a gentle laugh. A tone and a gesture turn a situation quite risqué by Hollywood's 1937 Puritanism into a moment of unexpected friendliness. Her good-bye to Varville is just slightly exaggerated—not enough to put off the Baron, but enough to let us know that her attachment is not deeper than it should be. This degree of irony makes it a pleasure to be included in the joke.

Our attentiveness to degree is refined by the narrow gap between manners and feeling. The Marguerite Gautier who charms the world she inhabits is not so different from the Marguerite Gautier who tunes her being to love. In *Camille*, the tension of Garbo's performance is created by the closeness of her private and public characters rather than by the exhausting transitions of Grusinskaya and Christina. At an auction, she meets Taylor and is again touched by his sincerity. Sharpened by her handkerchief-covered mouth, her eyes focus on Armand and love. Then, a toss of her head and a joke about death defuse the intensity.

Garbo avoids the trap of the portentous, again by playing against the obvious cliché resonances of the role.

The first love scene exploits this careful preparation. Garbo's worldly tone is breached, and the intimacy instantly envelops us, precisely because we have been on the verge of sharing it since the beginning of the film. Cukor's mannered mise-en-scène sets a diction appropriate to the tone eventually taken by the scene. Garbo has retired to her boudoir after a fit of coughing. Taylor appears in her mirror reflection. Candlelight and lace curtains draw them together in the frame.

This scene's high-accent lighting is a shock after the film's previous brightness.

As Garbo turns to rejoin the festivities, Taylor kisses her hand. "What a child you are."

A condescending line she utters without condescension becomes a declaration of love. In this same way, her readings during the first love scene with Barrymore in *Grand Hotel* connected words to the uniqueness of her personality rather than to the accidents of situation. "What on earth am I going to do with you?" receives the same treatment from her. When Taylor reiterates his protestation of love, she allows a bit of gentle irony to inflect "That may be true, but what can I do about it?" With her face nestled against the top of the chaise longue, she is brought into close contact with the interior of her being, recalling her relationship to objects in the memory sequence of *Queen Christina*.

Now she truly entertains the notion that her would-be lover is sincere and indeed worthy of sharing her privacy. The focus increases as she raises her head, arching her neck with an extravagance that draws our belief in her abandon just as it draws the kiss of her leading man.

"See, I'm not laughing any more." Her voice, breathy, half-whispering, complements the disquieting pattern of her head and torso.

Essentially the same situation is repeated a few minutes later, and yet varied by Garbo to deepen the feelings. She has come to Taylor's room to see if he is truly going away, and the inevitable protestation of love is sounded. She reads his expression without shifting her gaze, but through the barely perceptible movement of her own face. She seems to be doing a version of this man who promises her tranquillity, care, and love.

Her penetration of Taylor is the model for our scrutiny of her Marguerite Gautier. The scene works toward self-surrender, and almost founders on the triteness of the dialogue: "You can't be sensible, Armand." . . . "I want too much." . . . "So do I." Just before the silly "so do I," Garbo stiffens her back, moves a fraction of an inch toward Taylor, changes her voice register, and, beyond the poor scope of the words, successfully acts her transition to hope.

"How can one change one's entire life and build a new one on one moment of love? And yet that's what you make me close my eyes and do." Preposterousness is not skirted by this prose, it is courted. "Then close your eyes and say yes. I command you." . . . "Yes, yes, yes."

Again, the actress saves it all from disaster between her first "yes," enunciated with sentimental excess, and the second one—toneless, a throwaway, a departure from the stale rhetoric toward the wordless self. Body tension and verbal tension belong to the apparatus of focus. They give a duration and rhythm to our watching. The contemplation is so intense that the clarity of the image contemplated must be varied for relief.

Garbo's Marguerite is not flawless. Not even she survives Lionel Barrymore's Duval père, and lines like "I don't suppose you can understand how any woman, unprotected as you say I am, can be lifted above self-interest by a sentiment so delicate and pure that she feels only humiliation when you speak of such things." The music she found in a solitary syllable is drowned out by this cacophonous tongue twister. More important, her Marguerite is far too wise to think, let alone say, such a thing. This moralistic nonsense is part of a conventional society that Garbo never inhabits. Her talent is always geared to freeing our imagination from precisely such judgments. She gives us the strength to know that the only true humiliation comes from within. She proves this moments later, just when the scene seems to have completely eluded her grasp. Realizing what she must do to end her affair with Taylor, she suddenly drops to her knees on "Oh . . . I knew I was too happy." Barrymore makes the same mistake we do in assuming that she has weakly succumbed to anguish. "How can I ever repay you for all you're doing for me?" In the close-up of her head nestling on her arms, Garbo possesses the space of the frame. She calls forth the strength of the table by drawing the integrity of the spatial pattern into her mind through her eyes.

She looks up at Barrymore, her face sharply focused by the opposing directions of her gaze and her arms, with an expression of comprehension and seriousness and not without a trace of rancor.

"Make no mistake, Monsieur. Whatever I do, it's nothing for you—it's all for Armand." Her voice has dropped by octaves. The words are unweighted, and the simplicity of their inflection sets off the tension of the eyes/arms scheme.

The interview with Barrymore is poorly resolved, with bathos galore, and is uncharacteristic of Garbo. Her coactor ends on a note of the highly ridiculous by deciding to invoke God's blessing on "Margaret" Gautier instead of our familiar Marguerite. Yet Margaret-Marguerite survives the weakness of this central episode, Barrymore's orneriness, and her own inability to transcend dialogue that is meretricious even by MGM standards. It is misleading to dwell on these shortcomings, for the film offers her some of her most interesting opportunities and configurations that, in the context of the total performance, function like the best deep-focus shots in the films of Renoir, Wyler, and Welles. Garbo brings to the surface data that makes us bore within to see the expressions she hides, to hear the words she doesn't need to say.

She combines hardness and softness, laughing desperately with the remarkable Henry Daniell when Taylor, "the great romance of my life, who might have been," is left ringing her door bell.

In the richness of her double nature, she is truly with both men at once and betrays neither. In a subsequent scene, Daniell gives her money despite her imminent departure with Taylor. Garbo bestows a gentle kiss and receives a slap in return.

Disappointment rather than the expected embarrassment is modulated into prefigured satisfaction with her new lover.

Garbo manages this range in a single shot because of the simultaneity of her Marguerite Gautier. The links between opposing or divergent states are made feasible by the characterization's great "depth of field." *All* of her Marguerite is always on view in the range of its paradox, its ambiguity, and its extensions in public and private realms.

This promptness of being is unsettlingly exercised when she convinces Taylor she no longer loves him. She leans back, sarcastic, superior, distant, shoulders brutally exposed, coiffed with merciless corkscrew curls (in a film where most of her hairdos are soft).

Her brittle laugh greets Taylor's evocation of a simple life.

Then, she pulls Taylor to her with what is perhaps the most sudden movement in any of her films, recapitulating all those marvelous shots when a man's head and shoulder frame love on her face.

This is the first and only time in *Camille* Garbo uses the familiar BIG look. Anguish was her caricatural trademark, but its emblem explodes in *Camille,* the only film that so consistently exhibits her lightest manner. The principle of focus is again put to work as Garbo shifts radically from insincerity to passion, then to renunciation and grief at their purest. The juxtaposition of extremes in her Marguerite wrenches our sensibility to meld it with the amplitude and clarity of her feeling. The waves of sadness that welled from her Anna in *Love,* Diana in *A Woman of Affairs,* or her suicidal Grusinskaya—in fact from all of her films—reach their crest in this shot. By turning her face into Robert Taylor's cheek, she charts the geography of love lost.

Garbo is always cast as a woman desperately in love and Marguerite is her most "loving" role, literally loving to death, with some small help from tuberculosis. Garbo dies in six of her films, but only *Mata Hari, Camille,* and *A Woman of Affairs* (the bouquet sequence is a death scene manqué—she later runs her Hispano-Suiza into a tree) grant her that actress's plum, the protracted agony and demise. Yet, whether in roles that kill her off rapidly or let her live on, there is a sense of giving up and an echo of farewells that come from wisdom not melodrama. Garbo's generosity contains the slipping away of things and people; her gaze unites presence and inevitable absence.[5] Standing in the snow near the end of *Inspiration,* in the prow of the ship in *Queen Christina's* fade-out, hovering

[5] Alistair Cooke, *Garbo and the Night Watchmen,* p. 143, in one of the best love letters a critic ever wrote to Garbo, describes her fatalism in *Anna Karenina:* "She sees not only her own life, but everybody else's, before it has been lived."

over the wounded Herbert Marshall in *The Painted Veil,* or as Mata Hari, reassuring the blind Ramon Novarro just before marching to her own execution, she applies acting to an area of understanding that tolerates life and death in their simultaneity, as states in permanent, mutual qualification. Garbo suits films precisely because her embodiment of transitions and continuity sustains the unfolding nature of the medium. Her acting does not freeze attitudes, it propels them in the ever-changing context of the shots and the configurations provided by the performer.

Cukor and Adrian are sensitive to the plasticity of Garbo's death-in-life/life-in-death.[6] The sequence at the gambling house displays a costume that bespeaks the grave.

[6] Cecilia Ager, an eloquent Garbo-maniac, describes the costumes in *Camille,* among other things, in Alistair Cooke, *Garbo and the Night Watchmen,* pp. 297–298.

And her face is not more alive for its bright illumination.

Her arched neck is swathed in black for a mock embrace that ironically recalls the first love scene in Marguerite's boudoir.

In the film's finale, the pattern is reversed; vitality becomes a function of death's proximity. Garbo polarizes her previous resignation with girlish hope; her sophisticated languor of the gaming scene is replaced by febrile activity. And what an inspiration to emphasize, in her encounter with Gaston, the morning light, the flowers, the radiant smile. (Rex O'Malley achingly matches Garbo's light tone.)

Moments later, Prudence, the cruel gossip, forces Marguerite to abandon hope that Armand will return. First she is resigned to her loss,

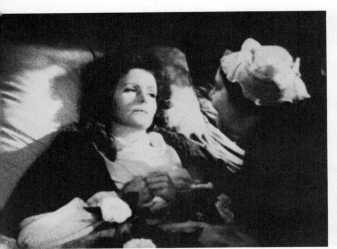

then incredulous at Nanine's assurance that Armand has indeed returned.

She passes through joy to anxiety about her appearance, and finally to imprecations to be helped out of bed.

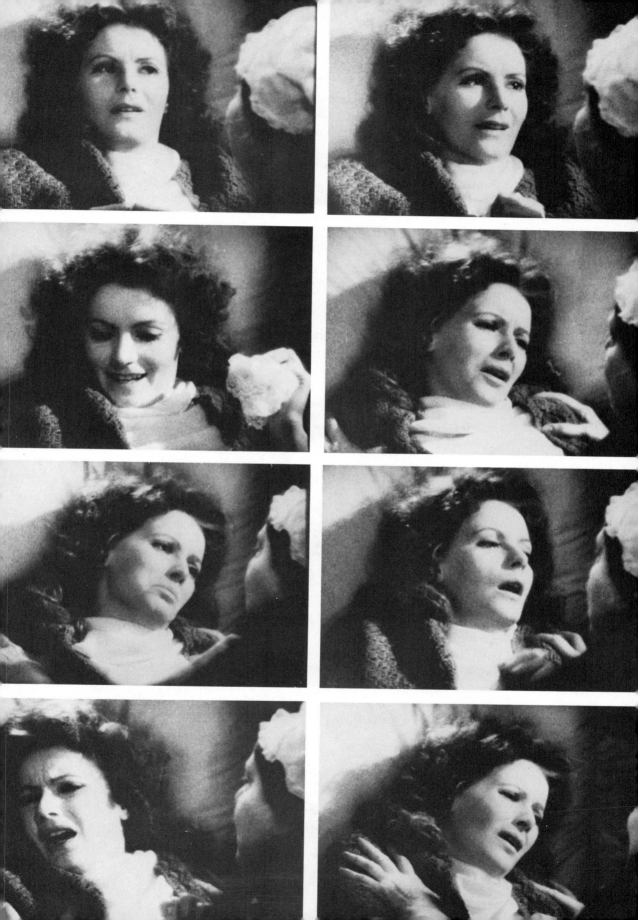

This shot, lasting about forty-five seconds, has a certain priority in the Garbo canon. Its placement at the film's climax is a significant element to our response, but more influential is the spatial context with the pillow delimiting, confining, obliterating our range beyond Garbo's features. Our perception of violent movement is again controlled by the near impossibility of movement. Few close-ups tolerate such a taxing rendition of activity. Quite apart from the emotional or thematic context of the shot, we are upset by the constant recomposition and reorganization of a face so familiar to us in its serenity. We bear down on Garbo through the merciless lens, and she does not flinch from our proximity. She seeks out new soprano whisperings in her voice.

In the last frame enlargement of the series, we are embarrassed by the disclosure of a Garbo so frighteningly vulnerable (quite unlike vulnerable Gruisinskaya). Our sense of it is compounded by its place in a performance posited on our apprehension of frivolity, as in a kind of quick waltz. The tempo and lightness of social Marguerite are somehow incorporated into this shot as Garbo darts all over the frame. Helped to her feet by Nanine, a rapturous smile caps her anguish.

She is reunited with Taylor and the softness of her smile and face envelops us as it does him.

To signal death, she opens her eyes—nothing more,

and the film is resolved in an image of ravishing tranquillity that we will all take to our graves.

    Camille contains the most protracted death scene in all of Garbo's films, and it is something of a test. Just as Gish submitted us to the unendurable agony and sweetness of Mimi in *La Boheme,* and Davis lucidly points our way to the "dark victory," so Garbo reveals her essential method *in extremis.* Her gentle smile subsumes the paradoxical border between life and death, a paradigm for all those borders she is used to crossing. She challenges our conventional perceptions of space, body, sexuality, voice with versions that establish harmony in ambiguity, that grant shape to antithesis, that forever bridge those unsettling gaps between feeling and logic. Everything fits inside the palpable eccentricity of her being. The gifts she bestows on us, from Diana's flowers to Marguerite's joy, are abundant. Knowing how to receive them is proving that the star's magic and wisdom are ours.

8.
A Star Is Made:
Davis, Warners, and
Wyler

We adore stars, not paradigms. Exemplars do not bestow the gifts of sight and insight so abundantly offered by the unique Gish and Garbo. In a sense, we learn more about twenties taste from Mary Pickford's pluckiness than from Gish's agonies. Norma Shearer's popularity has a more obvious relationship to a house-wife's dreams and fears during the Depression than has Garbo's introspection. Yet, for all their individuality, Gish and Garbo possessed qualities and were produced by circumstances we assume are pertinent to the general phenomenon of stardom. Most obviously, they were immediately identifiable as beautiful. Beauty in the eye of the beholder notwithstanding, their features stand the test of precedent, of Western iconography. Gish's face would clearly have inspired a Lucas Cranach or a Botticelli. Garbo, exempt from context and period both morally and visually, is the sum of those symmetries and harmonies sought by the great portraitists of women from Pollaiuolo to John Singer Sargent.

Besides having beautifully photogenic faces, with regular and pristine features, at the outset Gish and Garbo received the kind of encouragement from directors, studios, and public that favors career development. While it is hard to document the impact of Lillian Gish in those first years, her ever increasing importance to Griffith, the financial success of her films prior to *Intolerance,* the great popularity of *Broken Blossoms* and *Way Down East,* and the consistency of her playing in all the major vehicles from *The Birth of a Nation* to *Orphans of the Storm* suggest that her appeal only required expansion through the director's technique and vision for it to be fully appreciated. Stiller's adoring close-ups of Garbo in *The Saga of Gösta Berling,* Pabst's *Die freudlose Gasse,* although she was almost completely buried in its proletarian miseries, and her rapid American conquest, after a debut in a misnamed "Torrent," recall an immediate response to her presence independent of the unearthly intimations of self-awareness that were to surface in *Love, A Woman of Affairs,* and most of her sound films.

And Bette Davis? What is the sex appeal of "a little brown wren"? "She has about as much sex appeal as Slim Summerville." . . . "Can you picture some poor guy going through hell and high water in a picture and ending up with *her* at the fade-out?"[1] The mere fact that this is the genesis of the Davis story is a comment about her physical impertinence. Although posited to some degree on anomalism, stardom does not completely account for the photogenic quality of a woman whose attractiveness comes more from an effort of will than from nature. We learned to find beauty in her popeyes, particularly after William Wyler framed them—but it was a lesson, not an illumination. It is unlikely that anyone else's route to superstardom was as long and tortuous as Bette Davis's. Her career is abundant proof that each star redefines the species.

In 1930 a modest success on Broadway gained her a Hollywood contract. With the advent of sound the industry desperately needed performers who could talk, and what passed for talking in those first, post-silent years, makes one

[1] These judgments are requoted in Whitney Stine, *Mother Goddam, The Story of the Career of Bette Davis,* pp. 7–13.

wonder if there had not been some terrible epidemic of ear disease in Southern California. Bette Davis talked, but in tones ranging from the stagy to the unintelligible. It took her seven or eight years and more than thirty features to gain the precision and control of voice manifest in her mature work. George Arliss reputedly gave her pointers in speech, but his capital *T*s, semicolons, and commas are not part of the vocal technique of the virtuoso whose whisper is a death sentence in *The Little Foxes* (1941), and who, in *Watch on the Rhine* (1943), manages to make herself sound as if she has spent seventeen years abroad without *completely* losing her Yankee accent. And if Margo Channing owes something to a throat ailment and something to Tallulah, she owes even more to a sense of syllables and creative speech that is closer to Greta Garbo's than to Ruth Chatterton's.

None of this is apparent at first. Her fast talking is exciting, yet it is hectic, uncontrolled, distracting, and not particularly attuned to the films she plays in. Joan Blondell's rapid-fire delivery jibes with directors like Archie Mayo and Michael Curtiz who exemplify the hardness and clarity of the Warner Brothers style in the thirties. Davis is fast enough, but so neurotic that she often clashes with the straightforwardness of the studio product. She is terrific in *Jimmy the Gent* (1934) and *Front Page Woman* (1935), but no more terrific than Blondell would have been and was in all too reasonable facsimilies. A touch of madness particularizes her work in *The Rich Are Always with Us* (1932), *Bureau of Missing Persons* (1933), and *Fog over Frisco* (1934), but no one could project a great career on this evidence. The famous Davis energy and the intensity of her most accomplished performances is more of a liability than an asset in its unharnessed state. Davis flails and flutters, confusing our eyes with nervous gestures and our ears with mannerisms and artificialities that fail to distinguish nerve from nervousness. Her rise in films and the power of her response to the medium are directly related to an ever increasing refinement of her identity. It's a slow process, frustrating in its intermittence, its dependence on unflattering contexts, and on roles that suit her uniqueness in the most capricious way. Gish was cherished and nurtured chez Griffith, and Garbo was put on her solitary MGM pedestal. Davis raced with the other contract players at Warners, fought tooth and nail, sued her bosses and lost. She made thirty-five films in about seven years—some good, most bad—and even won an Oscar for a seriously flawed performance in an unequivocally dreadful vehicle. Perhaps all this activity was necessary. Would *Jezebel, Dark Victory, The Letter,* and *The Little Foxes* have been the same without it? Certainly the weight of the dross, the accumulation of years as an actress rather than a star, accounts for Margo Channing's center of gravity. That is justification enough for having to support George Arliss and Ruth Chatterton, and being directed by Alfred E. Green seven times, to mention only some of the most obvious indignities she suffered. The fact that she survived, and the duration of her survival, sustained her eventual stardom. But more significantly, it focused her talent for its eventual test with William Wyler.

THE STAR AS APPRENTICE

Bette Davis, in generously crediting George Arliss for giving her her first significant role in *The Man Who Played God* (1932), as well as for counseling her on diction and grooming, exhibits a loyalty and generosity of spirit unwarranted by the results. Her good grooming does not extend to her gaucheries.

The vitality is there, and so are the eyes, yet not even good camera angles could rescue her from ELOCUTION and the staginess of her mentor's film. Davis the star, as cinematic in her acting as Gish and Garbo at their most metaphoric, did not learn her best movie lessons from Mr. Arliss. The Warner Brothers' salt mines were healthier for her than Arliss's "good taste," although they could not always be counted upon to be salty enough. Another drawing-room film, *The Rich Are Always with Us,* is responsible for one of her most peculiar screen names, Malbro Barclay. That's a high point even for someone who will one day play Stanley Timberlake in *In This Our Life* (1942).

Garbed by Orry-Kelly and photographed by Ernest Haller, she profits from the chic of a Ruth Chatterton vehicle and looks luminous, but she sounds just as silly as the film and Alfred E. Green allow. Warner Brothers deserved its reputation as the proletarian studio. It was certainly unable to put on the ritz.

More characteristic of studio and actress is *The Dark Horse* (1932), one of the few bearable Warren William films. His oily presence suits a political con man, and the bluntness of the satire suits the Warners up-and-at-'em ethos. Again, it is difficult to know how much of Davis vintage 1932 is savored for itself and how much we confuse it with better years; but the look is sharp, and the role, a smart woman, is hers. A high-toned and stagy accent doesn't diminish her toughness and determination.

And so it goes. Her *Cabin in the Cotton* (1932) vamp memorably tells Richard Barthelmess "I'd love to kiss you, but I just washed my hair."

Then followed *Three on a Match* (1932). She awkwardly played a tiny role, third banana to Ann Dvorak and Joan Blondell, that unaccountably combines cheese-cake (slip and bathing suit) with the prim, governess type.

Twenty Thousand Years in Sing Sing (1933), one of the best of Warners prison films, tightly arched by Michael Curtiz, teams her with Spencer Tracy who is unhampered by MGM niceties. In one of her most effective scenes she is confined to a bed, bandaged, and her power is operational because it is held in spatial check.

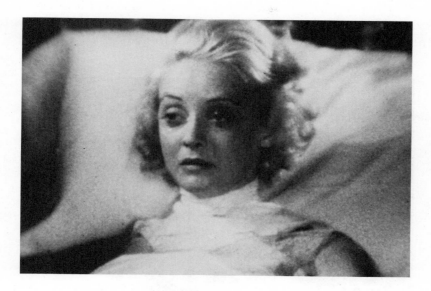

The final meeting with Tracy, just prior to his execution, represents a sympathy of concentrations never to be repeated.

This is arguably her best film until *The Petrified Forest* (1936), and her persistent accent problem (she doesn't go to the head of the class in Ann Dvorak's school of molldom, but by 1937 she will manage to form her own curriculum in *Marked Woman*) is unimportant when measured against the film's consistency and the stars' responses. But it's back to *Parachute Jumper* (1933) and Alfred E. Green, and *The Working Man* (1933) and George Arliss. In *Bureau of Missing Persons* (1933), Pat O'Brien invites her to "tie on the nose bag," and Glenda Farrell proves herself more attuned to this register of Warners quickie.

In *Fashions of 1934,* bewigged and glamorized beyond recognition, Davis is even denied the distinction of being a human harp in Busby Berkeley's "Spin a Little World of Dreams" number.

She is practically NOT in the film at all, despite second billing to William Powell. The contract system, with its possibility of apprenticeship, is one of the great casualties of the end of the studio era, but the frequent waste of Davis tries the limits of our patience.

Davis's films of this period can be conveniently grouped into three categories: (1) the incompetently directed *Parachute Jumper, Fashions of 1934, The Golden Arrow, Satan Met a Lady,* and so forth, where the roles call for none of her special qualities; (2) interesting little films that exploit her intensity in suitable if secondary roles, such as opposite Jimmy Cagney in *Jimmy the Gent* (1934),

a manic playgirl in *Fog over Frisco* (1934),

a fast-talking reporter in *Front Page Woman* (1935);

(3) big opportunities that reveal, even in their rough state, the characteristics that will make her stardom grow. Even a rapid examination of this third group allows us to reconstitute her progress toward self-possession, maturity, and William Wyler.

"A VITALLY TEMPESTUOUS CREATURE"

In 1933 *Ex-Lady,* Bette Davis's first starring film, seemed inauspicious. Reviews were bad, and she has referred to her role as "unsuitable" and the whole experience as "a disaster."[2] Yet, because she is the nominal star of *Ex-Lady,* she is provided with the kind of character-building scene that contains as much, if not more, of the vintage Davis, as much as, if not more, of her best flamboyance of the apprentice years. This is, perhaps significantly, a wordless bit of business. Having just seen her husband drive off with another woman, she enters her apartment, lights a cigarette, tosses her hat on a chair, pours herself a drink, and spills some on the table.

[2] Stine, *op. cit.,* p. 49.

It is all executed with a remarkable lack of fuss, with a rhythm that integrates body, object, and frame with a sureness that speaks of self-mastery. The Davis manner, so often described as a function of the angularity of her gesticulation, is here subsumed in a concentration made visible by the clarity and flow of her body through the shot. And it is precisely these qualities that will characterize her greatest achievements: her Leslie Crosbie, her Charlotte Vale, and her Margo Channing.

Later on in her career, when her self-mastery is postulated as a given, its loss becomes a meaningful cinematic sign. Her early reputation, despite annunciatory moments such as the one in *Ex-Lady*, was made by the noise and violence of an explosive temperament, an eruption of the self in cataclysms both thrilling and perilous. *Bordertown* (1935) exhibits the polar aspects of her presence. Archie Mayo is at his most relentless, and Paul Muni, before he was billed as "Mr.," is a perfect match for the Davis tensions. With eyes flashing, her face and body defy the strictures of her bungalow, of morality, and destiny. She lashes out at her adversaries, her audience, and at her houseboy, when she is stood up by Muni.

Then, prowling around his desk, she measures out the space between them in a confrontation of equals and shrieks, "I committed murder to get you. . . . Sure —me—me!"

Her *me* is as full of itself as it ever will be, and her abundance of egotism becomes an irresistible force. The Davis refinements will throb on this core of physical and psychic strength. Some are already exhibited in *Bordertown:* fleeting remorse in a rare close-up,

a mad scene on the witness stand, modulated from longing for Muni through daze to hysterical breakdown.

Mildred in *Of Human Bondage* (1934) is the kind of role designed to showcase a hyperkinetic actress who inclines toward exaggerated bitchiness. It singled her out of the ranks as did no previous film. Her work in it is paradoxical. No one could play Mildred as Davis does. This is not another Joan Blondell role. She was accorded the ultimate compliment of being borrowed by RKO for the part, proof that some people were aware of what she alone could contribute, and as good a mark of stardom as any. Her unique qualities are visual as well as emotional. She is a full-fledged movie actress in *Of Human Bondage*, a fact not abundantly clear in *The Man Who Played God* or *Fashions of 1934*. The tough humor of her waitress, and her come-hither cruelty during her first date with Leslie Howard are lodged in the sharpness of her features, the length of her neck, and the size of her eyes more than in her inexpert cockney accent.

Phonemes may be painfully awry, but her hard voice is exactly right; and the *look* is maintained despite mistakes of commission, whether she is wheedling, defiant, seductive, mean, down and out, or dying.

The rawness of Davis's Mildred is unflatteringly and inexpertly exposed in a caricature of sexuality.

Yet it permits her, a moment later, to sustain an outburst of vituperation that makes us flinch at its intensity.

The character's strength draws out the actress's primal force, to which we respond despite an uneven portrayal, tonal imbalances, and a body and voice that have yet to find their shape. No one who has shared her superb tongue-lashing with the camera and Leslie Howard can doubt that Davis's screen personality will be defined once that force is put under leash.

Due to studio mismanagement or her own immaturity, the promise was not to be kept fully for three or four more years. In *Dangerous,* for which she received her first Academy Award, she is more hysterical than in *Bordertown* and *Of Human Bondage.* Alfred E. Green is a poor exchange for Archie Mayo, and the vehicle is hackneyed even by Davis's 1935 standards. The level of its rhetoric is located when the heroine's fatal kiss is "illuminated" by a bolt of lightning.

Perhaps lightning is not inappropriate for a character referred to as "a vitally tempestuous creature" and "a comet." These are apt descriptions of the Davis persona, tempered to clarity at the highest pitches of intensity. Her award for *Dangerous* is often explained as a consolation prize after her disappointment over not even being nominated for *Of Human Bondage*. (It is curious that both Davis and Hepburn won their first Oscars for such dreadful films—*Dangerous* and *Morning Glory*—playing actresses, and scarcely giving their best performances.) I would suggest it is rather the industry's acknowledgment of that persona, with its concomitant stardom.

Quite remarkably, her next film, *The Petrified Forest* (1936), cast her against type. Reminiscent of the sweet young things she first played, Gaby Maple gives us some indication of Davis's filmic versatility, her ability to incarnate an attitude not naturally her own. She is beautifully photographed by Sol Polito, and her characteristic nervousness and bulging eyes become the curiosity and ingenuousness of the lonely, imaginative girl. When she gets angry, the remnants of her stagy diction disappear. Her fresh, wide-open face glows during a reading of François Villon's poetry and in cherishable two-shots with Leslie Howard.

The "little brown wren," when properly lit and coiffed, and matched by an authentic movie star, looks like one herself. Davis will always rise to the level of a given context, and Leslie Howard's arms, a gun battle, and talk of love and France offer a worthy context indeed. In *Marked Woman* (1937) and *Kid Galahad* (1937), she continues to demonstrate qualities of concentration, adaptability, and strength that are brought to fruition by the fine hand of William Wyler.

SEEING EVERYTHING WITH WYLER

In his seminal article on William Wyler, André Bazin[3] concludes that acting has first priority in this director's films. The Wyler mise-en-scène focuses the center of the dramatic interest on the performers. The most vivid example Bazin offers is of Bette Davis during Herbert Marshall's heart attack in *The Little Foxes*. This specific shot is organized by Davis's near immobility, and our perception of her as the frame's controlling factor. A slight turn of the head and a stiffening of the body are punctuated by Marshall's frantic passing in and out of our field of vision. His violent movement is barely seen; the rigid intensity of Davis's hatred and avarice fills the space.

[3] André Bazin, *Qu'est-ce que le cinéma? 1. Ontologie et langage*, pp. 150–154, 165–166.

While giving due credit to *The Little Foxes* as pure cinema,[4] in the cause of argument Bazin perhaps overstates the theatricality of Wyler's aesthetic. As this last shot illustrates, the frame as an ideally movable proscenium is not the director's standard. Yet more disturbing is the fact that Bazin completely overlooks the actress, the specifics of Davis, the weight of experience she brings to the shot, the elements that condition our viewing and are part of Wyler's mise-en-scène. If, as stated by Bazin, Wyler's goal is to permit the spectators *"de tout voir,"*[5] the actress who most efficiently complements that intention is Bette Davis. Even a sublime miscalculation like her Mildred is an effort to show everything. The director seems to have taught the actress that finding her place in the frame is the basis of her screen being.

The Davis pattern is a constant among the variables of the three films she made with him. In *Jezebel* (1938) she tries on the absurd red dress while trapped in a more absurd crinoline.

Julie's willfulness is concentrated in the comic frame within a frame; a film about conventions and their flaunting is gathered to itself in this unconventional shot. The star's underwear is exposed front and back, and the star's familiar energy is trapped in this dressmaker's parody of femininity. Both the parody and the centrality are pursued in yet another mirror shot: Davis is teasing Henry Fonda (he

[4] *Ibid.*, p. 173.
[5] *Ibid.*, p. 160.

pounds on her door with a cane), her hair is pinned up, her coy expression is frivolously multiplied.

This ironic pinpointing of Davis was initiated at her entrance when, eyes characteristically bulging, she shouts to her young slave, "Don't stand there with your eyes bulging out." It extends through these first sequences to her unleashing in the film's centerpiece, the Comos Ball, perhaps the best scene of massed movement in Wyler's career. From Davis's defiant arrival,

Wyler pits her singularity (notably qualified and literally governed by Henry
Fonda) against the ballroom, the area of the dance floor, and the white dresses of
the other young ladies. The director weaves volition in space. The symmetrical
establishing and closing shots

are parentheses for intervening close-ups of the embarrassed Davis's struggle
to leave.

She is caught in Fonda's embrace, in the circling waltz, and in the frame-filling sweep of the infamous dress.

The character's dominance, so surely posited in the sequences prior to the Comos Ball, is dislocated in the expanse. Cocksure and thoughtless in petticoats, hair curlers, and the wrong dress, Davis will spend the rest of the film looking quite different. The eccentricities of character and space suggested by the Comos Ball initiate a redefinition of both.

That process begins when Fonda breaks their engagement. Her face and eyes follow his departure as the camera would in a pan shot. Irony is softened when the actress begins to see with the clarity of the lens.

When Davis appears to Fonda after his long trip to the North he exclaims, "You're lovely." This time in white, and rooted to the floor much as she was in Mme. Pollard's fitting room, she is precisely that, collecting herself in ecstatic calm. The focus of her loveliness is sharpened when the dress puddles around her, its soft tulle setting off the strength of her line.

The space of *Jezebel* radiates from Davis no matter where she is in the frame, and our ability to locate her with such flexibility is related to the establishing shots of emblematic centrality. Completely vulnerable following her broken engagement, she is crowded into the foreground by the banister. Her hectic ascent of the staircase is countered by Fay Bainter's solidity.

(Bainter was judged best supporting actress for her work in *Jezebel*, and an Academy Award, usually granted for lots of carrying on in a secondary role, was won by someone who truly supported the star. Her grace is a mark of authentic refinement rather than conventional politeness.)

Near the film's end, displaced at Fonda's bedside by wife Margaret Lindsay, Davis recedes in the frame, almost thrust from it by another aggressive banister, an upright column, and Donald Crisp's back and shoulder.

Such diagonals are easily identifiable characteristics of Wyler's style. For him, zigzags and stacking indicate varieties of tension. In *These Three* (1936) staircases caught his characters in ambiguities of hierarchical spatial relationships, or simply distinguished between the actors posed at the extremities of the frame as coordinates for the enclosed structures.

Dead End (1937) is Wyler at his most vertical; its set rises from the river to the street to tenements to skyscrapers.

Elevation is scored by the opening and closing shots of *Dead End,* and the various stairway sequences: Marjorie Main telling son Humphrey Bogart he should "die," ritzy Wendy Barrie on the unfamiliar tenement landing, and Joel McCrea's extraordinary up and down chase of Bogart and Allen Jenkins.

Wyler's design for *Jezebel* is completed on a staircase, and the strength of the design effectively transcends the silliness of the film's elements—a belle at the ball in a red dress, magnolias and mint juleps, and the star's occasional lapses in her accent. Davis pleads with Lindsay to be allowed to accompany fever-stricken Fonda in quarantine. The star's face, exposed by a coiffure that has evidently not been abetted by curlers and mirror and brooks no frivolity, is now relieved of Julie's initial mindlessness.

The various camera positions relentlessly root the sloping planes in a will that is no longer willful, and we are grateful to melodrama for providing patterns so worthy of a star's belief and fortitude.

Her face resumes its centrality on her way to Lazarette Island; first, in gratitude, as she sweeps out of the door,

then riding in the cart with Fonda's head cradled in her lap. The face of a star matches the blaze of a bonfire.

Was *Jezebel* the turning point? Did Davis need to undergo the rigors set by Wyler, the taskmaster, before she could attempt to win her dark victory, or to sail forth to seek and find as Olive Higgins Prouty's voyager? Certainly her mad scenes in *Juarez* (1939) are exhibitions of a virtuosity quite beyond the elemental passions of her earlier performances. She rages at Claude Rains's Napoleon III.

Veiled by his cigar smoke (an uncharacteristically pointed effect in the characteristically leaden William Dieterle "biopic"), her face is thrown out of kilter, and its shapelessness is extended by her body that is lost in the voluminous cloak.

Her vacant stare and mindlessly fingered necklace do not simply suggest madness, but quite precisely posit the alienation of an empress.

As another monarch, in *The Private Lives of Elizabeth and Essex* (1939), she has a different manner, and this is one of the best examples of her vocal bravura. The range of her tonal colorations matches the range of her roles during her peak years. Her diction, no longer from the Arliss school of enunciation, is unmistakably Davis whether as baritone Elizabeth, contralto school teachers in *All This and Heaven Too* (1940) and *The Corn Is Green* (1945), mezzo soprano modern women in *Dark Victory* and *Old Acquaintance* (1943), or silvery coloratura Fanny Trellis in *Mr. Skeffington* (1944). Whatever her accent, Davis finds a sound for the role that bridges portrayal and persona. Muni's voices submerge the actor in fussiness; Davis shows her agility in a variety of registers. She itches and fidgets through most of *Elizabeth and Essex*, but her voice, weighted to her toes, gives a firm base to her flailing. Then near the end of the film, the pattern emerges in her despair after ordering Essex's arrest.

We see it in the pathetic primping before her final interview with him in the Tower,

her tragic mask, a tear, and the concentration of all her activity in resignation that is both queenly and womanly.

At no time previous to *Jezebel* does Davis suggest to us a sustained belief that her energy can be held in check. Her strong roles were hammer blows, and we cheer a champion's haymaker. Wyler reverses the assault, directs it within the actress, compressing her power so that its release becomes a meaningful cinematic sign. Davis's shoulders and arms will challenge the extremes of frames in her films after *Jezebel*, but she will collect her tension at the centers of other frames, and charge their remaining space with her density.

In *Jezebel* Davis's face was set against a bonfire; it defies the moon in *The Letter* (1940). The long staircases of the Deep South are reduced to a few steps descending from British colonial verandas. Wyler flourishes in *The Letter*'s smaller dimensions. The actress's performance suggests the sharpening of technique and the increased sense of measure apparent in the intervening *Dark Victory, The Old Maid* (1939), and *The Private Lives of Elizabeth and Essex,* and *All This and Heaven Too.*

The opening tracking shot (albeit a tricked-up one), slips past natives sleeping in a hut, to a bird, a veranda, and a crime of passion. It is exemplary of Wyler's obsessive juxtaposition of conflicting areas of meaning and space within a given shot.

This scope of vision is recalled at the film's end when the camera passes over the wall from Davis's corpse toward the party inside the house, and then cuts to the dark room and the heroine's shawl.

The images of the lace fluttering in the breeze and the moonlight slatted on the floor subsume the film's formal ambiguity. Davis's face is repeatedly broken by lines of light and shadow and by the light that passes through blinds. We find her behind the folds and perforations of her lace shawl.

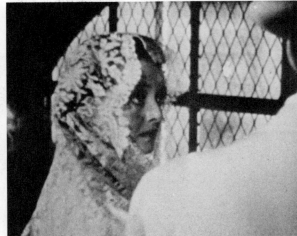

The Letter asks us to ascertain the actress's location. The tropics' slats and blinds, opening, closing, forming zebra stripes on furniture and face, precisely delimit the light without diffusive Sternbergian effects. They help us to see even if we are not looking through them. Leslie Crosbie's lawyer and her husband scan her face for the elusive truth. The audience of *The Letter* is caught in a visual inquiry, its characters in a moral and legal one. The clash between the image's clarity and the situation's ambiguity is rendered by Davis and Wyler. The conventional breeding and grace suggested by the heroine's voice are countered by her body's sensuality; the director's setups trace divergent meanings for the movie audience and the characters within the film. The ultimate shape of antithesis will be revealed at the film's climax when Leslie Crosbie reaffirms her love for her husband, and a bare instant later sobs, "With all my heart, I still love the man I killed."

This double standard first emerges during Davis's recital of the murder. Ensconced on a couch, a prim English wife who has supposedly shot a man to save her honor, she is surrounded by husband, lawyer, and local official.

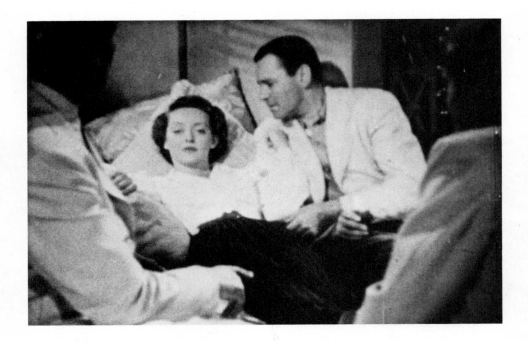

The courageous woman they see seems to us an odalisque, recumbent on a divan, settled into the comfort of the cushions. The image reeks of the sensuality that the voice denies. Toward the end of her narration, she rises and hesitantly re-enacts the shooting that we now witness from her point of view.

Again it is her voice that sustains the burden of her lie. Here, and in her eventual confession, her back is either the focus of her co-players gaze or the fulcrum of the shot.

The motif of inquiry goes through rich spatial permutations in Davis's major scenes of confession. She faints when lawyer James Stephenson penetrates her lie and she plays the remainder of the sequence on what seems to be the examining table of the jail's infirmary. Actress and director conspire toward a gradually heightened display of her presence, and then its withdrawal. At first we hear her most purring voice and marvel at her arm and hand defining the dimensions of the frame and the situation.

As she passes through other degrees of revelation, Wyler both opens up the space for her and pins her down with the camera's varying point of view.

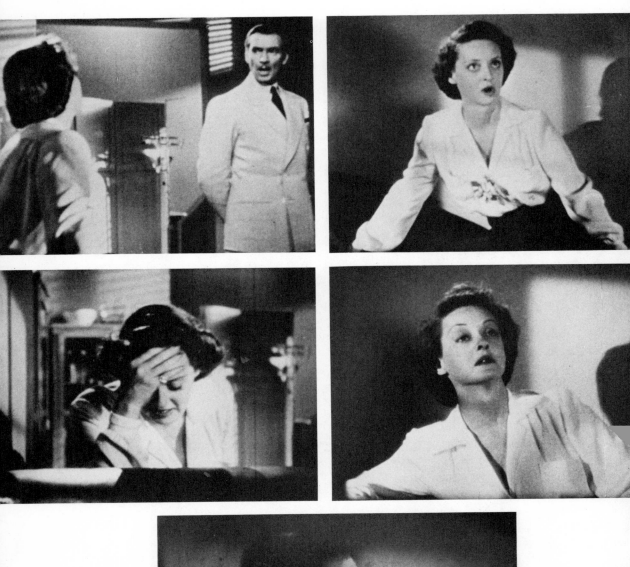

At the scene's end Davis's face submits to the dynamics of Stephenson's shadow. The actors' concentration and our own are caught in that last bit of shadowless area on her face.

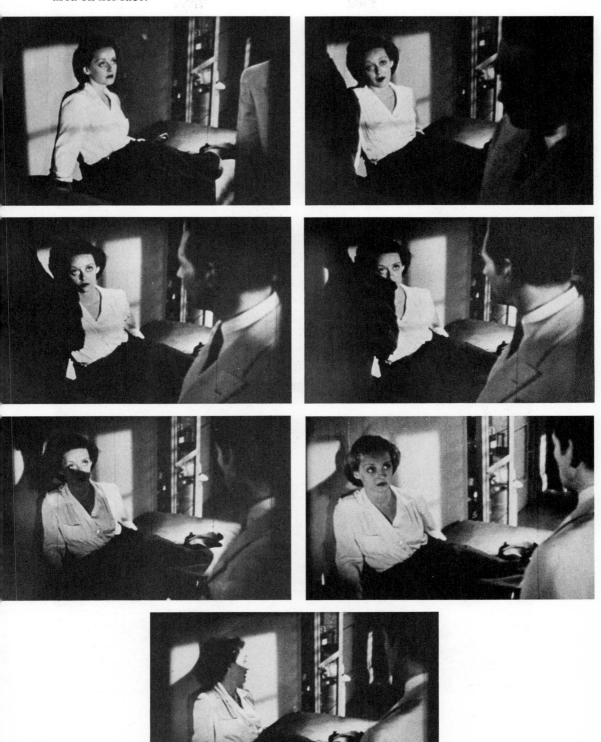

A different strategy of deployment is used when husband Herbert Marshall learns the truth. Wyler, ever faithful to his couches of domestic drama, traps Marshall on a zebra-striped sofa between the complicitous Davis and Stephenson.

Davis's weary face supplies the counterpoint to Marshall's anxiety in the shots over Stephenson's shoulder. In a languorous pose reminiscent of her false confession at the film's beginning, she recounts the details of her love affair.

She then prowls the room, straining its space to match the tension and disorientation of her marriage.

After Marshall's departure, she realizes that she will indeed be forgiven by her wronged husband, and the scene is resolved in the involuntary seductiveness of her body.

The closing in on Davis is logically focused in her eyes. Those enormous eyes are integrated into the film's visual and dramatic designs, its opening and closing blinds.

The heroine is played by an actress whose eyes are a caricatural feature (and whose adversary in *The Letter,* Gale Sondergaard, is said to have "eyes like a cobra's").

She wears glasses to make lace, which is a symbol of composure in a woman who kills in a jealous rage. Davis's eyes are paradigms for the depth of Wyler's shots. What demands they make on us! Their power is frightening. (In *In This Our Life,* 1942, and again in the outrageous *The Anniversary,* 1968, she demonstrates that even one eye is more than enough.)

Children are initially threatened by Bette Davis, and their fear must be a reaction to the force of her glance. The magnification of close-up consecrated the eyes as a distinctive element in screen acting from the days of Bara, Pickford, Gish, and Swanson. Davis's physically prominent eyes become a field of significant activity when she is properly photographed. A quick fluttering of her eyelids betrays an anxiety she suppresses in the rest of her body when she learns she is to be incarcerated prior to her trial.

In prison, during her interview with Stephenson, she prefaces her fainting spell with an odd set of the jaw and a most unusual, unnatural eye movement that make us fear that the orbs are too weighty for their sockets.

And if the tracking shots defined Wyler's understanding of the film, Davis's art shines in a murderess's eyes, challenging a moon whose appearance is as abrupt as her pistol shots.

Her eyes catch another reflection of the moon in the dark garden of her own death.

The Little Foxes (1941), while exploring more of the house than the play does and ranging into Southern town and city, draws from its theatrical source the integrity of a single set with an appropriate sense of "houseness" for a work about property and money. Wyler's framed images close in on the characters and their furniture, trapping them with each other in configurations of power and subservience, and they do so in ways that would be quite impossible within a fixed proscenium. Obsessively bound together in space by this director, the "little foxes" find their dreadful intimacy contained in a movie camera.[6]

The Little Foxes is a film of duets, trios, quartets, and small ensembles, which fully exploits an enviably collaborative cast, in particular, Herbert Marshall, Patricia Collinge, and Charles Dingle. (*The Collector*, 1964, essentially a two-character film, will be the ultimate test of Wyler's tight framing.) Wyler begins with the windows. In the first sequence Patricia Collinge leans out of hers.

[6] Otis Ferguson, more uncannily right and eloquent than we have a right to expect a daily critic to be, predated Bazin in his understanding of Wyler. "Herbert Marshall has come out to lean his weak fury against the banister, Bette Davis has come home from the battle-line, entering from the door across the space below, preoccupied and busy with gloves and stuff, to take five steps, six, seven (we know he is there, we are waiting) and another step and, *stop*. The dramatic part of the scene lifts up like a full chord in the orchestra, and we think, it is this woman who has looked up with her hard nervous eyes to find this object of hate. But it is actually the man who devised this much, to put her in the center of the screen, to warn us in advance, to give us that sense of an even count up to the point of collision, and then, seven, eight, collision. And that man is the director; it is in a picture like this that you can see him at work." *The Film Criticism of Otis Ferguson*, p. 385.

Teresa Wright sits on a sill to hear her aunt play the piano, Charles Dingle comments from another window, and, finally, Davis, on an upstairs porch, arranges her hair.

Wyler defines the spatiality: boxes within boxes, boxes stacked on boxes, characters pacing within them. The outdoors of the beginning is not merely "cinematic" or picturesque, or a gesture to "open up" the play. It provides a threshold for the prisonlike interior, a model for Wyler's favorite context—the movie frame—and a prefiguration of the film's final window frame in its last shot.

The intricacies of the intervening compositions force our eyes to dart about as we constantly readjust the links between people and things just as the characters vie for positions of superiority. At the dinner party for the visiting Chicago businessman (Davis's ambition to go to Chicago in *The Little Foxes* becomes the major theme of her Warners swan song, *Beyond the Forest*, 1949; the stiff self-possession of her Regina Giddens, in the first, and the freewheeling hysteria of her Rosa Moline, in the second, illustrate polar extremes of the actress's manner), the star is perversely reflected at the frame's center.

Wyler adroitly reorganizes the planes of table arrangement through visual-aural disorientation. Charles Dingle is presumably talking to someone in front of him, a character we see over his shoulder. The connivance and the deviousness of Regina Giddens and her brothers are rendered by this obliqueness. (Wyler had already displayed his dextrous "slight of mirror" in *Dodsworth,* 1936.) A later scene quite explicitly uses involved mirror play to realign faces at once separate, averted from each other, and almost superimposed in this depiction of a quasi-incestuous, wheeling-dealing family.

Even the reflection of a single face stresses indirectness through the angle of the shot and the tilt of the head.

The mirror is not, however, the film's dominant structural motif. The characters' awryness may be captured by it, but they are more richly served by the furniture that has been molded to their prepossession, and the house, which is a grander image of their ambition. The parlor couch receives particular attention first at the dinner party.

The low angle shot over Charles Dingle's leg stresses Davis's recumbency as a peculiar quest for softness and comfort by a woman whose hardness gives the fiction its texture. The couch's undulating back both supports and exposes the character. This very couch is the arena of Regina's sudden triumph during her husband's heart attack.

It is the setting of an even sweeter victory over her brothers, when the backs of the settee and the actress combine in a positively totalitarian diagonal.

In *The Letter* Leslie Crosbie's overstuffed sofa stresses conventionality. In *The Little Foxes* a new shape and the actress's newly emphasized spine project the satisfaction of the proprietary, of a dominion whose power is terrifying through its disproportion to the spaces of the film—a sofa, a room, a house.

The part of the house most suited to expressing the exertion of power is the central staircase, the passage from the privacy of bedrooms and hellish marriages to the politeness of drawing rooms and dinner parties. This is the ladder upon which to measure the characters, rising and falling in relationship to each other. Wyler knows that we see better when looking either down or up. This accounts, in part, for the frequent low or high angle shots. In his quest to "show everything" he finds the staircase particularly useful. It actually possesses the symbolic qualities of a solid, vertical or diagonal shape that can only be traced in thin air by an oddly angled camera. It gives mass and substance to hierarchies often sketched in space between the lens and its subject. The relationship of the staircase to sight is established in one of the film's most uncomfortable sequences (a true distinction since discomfort is the reigning mood). Patricia Collinge receives a slap in the entrance hall, and her embarrassment is witnessed by Teresa Wright from the upstairs landing.

The sudden shift of level is as rude as the slap and as revealing to us as it is to Wright, whose education in familial realpolitik is. one of *The Little Foxes'* prime subjects. Those stairs sharpen everyone's eyes: sister and brothers try to out-maneuver each other.

A husband momentarily triumphs over his wife.

Near the film's end Wright again sees the truth from that vantage point.

It's there that Davis must ultimately accept abandonment and loneliness.

All of the framing devices in *The Little Foxes*—the windows and mirrors, the furniture, the oval staircase—have Davis as their ultimate focal point. Her barest movement and her more shocking stillness both fix our attention and guide it to the complementary areas of the space she occupies. The standard of sharpness she sets summons images beyond those we see before our eyes. An almost languid pace recalls her jagged frenzy of the early thirties. An occasional arm stab is a remnant of once profligate gesticulation, touching as it now punctuates the inexorably measured unfolding of her Regina. Neither Herbert Marshall's outburst nor her hatred disrupts her swaying ascent of the stairs and the icy delivery of "I hope you die. I hope you die soon. I'll be waiting for you to die."

The crook of Marshall's arm and the expanse of lace expose the set of her shoulders and a deadly assured expression. Her voice appropriates the completeness of the image, conveying the depths of her loathing. Trust is the clue to Davis's success in wedding form to persona. Her reputation for strength and spirit invests Regina with a known quantity, an extrafictional graft of past achievement and experience. Yet it is her ability to illuminate the film with the hardness of her gaze that controls its shape. Whether she is staring at her despised husband or at the emptiness of her own future, her vision defies pretense.

She sees all, just like Wyler's ideal audience. The freedom of directorial perspective and the accuracy of the actress's glance meet at the centers of images that are tuned to the movement of the camera and the throbbing stillness of Davis's being. The gap between Mildred (*Of Human Bondage*) and Regina is enormous. As Davis traverses it, our eyes bulge to match her own.

9.
"I detest cheap sentiment": Davis and the Tearjerker

Never was an actress less suited to bathos than Bette Davis. She has always trumpeted her disdain for the poor dear good girls, and her public remembers most vividly the flashing eyes of the vixen, the woman on the prowl, who is ever ready to take on life, indeed, to shape it. The swagger of her Mildred in *Of Human Bondage* is modified via *Jezebel* through its ultimate refinement in Margo Channing in possession of her living room, hall, and staircase. Our awareness that this is the manner to which she was born is heightened by the control and variants of the manner. Yet it can be argued that her finest achievements are those performances that run quite contrary to her natural ferocity and strength so emphatically exploited in *Bordertown* (1935), *Dangerous* (1935), *Marked Woman* (1937), *Jezebel* (1938), and *The Private Lives of Elizabeth and Essex* (1939)—to name only a few of the most obvious examples. Finding a new brand of strength, she invests the vulnerable romantic heroine with a character so at odds with the conventional manifestations of the type that the mold must be refashioned, and the public, perhaps without truly noticing it, accepts a steel-trap discipline to control the flow of suds. In fact, suds they are no more, for in the best of the Davis women's films the sentimental ploys are given shape and elegance. The vehicles become precisely that: vehicles sturdy enough to contain the Davis presence and the Davis technique. Above all, they show an actress willing to eschew easy solutions. The facilely wrung tear is sacrificed, but something much more durable takes its place. The structure of a complete performance emerges from these films unburdened by the triteness and banality of the plots.

Garbo achieved this in such films as *Wild Orchids* and *The Mysterious Lady* with a totally different kind of projection. Garbo always seems to be inventing it as she goes along, eluding our grasp, and our insight flashes along with the actress's. Only through retrospect can we make some attempt to reconstruct the performance, indeed to remember a bit of what we have seen. Davis does the opposite. She is like an expert novelist, anxious that her own awareness be shared by her "readers." Part of her natural aggressiveness is reflected in the process through which she thrusts a portrayal upon the public. She trusts its intelligence, its ability to follow her sense of a role and a situation; therefore her best work is marked by its consistency, by its very inevitability. There is a chasm between the predictable and the inevitable, between a response that is standard or hackneyed, and the one that is necessary to an established pattern emanating from imagination and refined by intelligence. The spitfire is consciously transformed into the long-suffering heroine, a late-thirties and early-forties variant on the victimized creatures so ennobled in the silent era by Lillian Gish. Just as Gish, through her energy, was able to redefine the romantic heroine in the frame of melodrama, so Bette Davis can stand her upon a pile of ladies' magazines and all-too-popular novels—a personal and strong heroine despite the instability of the pedestal.

The best of her women's films come from her most fruitful period at Warners, after her undisputed establishment as queen of the studio and her second Oscar for *Jezebel*. Her confidence is expressed in a willingness to do things in a free, unexpected way. Gone are some of the wonderful excesses of the early years, but in their place is a control without the rigidity that too often characterizes maturity in acting. Davis is able to do all she wants, yet the freshness and vitality of her work in *Twenty Thousand Years in Sing Sing* (1933), *The Petrified Forest* (1936), and *Kid Galahad* (1937) are more than memories. They animate the core of her later films.

A FACE FOR DEATH: *DARK VICTORY*

Edmund Goulding directed four of Davis's films, and in all of them he cast her in sympathetic roles. By the late thirties the women's picture had become his specialty. His reputation for being an actress's director is more and more justified with the passage of time. His contribution to *Grand Hotel* has already been amply discussed (see p. 137ff). His taste and sensitivity are enormous assets to Jane Bryan (*We Are Not Alone*, 1939), Dorothy McGuire (*Claudia*, 1943), and Joan Fontaine (*The Constant Nymph*, 1943), and supporting actress Oscar winners Mary Astor (*The Great Lie*, 1941) and Anne Baxter (*The Razor's Edge*, 1946). Goulding's films with Davis are variable. She is done in by the staleness of *That Certain Woman* (1937), written by Goulding, and a remake of a 1929 Gloria Swanson vehicle, *The Trespasser*. Davis intelligently ceded *The Great Lie* (1941) to Mary Astor[1] in a more interesting role. *Dark Victory* (1939) and *The Old Maid* (1939) are, however, examples of the director's best manner.

Goulding, Garbo, and *Grand Hotel* are useful as standards for measuring the qualities of *Dark Victory*. (A delightful coincidence—David O. Selznick urged the role of Judith Traherne on Garbo in 1935.[2]) Some of the MGM gloss and pace were exported to Warners in this film, and Goulding must have been partly responsible for it. The gloss and pace were deadly when applied to Norma Shearer and Joan Crawford, but Garbo throve on elegance and long time spans. Surprisingly, Davis's nervous excitement is also beautifully set off by Goulding's grace. There is even some analogy to be drawn between the handsome superficiality of George Brent and of John Barrymore, both being silent foils for the solo arias of the actresses. And one final reminder of Garbo and *Grand Hotel*—both actresses first appear raising their heads from pillows (see p. 140).

[1] Mary Astor, in *A Life on Film*, gives an illuminating and detailed account of what it was actually like to act in films.
[2] Rudy Behlmer, ed., *Memo from David O. Selznick*, p. 75.

The comic tone of Judith Traherne's hangover could not be more distant from Grusinskaya's weltschmerz. Yet the character's essential aloneness, so swiftly established in the first shot of Garbo in *Grand Hotel*, is also posited by this *Dark Victory* close-up. What is more, the close-up is a relatively infrequent element in the rhetorics of Davis and Warner Brothers. Its priority and subsequent use in *Dark Victory* are pertinent to the character's development and, particularly, to the film's climax. The close-up belongs to the style of this film because it is relevant to the heroine's need for identification, an identification in solitude. It is something akin to the drawing-in process of *Grand Hotel*.

Drawing-in is rendered in a scene characteristic of Goulding, a director who extracts the most from small spaces and situations of confinement. It is Davis's first encounter with George Brent (the doctor). Figuratively trapped in the doctor's office, she is forced to stop her nervous side-stepping of the issues of her health and her madcap life. Goulding uses every bit of the office. The characters sit on several chairs and the arms of the chairs, they lean on the desk, stand by the window and the door, and pace back and forth. The shades are drawn and opened. The angles are constantly varied and it seems as if all the permutations of the two-shot are employed. The activity is wonderfully filmic. It expresses entrapment in space, a point that is emphasized when Brent stops Davis at the door with "You're frightened."

The central shots of the scene are two close-ups of Davis, the first an ingenious and affecting appropriation of her trademark: setting a speed record in cigarette lighting. The gesture was not seized upon by Davis's impersonators without cause; she knows its value both as prop and as focusing element. The spectator's eye follows her hand to the center, a triangle of expression formed by mouth and eyes. In *Dark Victory*, the ritual is integrated into the drama; the gesture tells "Doctor" Brent her motor control is not all it should be.

Audience and doctor know that when Bette Davis can't light her own cigarette something is seriously amiss. A moment later she tries to light Brent's cigarette with the same lack of success. This extension of the actress's persona into the role is bolstered by the brittle voice, the breakneck diction. Goulding is pursuing his quarry, and finally cages her in a particularly inventive close-up that is held for such a long time that its spatial value can escape no one.

This shot is ostensibly from Brent's point of view, but the radical angle of the face also captures the character in the act of reflecting and of confronting herself. The close-up per se isolates the profile; the angle gives an over-the-shoulder effect without hiding the expression. We are thus simultaneously permitted to see the actress and to see from her point of view.

This kind of concentration on the star's face is reiterated at the moment when Judith Traherne learns she must undergo brain surgery. The notion of self-confrontation is obviously conveyed by a mirror.

Davis passes from hysteria to consciousness of her predicament, again expressed in those wide-open eyes. They strain to take in the whole reflected image, avid for knowledge of her true identity, but her avidity will be satisfied only when she accepts that identity through the focus of death.

Dark Victory is happy in its use of such accouterments as a cigarette, a mirror, a hat to sustain the actress's performance.

Davis does not truly require props or special costuming, but a bit of help goes a long way. The hat she is wearing when she discovers her true medical history ("prognosis negative") is somehow disproportionate without being ridiculous, and it gives her personality an edge, emphasizing the triangular shape of her face and bringing even more sharpness into her eyes. This focus is pushed further when she challenges Brent and Geraldine Fitzgerald with her knowledge of the truth.

This face is not the allegorical emblem à la Lillian Gish, nor is it Garbo's surface of paradox and ambiguity. It is possessed by a will and an intelligence that concentrate physique, pattern, and moment; it comes out of the frame with the force of the early Davis; it embodies the refinement and refusal of irrelevancy she developed with Wyler. The actress's belief in the situation is instantly transmitted to the spectator by the intensity of the configuration, an alliance of expression and space that allows us not the slightest latitude. Davis's Judith Traherne becomes ours. No other interpretation is imaginable, so unswerving and sure is the version she created in *Dark Victory*.

The film's climax—of course, the sequence toward which everything else is drawn—is the most dangerous for actress and director. If the central issue is the heroine's death, its rendering is fraught with opportunities for the insufferably banal—a protracted expiring with gobs of self-sacrifice and self-congratulation, and a good cry was had by all—and it must be admitted that pitfalls are not avoided. The heavenly choir that accompanies the fade-out is singularly inappropriate—inappropriate, that is, to the Davis way of playing a long death scene.

But Davis makes preparations. A sign that death is near brings on a moment of panic unblemished by histrionics. She almost turns away from the camera.

In situations like this, Davis knows that less is more, and again, an actress famous for the broadness of her personal gestures, underplays with precious restraint whenever the script is strong enough for her to do so.

The entire final sequence of *Dark Victory* is salvaged, indeed, made memorable, by her holding back, her reserve, and her refusal to indulge in the almost unavoidable tear-jerking context. Geraldine Fitzgerald supplies the breakdown, and Davis offers comforting arms accompanied by a face with eyes blinded but still searching out the truth, reminiscent of the mirror scene.

She needs no quivering mouth or lacrimal cascade; in her farewell to her doctor husband (he is ignorant of her imminent death), she presses her cheek to the firm outline of Brent's shirtsleeve.

What she must do borders on the insufferably noble, but the serenity and grace she summons relieve this sequence of its preachy moral burden. Goulding and cameraman Ernest Haller help her to realize her decision to look beautiful. For it is a decision. Davis does not bring to her films a photographer's ready-made dream of a face, such as the madonnalike perfection of Gish or the unnerving harmony of Garbo's features. She reshapes her face to the part, and although Gish and Garbo do so to some extent, they never truly escape their intrinsic beauty.

Two scenes from *Dark Victory* demonstrate the extremes of Davis's facial control. At her party, after what she supposes was a successful operation, she is literally bursting with joy, and her face is too full for the composure "beauty" requires.

But this lack of composure and this bursting face are just as appropriate to Judith Traherne as the almost startling loveliness she acquires in the film's last moments. She asks her friend to leave so that she may die alone, and we wonder if there has ever been a more beautiful chin and jawline.

The best is saved for the famous final shot and the culmination of the heroine's looking ahead, her attempts to grasp the future. Blind, she now sees without the exertions and uncertainties that previously filled her eyes. The self that sought to penetrate the mirror is contained in the calm of this wonderfully framed face, which is given significance by shadow and the chenille bedspread, by the unusual side angle, and by Bette Davis, who knows that she has to look her best, her most beautiful, in order to greet death with the proper dignity.

The shot goes out of focus at the very end, thus creating its own time—lingering, triumphing over the heavenly hosts—and reminding the most skeptical viewer that there is a way to deal with the sentimental. Looking banality squarely in the eye, Davis proves that thought transforms it, in fact, can exploit it to provide models that are adequate to the force of the thinker. The integrity of her conception leaves no room for blubbering. Each scene is invested with a tautness that radiates from her face and her body, overlaying the pseudoseriousness of *Dark Victory* with a tear-proof surface to which it has no right. It is her bravery and strength, not Judith Traherne's, that constitute the film's real victory.

DECORUM AND FEELING

The processes of self-understanding Davis undergoes in *Dark Victory* are further articulated in *The Old Maid*. Unable to cope with the spatial and temporal displacements of the first half of the film, Goulding does not match his success in *Dark Victory*. But later, limited to a few rooms and a short time span, he finds the kind of concentration that so richly focused Grusinskaya and Judith Traherne.

Davis's illegitimate daughter believes her to be an old maid, an illusion the character maintains for propriety's sake. Davis is particularly harsh with the girl so as to avoid revealing the truth in a gush of maternal solicitude. Throughout the last half of the film, she repeatedly overhears her daughter's expressions of resentment, and this situation neatly links her pain and love.

The formality of ambivalence is exploited when, alone in her sitting room, her face cut in half by a shadow, Davis passes from an indulgent mother's tenderness to an old maid's sternness.

Tenderness served up with this amount of style is an extension of Judith Traherne's toughness of spirit, and no less tender for it.

From *Dark Victory* until her departure from Warner Brothers in 1949, Davis portrayed the courageous, long-suffering, and essentially sympathetic heroine in roughly half of her twenty-three films. Errol Flynn accurately describes her in *The Sisters* (1938): "You have a very exciting serenity." It is precisely this paradoxical excitement in serenity that lies at the center of her performances. Her

Carlotta in *Juarez* (1939) is remembered for her two mad scenes (see pp. 234–235), but her prayer for a son is an image of beatific patience.

This degree of calm becomes the pattern for her work in *All This and Heaven Too* (1940), a veritable exercise in underacting. Involved in a platonic romance with Charles Boyer, she trusts her mind to convey emotions that cannot be manifested openly. Without sighs, tears, or breast-heaving, she exudes a grandiose self-assurance and a knowledge that she is deeply loved. Her face takes on a treasurable, masklike quality, as seen here just after she has received a compliment from Boyer. Her hair is parted in the middle and her forehead bares the security of her moral commitment.

The clear lines of countenance that brooks no dishonesty, and the firm conviction that sloppy gestures and facial contortions will pander to the material, these are the special talents Bette Davis brings to her best women's films. The crispness of her manner successfully challenges and submerges sentimentality into the truth of sentiment.

The plainness of Davis's Henriette in this film is set against rival Barbara O'Neil's florid beauty and Boyer's extraordinary sensuality.

In *Mother Goddam* by Whitney Stine,[3] the actress complains of the unrealistic situation of Boyer's spurning such an attractive wife; yet Davis's refusal to appear glamorous or fleshy draws emotion beneath the surface and makes convincing the notion of a man who kills for platonic love. Hairdo and costuming have something to do with it, but much credit must go to a star-actress who, for the duration of a very long film, refuses to think of surface beauty.

Her self-possession serves a variety of situations and moods. When, on the witness stand, she learns of Boyer's suicide attempt, she tests her face's tensile limits without losing control.

When she is on her way to his bedside, memories and anxiety are lodged in the subtly varied set of her eyes—a variation perceptible only because the surrounding frame of the face has remained so constant.

[3] Pp. 129–130.

In this film of silences and unplayed love scenes, the final encounter between Boyer and Davis is a wordless juxtaposition of close-ups. He has poisoned himself to avoid a murder trial that would implicate her. The police have brought her to him in the vain hope that evidence of an illicit relationship will emerge. The lovers merely look at each other, and that looking, which has been sustained throughout the film, is recapitulated by actors who know the value of absolute composure.

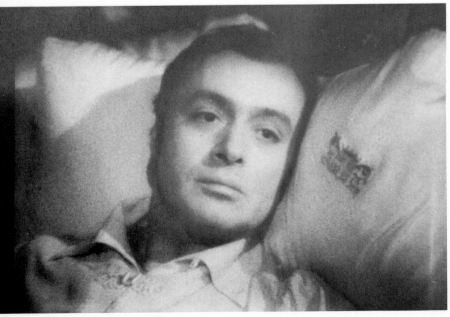

Davis's constancy of expression is dramatized at the film's end. She has recounted her story to schoolgirls, who dissolve in tears. As she looks out of the window, Boyer's voice is superimposed on the sound track and snowflakes texture her face.

The aural, visual, and emotional levels of this shot reveal the function of the fixed shape of Davis's face in director Anatole Litvak's graceful setups and in the film's romantic excesses. The more she is fussed at, the less she has to fuss; her own tears are withheld when everyone else's (including our own) are freely flowing.

Davis preserves her integrity in all her tearjerkers. In *The Corn Is Green* (1945) she is a schoolteacher, at first joyful, and then resigned to her fate.

On her way to give herself up to the police in the fade-out of *Deception* (1946), she is told that she must be "*so* happy."

In the disastrous *Winter Meeting* (1948), the line "I'm so horribly unhappy" is completely thrown away.

Davis has said[4] that the lady novelist of *Old Acquaintance* (1943) is the heroine closest to her own personality, and we are forced to believe it when she wryly sums up her no-nonsense attitude to the posturing of this sentimental film: "It's late, and I'm very, very tired of youth and love and self-sacrifice." A dose of skepticism is precisely what permits actress and audience to engage in the sentimental without that terrifying loss of self that is endemic to the mode. While indicating the dangerous areas of mawkishness, Davis enacts the superb tests of decorum and feeling—earning "all this and heaven too," and touching with her voice, her body, and her hands "where the corn is green."

4 Stine, *Mother Goddam*, p. 173.

BUT JUST A FEW TEARS: *NOW, VOYAGER*

Dark Victory, The Old Maid, and *All This and Heaven Too* are merely warm-ups for the emotional calisthenics Bette Davis is put through in *Now, Voyager* (1942), and the situations of the earlier films seem like paradigms of classical restraint when compared to these "Perils of Aunt Charlotte" concocted by Olive Higgins Prouty. In *Now, Voyager,* Davis must survive a complete change of personality and a star-crossed love affair, and overcome a brutally tyrannical mother and a particularly talented child actress. She triumphs over the collection of absurdities that pass for the peripeties of this "modern psychological drama." It is a triumph that insures *Now, Voyager's,* place among the most satisfying of her films.

The great enigma of *Now, Voyager,* is Irving Rapper. Rapper's reputation rests on the four Bette Davis films he directed, two of which, *Now, Voyager,* and *Deception,* are in the major film category. Despite the most slighting nod given him in the actress's autobiography, one suspects that he was a better director than he is given credit for. It is likely that Davis had much more to do with directing in *Now, Voyager,* than stars normally have, but that cannot explain the ensemble elegance of *Deception* or the exquisite performance of Jane Wyman in *The Glass Menagerie.* (Yet Gertrude Lawrence's dreadful errors of characterization in the latter film do make one wonder.) And if Rapper relinquished the reins to the star in *Now, Voyager,* the results suggest that abdication is sometimes an act of great creativity. Whoever is responsible, *Now, Voyager,* has the consistency of style and even more surprisingly, the taste that gives continued pleasure to its viewers.

The film's organization threatens to be a drawback, for it is impossible to sustain the tension of the first sequences, which involve Davis before she has changed from ugly duckling into swan. If the much longer swan portion develops its own interests, it is only a tribute to the actress's ability to survive her own bravura. Davis on the brink of a nervous breakdown is a sight to behold, and she brings to her rendition of the frustrated, mother-hating virgin a tautness and a lack of compromise that, along with Margo's party scene in *All About Eve* and the Wyler films, constitute some of her best footage.

She has been summoned by skeptical mother Gladys Cooper to meet psychiatrist Claude Rains. Repression, fear, and embarrassment at her dowdy appearance are caught in her face as she looks away from a mother who commands her daughter's very glance. And how does she manage to make that famous gash of a mouth so small and pinched?

The over-the-shoulder shot neatly diagrams a domineering-mother/hysterical-daughter relationship. The lines of Gladys Cooper's body and Bette Davis's hands tell us all there is to know about Charlotte and her tormentor.

Shamed by Cooper's cruelly disparaging remarks, she varies the set of her eyes and mouth, increasing the compression of her features and thus preparing for the inevitable outburst that will come a few minutes later.

Alone with Claude Rains in her room, she initiates the second stage in the sequence of her breakdown, and the strategy of crescendo is neatly arranged: the interview downstairs and the bottled-up nerves, the loosening in the upstairs room and the recital of an abortive shipboard romance squelched by "my mother," and then a complete letting go with a goodly quantity of sobs on the repeated "my mother." The accompanying rain on the window is a pardonable de rigueur convention.[5]

[5] Rapper considers the use of rain effects his "trademark." Charles Higham and Joel Greenberg, *The Celluloid Muse,* p. 202.

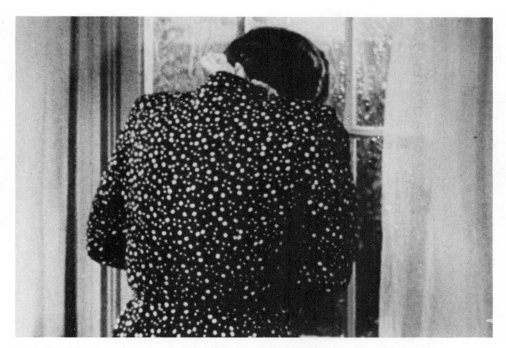

The shot of her back is significant in the Davis vocabulary. Many of the most highly charged scenes in this and other films find ways to withhold her such as with her face averted or her voice out of frame. Both she and her directors capitalize upon her potential energy, which is an inexhaustible store that must be dosed out to avoid stridency. Her turned back does just that without destroying the accumulative impact of the scene.

The third stage of her mounting hysteria can top the "my mother" bit precisely because of the strategy—the expert ladling out. This time she is goaded by her bitchy niece (Bonita Granville).

The transition from shakily pouring tea to coming apart at the seams is part of a structured and accessible emotional response, which is her ability to transmit feeling with the kind of sureness that elicits a controlled audience reaction. She pulls her trumps only when there is nothing else strong enough in her hand. The final shot of "my mother" and the final moment of the tea business distinguish between the power of the king and the ace of trump, and between the strategy and the finesse for rendering a nervous breakdown. The relatively slow pace is conducive to gradual development and runs counter to the rat-tat-tat Warner Brothers style; it makes palatable the excesses of *Now, Voyager*. That shaking hand, that wild mouth, and those bulging eyes rely on the previous patience of actress and director. What might easily have sunken to the grotesque is relieved of nonsense by the perceptible pattern of elaborately worked out alternate tension and release, a design that is quite obvious in great dancing but no less necessary to great acting.

Where is she to go from here? During an ocean voyage after a brief scene of recuperation at the sanitarium, the swan emerges at the top of a gangplank, and if a hat did the trick in *Dark Victory*, it is a stroke of genius in *Now, Voyager*.

The radical shadow bisecting the face in white/dark/white strata creates a visual phenomenon quite distinct from the makeup transformation of lipstick and plucked eyebrows. Our attention to appearance is imperiously summoned by the hat and its effect upon a Charlotte who, hatless in a Boston parlor, had no protection against her mother and niece. This shot does not reveal what we commonly call acting, especially after the most recent exhibition of that activity, but the sense of face belongs to a plastique pertinent to the camera. The viewer is allowed a different perceptual referent, a chance to come down from the nerve-jarring, first sequence and to use his eyes anew.

The cruise and Rio interludes are certainly the weakest segments of the film, for, aside from a few moments of anxiety about her recently acquired chic and love, Davis can do little more than look chic and in love. This wears thin because Paul Henreid is hardly a Charles Boyer, who could take the initiative when Bette relinquished it. (Davis is poorly served by her leading men in the major tear-jerkers, with the exceptions of Boyer, Claude Rains in *Mr. Skeffington* and *Deception*, and John Dall in *The Corn Is Green*.) These sequences do, however, introduce that particularly slurpy, Max Steiner theme music, and done in one shot, the first kiss is adroitly photographed in its passage from tears to the kind of gentle passion so common to the forties' style.

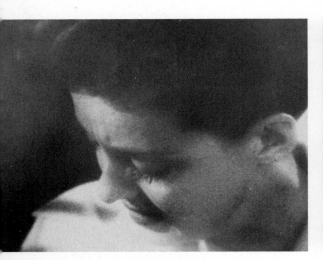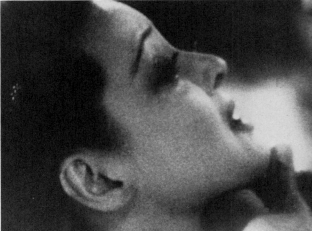

Henreid is barely visible in the shot; Rapper has the good sense to locate all the important events in Charlotte's face. True to the Davis manner of withholding, she emerges in profile only when Henreid takes her chin in his hand. Her fulfillment and the audience's are simultaneous. But just to remind us that we are watching Davis in a Warner Brothers film, there is no lingering. Throughout the film, there is a chance for development but not for slackness.

With Charlotte's return to Boston and mother, *Now, Voyager*, springs tauter still, proving the obvious point that co-players of equal energy make for interesting movies. Bette Davis meets her match in Gladys Cooper. Their reunion is one of the nicest bits of staging in the film: Davis, in black (with a cousin of the shipboard white hat sharpening her face), strides in; Cooper, majestically ensconced, disdainfully surveys her daughter's new-found glamour.

This spatial setup, with the directions a bit altered, has the same function in a scene in Irving Rapper's *Deception*.

Again, the seated character is the dominant one, and Claude Rains's Hollenius is every bit as classy as Gladys Cooper's Mother Vale. Magnificent in their self-assurance, both polarize Davis's energy; they are centers that give shape to the boundaries described by her gait. In fairness, it must be admitted that Rains is the center of *Deception* in more ways than one. But if Davis yields to his showier role, it is a conscious yielding and the fruit of an artistic partnership that sees them both to good stead in four films.

Such yielding is appropriate in her scene with Gladys Cooper in *Now, Voyager,* and Rapper wisely keeps his distance from Davis to avoid the impression that she is dominant. Charlotte is caught at the door while Mother is ridiculing her, and both actress and director show surprising and welcome stand-offishness.

Lowered lids and the briefest duration particularize a moment "pregnant with meaning."

Immediately after, another big opportunity is undercut by the camera's retreat. Charlotte has received flowers from Jerry (Paul Henreid), and Max Steiner's music ably shoulders the emotional burden.

The mother–daughter battle for independence is resumed in Charlotte's room, and the relationship in depth recalls the previous one. This time, a standing Cooper is much more vulnerable.

Davis displays self-assurance, and so much so that she delivers her defiant lines from off-screen to Cooper's back and arm.

Rapper understood that the scenes between the two Vales were the most exciting in the film, and he created a textural variety to guarantee their potency.

Mother is resting in bed subsequent to her self-induced fall down the stairs, and the focus shifts completely to Davis and her quietest, most graceful nuance of realization: "I'm not afraid."

The high contrast invests her features with a neatness that illuminates the barest of alterations in a mixture of surprise, satisfaction, and sureness unencumbered by a logical loathing for Cooper. The quietness works, and if Charlotte is one of Davis's most sympathetic portrayals, it is because of this reticence.

No scenery is chewed, even during the remarkable death of Cooper. "I didn't want to be born. You didn't want me to be born. It's been a calamity on both sides," says Davis. Soul-shaking words—soul-shaking enough to cause Mother to expire—but they are uttered with her eyes closed, and then her back turned to the camera.

Clearly Gladys Cooper's demise cannot be topped, so Davis remains in character and lets the situation play upon her face. She offers a receiving surface, and that is quite enough. She has just talked mommy dead, and no amount of guilty heaving and horror would convey the weight of this straightforward appraisal of the circumstances.

Her tears, a moment later, are over before we know it, and again, a scene threatening in its potential bathos is lent strength through spareness.

Bette Davis can cry. She doesn't do so very often in front of the camera, certainly much less often than one might expect a leading exponent of the tear-jerking women's film to do. Norma Shearer, Greer Garson, and Sylvia Sidney drench us with ten moist eyefuls for each one of Davis's tears. But tears do serve in moderation, especially when they conspire with particular lighting effects to modify the actress's face. Her reconciliation with and good-bye to Henreid at Back Bay Station call forth the glisten and the trickle. *Now, Voyager,* is a love story (among many other things), and the play of lights from the passing train on her tear-streaked cheeks is undeniably attractive.

Characteristically, the camera tilts down to the wilted camellias, and although the metaphor is trite, it does continue the established pattern of withholding the star ever so slightly, and of refusing indulgence in the plenitude of Davis's expressive features.

The rest of the film shifts to the relationship between Jerry's unhappy daughter (played by Janis Wilson) and Charlotte, and now tones of maternal generosity and understanding are applied to the portrait.

It is up to the child to provide the hysteria, and Davis knows when to back off. Her super-self-assurance is perhaps not showy, but it is pointed to the film's final sequence. The hysterical tightness of the beginning has been transformed into the expansive awareness of a woman who declares, "Oh, Jerry, don't let's ask for the moon. We have the stars."

This line is one of the most famous in all of Bette Davis's films, and I am always surprised at the naturalness of its delivery. It is suffused with her knowledge that 118 minutes add up and constitute an entity, and that the shape and flow are worth more than any cheap effect. It rightly caps a performance in which strength qualifies weakness without denaturing it. Davis teaches us strength through her ability to stamp its quality on the attractive claptrap of *Now, Voyager*. Indeed, Davis calls for our strength along with our handkerchiefs, and we can see clearly even when our eyes are awash with tears.

10.
All About Acting

Movie acting accommodates the most arch self-referentiality. The preceding chapters have hardly stressed the naturalism of film portrayal. Gish, Garbo, and Davis repeatedly affirm their distance from the self-effacement of a strict likeness to reality. Stardom is a sphere of activity that calls attention to its procedures, and star acting of the highest order initiates the spectator into its most arcane rituals. When Gish fixes the smile on her face in *Broken Blossoms,* she performs a gesture that links the realms of character and actress and reminds us that a movie star is enacting a frightened fifteen-year-old. She does ·this by wielding her most pertinent tools—convention and mask. Over and over, Gish carries us beyond representation to an area of patent artificiality where the confusion of experience is reordered by the transparency of her playing. In *Broken Blossoms* she mothers her doll, in *Way Down East* she baptizes her dying child, at the revolutionary tribunal in *Orphans of the Storm,* in full view of the mob, she signals to her blind sister. It is a peculiar show for two audiences (three, if you count the movie patrons) that bridges historical and personal predicament. Such instances of Gish's theatricality—Mimi's death scene, Hester Prynne's public/private exhibitions on the scaffold—display a degree of exteriorization that accepts and exploits our awareness of an actress who is acting. The moments we remember best are those when a star crystallizes a performance in a blaze of artifice.

Garbo was often criticized for being mannered, a judgment I consider positive. Garbo is mannered with postures as convoluted and as revealing as the most artfully contrived canvases of Velázquez. The cadences of her gait supply the phony MGM sets with angles and perspectives undreamed of by Cedric Gibbons. Her speech and her being realign time, freely mixing doses of a lost past and an empty future in a present enriched by both.[1] Hooded eyes fill the space between her and the lens with a knowledge beyond words. *Wild Orchids, A Woman of Affairs,* and *Queen Christina* concentrate on Garbo's relationship to objects. She manipulates her Javanese costume, her bouquet, her love nest in configurations whose pictorialness supersedes plot and character. A particularly rarefied brand of mannerism emerges when traditional theatrical content and conflict are subordinated and a film's meaning is located in the connections between actress, ambience, and camera. The screen becomes a huge canvas of Garbo holding all the other actors in the palm of her hand. Even *Grand Hotel* and *Camille,* works

[1] In Alistair Cooke, *Garbo and the Night Watchmen,* pp. 143–144, Cooke was one of the most eloquent Garbo-maniacs in the thirties. His assessment of her acting in *Anna Karenina* is applicable to her work throughout most of her career: "She sees not only her own life, but everybody else's before it has been lived. This fatalism has happily passed over into her technique. And since the plot is now high hokum, the chief excitement is to watch how perfectly she now sees backwards, like a perpetually drowning woman, not only her life but her past: the way, at one point, she takes Fredric March's arm in the box, the way she looks down at the baby of a young friend, the way she picks up the field-glasses to watch March fall from his horse, the way—years ahead of the acting textbooks—she hides a broken moment not with a cute nose-dive into cupped palms, but with the five inadequate fingers of one bony hand;—her gestures, too, therefore have the same tender calculation, the same anxiety to treat people with perhaps too much care at the moment, because she knows what's going to happen to them in a year or two."

whose excellence is not limited to Garbo, are shaped by her esoteric presence, by Grusinskaya's exaggerations and Marguerite's smile. The mechanical dramatics of *Grand Hotel* are transfigured by Garbo's eccentric ballerina, as is the bourgeois ethic of *Camille* by the playfulness of her doomed cocotte.

Mannerism was not part of the Warner Brothers vocabulary in the thirties. The prevailing speed of their films, except for the musical extravagances of Busby Berkeley, inhibited silences, epiphanies, and spatial complexities. During the apprentice years Davis was kept hopping so fast that the surrounding space almost never adjusted to her presence nor she to it. When she got to play an actress, a manneristic impersonation for any actress, her Joyce Heath in *Dangerous* led us to believe that histrionic talent is something like an advanced case of the heebie-jeebies. As a second actress named Joyce, in *It's Love I'm After* (1937), she proved herself an accomplished comedienne by extracting the humor from her own caricatural gestures—flapping her arms, prowling over the sets, opening a door as if she wanted to destroy it. By that time she was able to control her persona with self-irony, and if the film had a bit more of Davis it might be more amusing today. Still, it features the treasurable tomb scene from *Romeo and Juliet* where Davis and Leslie Howard interlard Shakespeare with lines like "You reek of garlic."

The subsequent curtain calls of the acting couple are clearly reminiscent of Lunt and Fontanne in *The Guardsman* (who, by the way, have just finished performing a future Davis vehicle, *Elizabeth the Queen*). And Joyce Arden's face in a dressing-room mirror—hair tied back beneath a towel—is a precious first version of Margo Channing in her lair.

Davis has the time and space to explore the function of the acting self in her films with Wyler. Together they elaborate a screen being that is at once significant in a given fiction and reflective of the whole process of moviemaking. A director who uses film space as a refracted field—grouping sets, furniture, and people so as to explore the dynamics of relationships that exist only in art—finds a performer who energizes the field no matter where she is placed, and whose clarity of presence lights us through the spatial labyrinths without sacrificing a whit of their refinement. On Julie's staircase she sorts out desire and pride; she sits on Leslie Crosbie's divan clothed in British-colonial righteousness and voluptuous perversity. The power and defeat of Regina Giddens are caught in the curve of another couch and another staircase by this actress who is able to inhabit the most esoteric configurations and mold their contrivances to her distinct personality.

The qualities of poise and bravura Davis developed and the sense of her playing a role are important ingredients in most of her subsequent films in the forties. Watching Davis as she subordinates herself to other stars in *The Man Who Came to Dinner* (1942) and *Watch on the Rhine,* manages the ugly-duckling transformation in *Now, Voyager,* sings and dances in *Thank Your Lucky Stars,* ages in *Mr. Skeffington,* essays a dual role in *A Stolen Life* or plays comedy, first as a bride who came C.O.D. and later in *June Bride,* we are attuned to acting as a prodigious feat even when the actress is underplaying with exquisite restraint. The prodigiousness of the actress and her assumptions of characterization and existence are the core of *All About Eve* (1950). As Joyce Heath, Regina Giddens, and Fanny Trellis, Davis emphatically told us she was acting. In *All About Eve* she enacts her reasons for acting.

Claudette Colbert injured her back and deprived us of a Margo Channing we would undoubtedly still be cherishing, but she thrust Davis into a role that was as much a test and *summa* of her career as Letty in *The Wind* was of Gish's or Marguerite Gautier of Garbo's. All of the errors and the triumphs, the accumulation of years, the elaboration of an image before an audience, the sense of a private and public self in tender balance between the intimacy of the camera lens and the frightening expanse of silver screen are examined in *All About Eve*. The film's ultimate mannerism is in its focus on the screen actress as stage actress. (A similar kink in Antonioni's *Blow-up* locates the camera games in the perception and technique of a still photographer.) Davis, the film actress in Hollywood for almost twenty years and a superstar for more than ten of them, dominates the "theatah" of the role, the situation, the film medium, and her own starry identity by creating perspectives of execution, measure, scale, and frame. She amazes us with her dexterous passage between a role about performance and the performance of a role, and with her ability and courage to both use and demonstrate the tricks of her art and her life.

Trick No. 1 is pulled out in her first shot. When a Bette Davis performance in 1950 opens with a cigarette bit, something is being said about an actress whose name is not Margo Channing.

The offhand gesture is executed without the brittle nerves of her earlier Judith Traherne, and its rhythm is a variant on the familiar we cannot help but notice. One of the miracles of *All About Eve* is the way it uses the Davis presence, calling on our past knowledge of the "Queen of Warners," and our 1950 knowledge that she is queen of Warners no more. Davis is not playing herself in *All About Eve*. She is an actress, and for an actress there is no way simply to *play* herself. But she and director Mankiewicz cull from the Davis emblem hints that entice us into conjecture about who is really puffing on that cigarette. Our conjecture is enough to give Margo an unfaltering beat. The role pulses in and out of fiction as the character herself challenges her own roles of actress and woman.

We have lived with Margo for many years and tend to forget how much Davis created in *All About Eve*. Contemporary audiences needed that cigarette. They certainly recognized the Davis face, but the rest was a bit of a surprise. Tallulah Bankhead, whose career was more than once linked to Davis's, lurks in these first shots. Tallulah created *Dark Victory* and *The Little Foxes* on the stage, and her insouciant image was perhaps at its most public in the late forties. The opening of *All About Eve* begs for comparison between two actresses known for their temperament, and Davis seems a newcomer to this brand of sarcastically cast glamour. In *June Bride* (1948) she wore smart but tailored clothes and sported a businesslike coiffure. Her poetess in *Winter Meeting* (1948) was intentionally dowdy. Her chic in *Deception* (1946) was supposed to represent "good taste" rather than pizazz. The only modern-dress role in the forties that required her to look terrific was the transformed Charlotte Vale of *Now, Voyager* (1942), and even there she looks terrifically handsome rather than glamorous. (Her cameo appearance in *Thank Your Lucky Stars*, 1943, is a *very* small exception.) The 1950 public's most recent memory was of Rosa Moline in *Beyond the Forest* (1949), the wicked witch of the north woods.

We had not before seen her gesture with such worldliness, refusing to have her drink watered.

Through all of this, she has not spoken. A patient camera helps create a new Davis—and for many the best and only Davis—out of an old cigarette, a Tallulah hairdo, an Edith Head gown, and an identity that now boldly emerges from the tearjerkers and the historical costume romances. With one eye cocked, she takes on life with the mixture of irony and self-scrutiny that were present in Judith Traherne, Regina Giddens, and Charlotte Vale but were to some degree dependent on roles and fictions. Now Davis deals in undiluted whiskey and undiluted technique. For Margo, the playing is the thing.

The film's mannerist intention is completely stated in Davis's next appearance. Wearing a dressing gown—her face smeared with cold cream, her soft hairdo now tightly bound—she thrusts this ensemble at the camera after it has been reflected in a mirror.

We see how the star got that way. The raw material beneath the glamour and the star mask finds its own style. A female *pagliaccio* tries out her grimaces in a nether land between stage and life, an antechamber where the two realms are held in stylistic tension. There is comedy in her *grande-dame*like "Won't you sit down, Miss Worthington?"

But it is followed by a tragic mask that is both tragically theatrical and a model of sincerity and genuineness in her reaction to Eve's bathetic tale. (This scene is the first of many that nicely disorganize the actor/spectator relationship.)

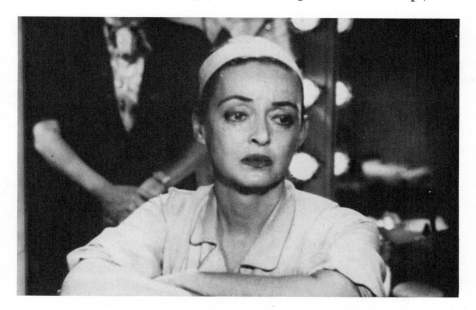

We are engulfed by the plenitude of her expression—the generosity of eyes, mouth, and feeling in the contextual emblem of a dressing-room face—and it is easy to believe that Margo Channing is a great actress. We are mercifully denied her performance in "Aged in Wood." Anything written by Hugh Marlowe's playwright (whose next play is enticingly entitled "Footsteps on the Ceiling") would have to be unworthy of the honesty and courage of such a performer. Garbo's Grusinskaya confined her best dancing to her bed and chaise longue, but Margo Channing turns her environment into a theatre, whether it be a seedy dressing room, a rehearsal stage, or her own living room. This is where we see the artist at work. After Anne Baxter's woeful recital and Thelma Ritter's homely reaction, Davis snaps, "There are some human experiences that do not take place in a vaudeville house."

Nothing is further from the truth, as Channing–Davis has just demonstrated. Covered with cold cream, surrounded by dirty Kleenex and assorted disorder, she shows that all experiences do indeed belong to the theatre. The actress and her craft are one.[2]

The mobility of Davis beneath the cold-cream mask is the clue to her Margo Channing. The tension of a pose is released by self-irony and self-parody, but never self-destruction. The sense of execution and the variety and range of performance are caught in the alternatives—poised and "put together" (as Thelma Ritter will say) at the Sarah Siddons Awards—put together quite differently in her dressing room, straightening her seams.

She grandly takes her curtain call (her feigned surprise is a directorial error) and then complains about her tight girdle.

[2] Joseph L. Mankiewicz describes Margo as "a woman whose need to act equates with her need to breathe. Who, when she isn't 'on'—just isn't, at all." *More About All About Eve*, p. 20.

She is half asleep during her unplanned, middle-of-the-night phone call (placed by Anne Baxter) to Gary Merrill, then, all too awake.

She holds forth in front of her own caricature.

The simultaneity of actress-woman is enacted long before it is elucidated in her confession to Celeste Holm. Much of the speech, with lines like "You're something with a French provincial office or a book full of clippings—but you're not a woman [without a man]," dates the film as embarrassingly pre–women's liberation, but it is beautifully executed. The space of the car, the hug of the coat, the centrality of the composition, and the mellowness of the tone help us through to the lifesaving punch-line: "Slow curtain. The End."

Margo knows how to deal with self-pity. So did Judith Traherne, Henriette Deluzy, Charlotte Vale, and Miss Moffat.

The film is entitled *All About Eve,* but there really isn't too much to know about Eve. Her duplicity is mechanical, her evil bald, and if she had truly been the subject of the film, we wouldn't lose as much sleep as we now do during those happily frequent Late Show reruns. We return with fascination to find out all about Margo because she makes finding out an ever-renewable process. The pattern of the actress testing herself in experiences and fiction emerges in the film's great set piece, the party. It is here that Davis closes the gaps, drawing us to disquieting boundaries and forcing us to behold the cost of pretense, its slippage, the nakedness beneath, and finally the reestablishment of a mask that enhances, rather than hides, the identity of its wearer. The initial banter with marvelous Thelma Ritter restates Margo's warmth and humor, which are qualities we never doubt, despite the criticisms her friends are about to heap upon her.

Davis has never been funnier than in the first part of the party sequence, debating with herself about having a piece of candy and succumbing to temptation with an enormous chew, while arguing with Merrill about Anne Baxter.

Fed up with hearing the praises of her rival, she again finds reality in the vocabulary of show biz: "Cut! Print it! What happens in the next reel?" At the same time, she manages a dig at her director-lover's recent Hollywood foray.

The first peak of the festivities occurs when Celeste Holm, noticing the din of jangling nerves, asks, "Is it over—or just beginning?"

Davis is clearly contemptuous of polite meddling. She is beyond social conventions and even common jealousy. She has the confidence and superiority of an artist being asked what his latest canvas *means*. The drink is downed; the star, whose walk is talk, takes a step up the stairs, turns, settles into a pose, and surveys her public: "Fasten your seat belts. It's going to be a bumpy night."

Davis plays the big line with the security of a great actress used to attention and applause, balancing the configuration of arms, shoulders, and head, and the complete possession of space with a voice that complements rather than translates the message of the visual presence. The line never fails to get its laugh, but, finally, it comes from the joy of relief that it all works so well and that its realization never disturbs the harmony of physique, environment, rhetoric, and situation. Acting her best while patently acting, Davis has never looked more beautiful.

The next portion of the sequence is a half-drunk adagio; her speech is slurred but her awareness is no less acute in the slow pace of the party lull.

Her eyes turn inward for reflection following the exhibition of self. This prepares the new and more accurate articulation about to come. In the kitchen encounter with Hugh Marlowe, to his idiotic "Margo, you haven't got any age," she retorts, "Miss Channing is ageless," and admits to being forty; "Four-oh" is a bit of truth-telling surprising even to her.

What Margo is learning is that she can tell the truth and be a great actress as well.

The best stage is her own staircase, with her cast-audience at her feet. The fine ear of director Mankiewicz, and his very personal sense of enclosure and intimacy, serve the film's core and Margo's deepest triumph. When Edmund Goulding or William Wyler confine actors they use the frame to play elaborate spatial games. Mankiewicz's setups are almost unremittingly eye-level and medium range. The tightness of his compositions reflects his view of characters in a universe of people rather than things. They may wear the proper clothes and sit on the right chairs, but the wearing and the sitting are usually subordinate to their relationships to each other. Goulding exploited the back of Barrymore's head to define Garbo's cheek; Wyler created significant shapes from an arm resting on a couch or the asymmetrical alignment of bodies. Mankiewicz crowds his actors together, and the resulting tension—verbal and formal—is his cinematic trade-mark. In most of his best moments, environment does not demand our attention. (Connie Gilchrist's kitchen in *A Letter to Three Wives*, 1949, is an inspired exception.) Margo's dressing room, and now her staircase with its steps that display the actors' faces with the most transparent clarity are his congenial milieus. We needn't have been surprised at his discomfort in Cleopatra's Egypt or the over-dressed dullness of *The Honey Pot* (1967) and *Sleuth* (1972). Celeste Holm, Gregory Ratoff, Gary Merrill, George Sanders, Anne Baxter and Marilyn Monroe are scenery enough.

The group first hears Sanders's quip about the "Theatah," and then Baxter's epiphany about applause "like waves of love coming over the footlights and wrapping you up." This is accompanied by the lush "Eve" theme from Alfred Newman's musical score, one of the film's glories. Davis's entrance deflates the effusion and occasions her first barb as a reaction to Baxter's cloying deferences: "Don't get up. And please stop acting as if I were the queen mother."

Then her acting skill is plied to denounce everyone present for conventionality and smallness of spirit. To the conciliatory Holm she says, "Please don't play governess," and, with eyelid virtuosity, she is lushly sarcastic: "I wish I'd gone to Radcliffe too but Father wouldn't hear of it."

To make sure we know we're witnessing a good show, the critic Sanders adds, "You're maudlin and full of self-pity. You're magnificent."

A measure of Davis's magnificence is in the drooping head, her willingness to show Margo undone as well as done up, and the fatigue and misery that goes with "Four-oh" as well as its mastery. This letting go, the relaxation of Margo's public face, is continued during her scolding by Holm: "Then stop being a star—stop treating your guests as your supporting cast!"

As star, Margo sometimes displays the cruelty of superiority, but more often it's wisdom. Telling her to stop being a star elicits her best act. Having passed through the excesses of parody and defenselessness, she collects herself, mounts the stairs, and when asked by Merrill if she wants to be put to bed, she turns, using the railing as if it were a piece of scenery (which of course it is), and pulls together the film's poles of affection and dissimulation. "Put me to bed, take my clothes off, hold my head, tuck me in, turn out the lights, tiptoe out? . . . Eve would. Wouldn't you, Eve?"

Perched on high, at the center of everyone's attention as a star should be, she regains the equilibrium of her talent. With her dress askew and her posture a bit awry, she delivers the lines with the aplomb of Leslie Crosbie and Regina Giddens, but with a softness that as well becomes the creator of Judith Traherne and Charlotte Vale.

Davis is happiest when playing a woman with brains. (One of the errors of the flamboyant *Deception* is the inanity of its heroine. All Davis's skill as an actress cannot make us forget the basic incongruence of her assuming the role of an indecisive woman.) At this point in *All About Eve*, we tend to forget that Margo has learned the truth. Only she and Thelma Ritter have seen through Baxter's facade of saintliness and competence. Margo's magnificent self-pity is replaced by a self without the slightest need of pity, much less tucking in. The evenness of her delivery, following the drunken slur and the parodic broadness, signals Margo's understanding in splendid isolation. She and her lover will separate and be reconciled as the film passes from crisis to happy ending, but she will never be more herself than she is at the top of those stairs—actress-woman on an appropriated stage.

The film's mannerism is extended in the next sequence where the performance is continued on a real stage, albeit a rehearsal stage. And to complicate the perspective, the actress who was looked up to and in command at the top of the stairs, is momentarily defeated on her professional stage in a high angle shot. But first she takes charge of the theatre during her fight with Hugh Marlowe. In their final exchange of insults, the playwright asks, "Just when exactly does an actress decide they're her words she's saying and her thoughts she's expressing?" Backed by flats, thrusting her body over the footlights and her voice into the auditorium, she shouts, "Usually at the point when she's got to rewrite and rethink them to keep the audience from leaving the theatre!"

This is the other extreme of Davis's expanse of presence—the fortissimo, the explosion of temperament that identified her most memorable work in the early thirties as Marie Roark in *Bordertown* and the vituperative Mildred in *Of Human Bondage*. After demonstrating two decades worth of self-possession at the end of the party sequence, she now sets off the fireworks and the pure energy that first launched her career. All of Davis is in Margo. A long string of films at Warner

Brothers exhibited her in a series of manners—noble in *The Corn Is Green,* vain in *Mr. Skeffington,* repressed in *Winter Meeting,* horrid in *Beyond the Forest.* Her body ranges from the moral tautness of Sara Muller in *Watch on the Rhine* to Rosa Moline's sloppy flaccidity. In *All About Eve,* without the distancing elements of period costumes or contemporary melodrama, teasingly skirting her own life and her own persona, Davis brandishes every weapon in her acting arsenal. She fits together the extrafictional and the artificial in the character's various degrees of intensity, each one recognizable as part of her acting vocabulary but summoned here with an alternation of utter seriousness, insolence, and off-handedness that are an actress's comments on her craft. The end of this sequence is fascinating in its reversal of the Davis image, her flailing arms pinned to a stage bed by Gary Merrill: "Margo, tell me what's behind all this."

"I—I don't know, Bill. Just a feeling, I don't know. . . ."

Her lack of focus in the second frame is a visual ambiguity that tolerates both the false admission that she does not know what she really knows about time and love and the real strength of her feeling. This actress is smart, but she does not live or act by brains alone. Her defeat will be of short duration—a bit of a sob in a long shot on a stage bed.

With all that has preceded as evidence of her strength, we never doubt that she will reconstitute herself, and she does—in the car scene with Holm, and toasting Sanders with a scallion in the Cub Room,

and sarcastically telling the ever-cloying Eve, "But I wouldn't worry too much about your heart. You can always put that award where your heart ought to be."

This advice from Margo, an actress who has repeatedly demonstrated a talent of heart, to Eve whose role is essentially heartless and for whom acting is subterfuge rather than revelation, reminds us of the reasons for Davis's stardom. The lessons of clarity she learned with Wyler come to their most stirring use in this very funny film about someone for whom art and self are not in conflict but are in the most subtle and vital stress of complementarity.

Davis will play another actress in *The Star* (1952), a film that is unsatisfying for many reasons, not the least of which is its contrary resolution of Margo's inquiry. Margaret Elliott is a down-at-heels Norma Desmond, unable to reconcile living and performing. In the film's "happy" ending, she gives up all hope of resuming her career and settles for anonymity and Sterling Hayden. When Margo becomes Margaret, style is abandoned for something often called "good sense," and as the ads would have it, "the woman is born." The message of movie acting's failure is supposedly transmitted by a Davis acting her head off. Margo keeps her head and her art.

11.
The Tunes of Acting

Davis offered us the richest of her bounty in *All About Eve*. Garbo "temporarily" ended her career after the woeful *Two-Faced Woman*. Gish left MGM after *The Wind*, which was a financial failure, made a talkie, *One Romantic Night* (1930), and has not starred in a film since. Yet as a featured actress Gish has kept her art intact. Her death scene in *Duel in the Sun* (1947), her facing down the villainous Robert Mitchum in *The Night of the Hunter* (1955), and playing the piano during an Indian attack in *The Unforgiven* (1960) make us yearn to see her in roles that would call upon yet more of her resources. And when, in *The Unforgiven*, she gently combs out Audrey Hepburn's hair, two of the screen's most extraordinary faces are united. The incessant revivals of Garbo's films—revivals that have nothing to do with historical curiosity—seem to prove that she acts for us today just as she did in 1937 and in 1927. Her eternal link to the camera is described by James Wong Howe who tells of the color tests he did of her in Paris in the late forties for the never-to-be-filmed *Duchess of Langeais*: "She was like a horse on a track: nothing, and then the bell goes, and something happens. When the shot was over, she said simply, 'Have you got enough?' And I said 'Yes,' and very matter-of-factly she remarked, 'O.K. I go home.' She did. And she was nothing again."[1] Never truly of her epoch, her stardom didn't cease because it had dated. Our regrets over Garbo's silence are only matched by our disappointment over the inexplicable waste of Bette Davis. Since she was a character actress even during her most successful years, we would have expected her to have been more durable commercially than stars who specialized in romantic heroines. Yet her films since *All About Eve* are as frustrating as those previous to *Jezebel*. There are instants ablaze with the wonderful absurdity of her energy or her passionate control—screaming "You've . . . killed . . . Fury" in *Another Man's Poison* (1952), weeping over her own horrible reflection in *Whatever Happened to Baby Jane?* (1961), ferociously underplaying and again helping someone toward a heart attack in *The Nanny* (1965)—but they simply remind us how silly and exploitative the vehicles are.

For Gish, Garbo, and Davis we are left with the might-have-beens and the aching possibilities that might still be realized. Gish and Garbo were at MGM at the same time. Would that the studio's munificence had united them. Or later, in the thirties, when talk of a Garbo-Hepburn *Mourning Becomes Electra* evaporated, why did not some enlightened producer group Garbo, Davis, Wyler, and Gregg Toland in front of those New England columns? Or imagine *The Three Sisters* circa 1940, with Gish a noble Olga, Garbo seethingly passionate as Masha, Hepburn a tremulous yet practical Irina, and Davis the most perfectly bitchy Natasha. . . .

"Wishful Thinking" is one game we play with our movie actresses. Another spectator entertainment is "See the Falling Star." *All About Eve* and *Sunset Boulevard*, both released in 1950, respectively star Bette Davis who, after almost two decades, had recently left Warners, and Gloria Swanson who, after a long hiatus had returned to Paramount, the studio that, starting in 1919, had molded

---

[1] In Charles Higham, *Hollywood Cameramen: Sources of Light*, p. 92.

her stardom in more than twenty-five films. Retrospection makes it so easy for us to draw conclusions about the declining studio system in 1950 and the essentially decadent films about aging actresses. Norma Desmond's dead monkey and her chin strap are closer to Margo's dressing room and hardheadedness than the distance between gothic flamboyance and the comedy of manners would seem to allow. Mankiewicz and Wilder take a long, last look at the stars, scrutinizing their simultaneous effulgence and dissolution.

The attraction of decadence lies in its measure, the effect of lingering and drawing out, and of ripeness perilously sustained. After having lived for years in a demented freeze-frame of her glory, Norma Desmond slowly descends a staircase in thrall to movie madness. A fifty-year-old, she imagines herself playing Salome, the teen-age darling of other decadent imaginations—Gustave Moreau, Oscar Wilde, Aubrey Beardsley, Richard Strauss. The actress-murderess plays the role of another avenging lover. The newsreel cameras reporting a *crime passionnel* and the voice of gossipmonger Hedda Hopper (a former movie actress re-turned movie actress) are subsumed in the final close-up of a face with two enormous eyes, truly the close-up of ending. As Swanson demonstrates both how she *is* and how she *was,* we savor the bitter aftertaste of beauty, an image that by standards of logic and precedent has overstayed its welcome. But such standards are made to be challenged by the disproportions of Gloria Swanson's colossal eyes and minuscule body, the accouterments of the diva and a directorial style more astringent than Norma Desmond's facial lotions. They are challenged by such time warps as Gloria Swanson playing Norma Desmond watching a more than twenty years younger Swanson/Desmond playing Queen Kelly in the aborted film of Erich von Stroheim, one of her co-stars in *Sunset Boulevard.*

The self stretches through time in the art of films, eternally young and old, going faster and slower than life in rhythms just as magnified and "unreal" as the giants on the screen. Only stars can bear the strain of this magnification, the flowering of one's being in expanses ironic to human stature and in spans that transform life into art. Leni Riefenstahl uses a slow-motion camera and radical angles to turn divers into birds in *Olympia.* Arthur Penn, with an optic of yet slower motion, investigates the stress of bodies in flight at the 1972 Olympics. Gish, Garbo, and Davis need less hardware for their revelations. Their gestures are projected onto enormous screens by powerful lamps, but also by their own strength. In conspiracy with the medium, they turn into flowers, they unravel time, feeling, and the secrets of their craft. We submit to their rhythm and their harmony just as surely as we sway to the urging of Fred and Ginger. We sing along with *Broken Blossoms, Camille, Now, Voyager,* and *Swing Time* and retain the melody of acting along with countless other memorable tunes.

Gish, Garbo, and Davis may never have shared a film, but they often shared partners. They star together in our imagination, woven into the single fabric of *The Movies* by Richard Barthelmess, Lars Hanson, Donald Crisp, Eugenie Besserer, Laura Hope Crews, Ricardo Cortez, Paul Muni, William Dieterle, John

Huston, Marie Dressler, Robert Montgomery, Conrad Nagel, Lewis Stone. Charles Boyer actually appeared with all three of them. John Gilbert makes love to Mimi and Anna Karenina, George Brent escorts a straying wife through a Chinese festival and diagnoses the fatal tumor of a debutante, King Vidor pursues one heroine over the cobblestones of Paris and another down Main Street in her vain attempt to get to Chicago. And if we link Garbo and Davis through Herbert Marshall's worried face, it is precisely because their images are impervious to change, forever alive in the kitchen of *The Painted Veil* and the parlor of *The Little Foxes*. We periodically rejoin them to explore the resonances and angles modified by *our* changing years, not theirs.

Filmographies

Within the year given, the films are listed by release.

The following abbreviations are used: Director–D, Producer–P, Cinematography–C, Scenario–S, Music–M; Metro-Goldwyn-Mayer–MGM, United Artists–UA, Paramount–PAR, Columbia–COL, Universal–UNI, Warner Brothers–WB, Twentieth Century-Fox–20TH, Seven Arts–7A.

LILLIAN GISH

1912

An Unseen Enemy (American Biograph). D. W. Griffith (D), G. W. Bitzer (C), Edward Acker (S). Dorothy Gish, Robert Harron, Harry Carey, Elmer Booth.

Two Daughters of Eve (American Biograph). D. W. Griffith (D), G. W. Bitzer (C). Henry B. Walthall, Claire McDowell, Elmer Booth.

In the Aisles of the Wild (American Biograph). D. W. Griffith (D), G. W. Bitzer (C). Claire McDowell, Harry Carey, Henry B. Walthall.

The Musketeers of Pig Alley (American Biograph). D. W. Griffith (D), G. W. Bitzer (C). Walter Miller, Elmer Booth, Marie Newton, Robert Harron, W. Chrystie Miller, Jack Pickford, Harry Carey, Dorothy Gish.

My Baby (American Biograph). D. W. Griffith (D), G. W. Bitzer (C). Mary Pickford, Henry B. Walthall, Lionel Barrymore.

Gold and Glitter (American Biograph). D. W. Griffith (D), G. W. Bitzer (C), George Hennessy (S). Elmer Booth, Dorothy Gish, Lionel Barrymore.

The New York Hat (American Biograph). D. W. Griffith (D), G. W. Bitzer (C), Anita Loos (S). Mary Pickford, Lionel Barrymore, Mae Marsh, Dorothy Gish, Robert Harron.

The Burglar's Dilemma (American Biograph). D. W. Griffith (D), G. W. Bitzer (C), Lionel Barrymore (S). Lionel Barrymore, Henry B. Walthall, Robert Harron.

A Cry for Help (American Biograph). D. W. Griffith (D), G. W. Bitzer (C), Edward Acker (S). Dorothy Gish, Harry Carey, Lionel Barrymore, Walter Miller, Claire McDowell, Robert Harron.

Oil and Water (American Biograph). D. W. Griffith (D), G. W. Bitzer (C), E. J. Montagne (S). Blanche Sweet, Henry B. Walthall, Lionel Barrymore, Charles H. Mailes, Walter Miller, Robert Harron, Alfred Paget, Dorothy Gish.

The Unwelcome Guest (American Biograph). D. W. Griffith (D), G. W. Bitzer (C). Mary Pickford, Claire McDowell, Elmer Booth, W. Chrystie Miller, Jack Pickford.

1913

A Misunderstood Boy (American Biograph). D. W. Griffith (D), G. W. Bitzer (C). Robert Harron, Alfred Paget, Lionel Barrymore, Charles Mailes.

The Left-Handed Man (American Biograph). Tony O'Sullivan (D), G. W. Bitzer (C). Charles West, Harry Carey.

The Lady and the Mouse (American Biograph). D. W. Griffith (D, S), G. W. Bitzer (C). Dorthy Gish, Lionel Barrymore, Henry B. Walthall, Robert Harron, Harry Hyde, Kate Toncray.

The House of Darkness (American Biograph). D. W. Griffith (D). G. W. Bitzer (C). Lionel Barrymore, Claire McDowell, Charles Mailes.

Just Gold (American Biograph). D. W. Griffith (D, S), G. W. Bitzer (C). Lionel Barrymore, Alfred Paget, Charles West, Joseph McDermott, Charles H. Mailes, Kate Bruce, Dorothy Gish.

A Timely Interception (American Biograph). D. W. Griffith (D), G. W. Bitzer (C).

Robert Harron, Lionel Barrymore, W. Chrystie Miller, William J. Butler, Joseph McDermott.

The Mothering Heart (American Biograph). D. W. Griffith (D), G. W. Bitzer (C). Walter Miller, Viola Barry.

During the Round-Up (American Biograph). D. W. Griffith (D), G. W. Bitzer (C). Henry B. Walthall, Fred Burns.

An Indian's Loyalty (American Biograph). D. W. Griffith (D), G. W. Bitzer (C). Fred Burns, Eddie Dillon, Dark Cloud.

A Woman in the Ultimate (American Biograph). Tony O'Sullivan or D. W. Griffith (D). Henry B. Walthall, Charles Mailes.

A Modest Hero (American Biograph). Walter Miller, Charles Mailes, Harry Carey.

The Madonna of the Storm (American Biograph).

The Battle of Elderbush Gulch (American Biograph). D. W. Griffith (D), G. W. Bitzer (C). Mae Marsh, Robert Harron, Henry B. Walthall, Kate Bruce, Alfred Paget.

1914

Judith of Bethulia (American Biograph). D. W. Griffith (D), G. W. Bitzer (C), based on the apocryphal Book of Judith and the play by Thomas Bailey Aldrich. Blanche Sweet, Mae Marsh, Henry B. Walthall, Dorothy Gish, Robert Harron, Kate Bruce.

The Green-Eyed Devil (Reliance–Majestic). James Kirkwood (D). Mary Alden, Henry B. Walthall, Earle Foxe, Ralph Lewis.

The Battle of the Sexes (Reliance–Majestic). D. W. Griffith (D, S), G. W. Bitzer (C), based on *The Single Standard* by Daniel Carson Goodman. Donald Crisp, Mary Alden, Owen Moore, Robert Harron, Fay Tincher.

Lord Chumley (Klaw and Erlanger). James Kirkwood (D). Henry B. Walthall, Mary Alden, Charles Mailes, Walter Miller.

The Hunchback (Reliance–Majestic). Frank Turner, William Garwood, Edna Mae Wilson, T. Haverly.

The Quicksands (Reliance–Majestic). Courtenay Foote, Fay Tincher.

Man's Enemy (Klaw and Erlanger). Franklin Ritchie.

Home Sweet Home (Mutual). D. W. Griffith (D), G. W. Bitzer (C), Griffith and H. E. Aitken (S), four stories based on the song as reflected in the life of the composer, John Howard Payne. Henry B. Walthall, Josephine Crowell, Fay Tincher, Dorothy Gish, Mae Marsh, Spottiswoode Aitken, Robert Harron, Miriam Cooper, Mary Alden, Donald Crisp, James Kirkwood, Jack Pickford, Fred Burns, Courtenay Foote, Blanche Sweet, Owen Moore, Edward Dillon.

The Rebellion of Kitty Belle (Reliance–Majestic). Christy Cabanne (D). Robert Harron, Raoul Walsh.

The Angel of Contention (Reliance–Majestic). John G. O'Brien (D). Spottiswoode Aitken, George Siegmann, Raoul Walsh.

The Tear That Burned (Reliance–Majestic). John G. O'Brien (D). John Dillon, W. E. Lowery.

The Folly of Anne (Reliance–Majestic). John G. O'Brien (D).

The Sisters (Majestic–Mutual). William Christy Cabanne (D, S). Dorothy Gish, W. E. Lawrence, Elmer Clifton.

1915

The Birth of a Nation (Epoch Producing Corporation). D. W. Griffith (D, P), G. W. Bitzer assisted by Karl Brown (C), Griffith and Frank E. Woods (S), Joseph Carl Breil (M); based on Thomas Dixon's story "The Clansman." Henry Walthall,

Miriam Cooper, Mae Marsh, Josephine Crowell, Spottiswoode Aitken, J. A. Beringer, John French, Jennie Lee, Ralph Lewis, Elmer Clifton, Robert Harron, Wallace Reid, Mary Alden, George Siegmann, Walter Long, Joseph Henabery, Raoul Walsh, Donald Crisp, Howard Gaye, John McGlynn, Ernest Campbell.

The Lost House (Reliance–Majestic). Christy Cabanne (D), from a Richard Harding Davis novel. Wallace Reid, Elmer Clifton, E. A. Turner, A. D. Sears.

Captain Macklin (Reliance–Majestic). John G. O'Brien (D), from a Richard Harding Davis novel. Jack Conway, Spottiswoode Aitken.

Enoch Arden (Reliance–Majestic). Christy Cabanne (D). Wallace Reid, Alfred Paget, D. W. Griffith, Mildred Harris.

The Lily and the Rose (Triangle–Fine Arts). Paul Powell (D), Granville Warwick [Griffith] (S). Rozsika Dolly, Wilfred Lucas, Mary Alden, Elmer Clifton, Loyola O'Connor, William Hinckley, Cora Drew.

1916

Daphne and the Pirate (Triangle–Fine Arts). Christy Cabanne (D), Granville Warwick [Griffith] (S). Elliott Dexter, William Gaye.

Sold for Marriage (Triangle–Fine Arts). Christy Cabanne (D). Frank Bennett, A. D. Sears, Walter Long, Mike Siebert, Olga Grey.

An Innocent Magdalene (Triangle–Fine Arts). Allan Dwan (D). Sam de Grasse, Mary Alden, Spottiswoode Aitken, Jennie Lee.

Intolerance (Wark). D. W. Griffith (D, P), G. W. Bitzer assisted by Karl Brown (C), Joseph Carl Breil and Griffith (M). Mae Marsh, Fred Turner, Robert Harron, Sam de Grasse, Vera Lewis, Mary Alden, Pearl Elmore, Lucille Brown, Luray Huntley, Mrs. Arthur Mackley, Miriam Cooper, Walter Long, Tom Wilson, Ralph Lewis, Lloyd Ingraham, A. W. McClure, Max Davidson, Monte Blue, Marguerite Marsh, Tod Browning, Edward Dillon, Clyde Hopkins, William Brown, Alberta Lee, Howard Gaye, Lillian Langdon, Olga Grey, Gunther von Ritzau, Erich von Stroheim, Bessie Love, George Walsh, Margery Wilson, Eugene Pallette, Spottiswoode Aitken, Ruth Handforth, A. D. Sears, Frank Bennett, Maxfield Stanley, Josephine Crowell, Constance Talmadge, W. E. Lawrence, Joseph Henabery, Elmer Clifton, Alfred Paget, Seena Owen, Carl Stockdale, Tully Marshall, George Siegmann, Elmo Lincoln, George Fawcett, Kate Bruce, Ruth St. Denis, Loyola O'Connor, James Curley, Howard Scott, Alma Rubens, Ruth Darling, Margaret Mooney, Mildred Harris, Pauline Starke, Winifred Westover.

Diane of the Follies (Triangle–Fine Arts). Christy Cabanne (D), Granville Warwick [Griffith] (S). Sam de Grasse.

Pathways of Life (Triangle–Fine Arts). William Christy Cabanne (D), Mary H. O'Conner (S). W. E. Lawrence, Olga Grey, Spottiswoode Aitken, Alfred Paget.

The Children Pay (Triangle–Fine Arts). Lloyd Ingraham (D), Frank E. Woods (S). Violet Wilkie, Keith Armour, Ralph Lewis, Alma Rubens, Jennie Lee, Loyola O'Connor.

1917

The House Built upon Sand (Triangle–Fine Arts). Ed Morrisey (D). Roy Stuart, Kate Bruce, Josephine Crowell, Jack Brammall, William H. Brown, Bessie Buskirk.

Souls Triumphant (Triangle–Fine Arts). Lloyd Ingraham (D). Wilfred Lucas.

1918

Hearts of the World (Comstock–World). D. W. Griffith (D, P), G. W. Bitzer (C), Gaston de Tolignac [Griffith] (S). Dorothy Gish, Adolphe Lestina, Josephine Crowell, Robert Harron, Jack Cosgrave, Kate Bruce, Ben Alexander, M. Emmons, F. Marion, Robert Anderson, George Fawcett, George A. Seigmann, Fay Holderness, L. Lowry, Eugene Pouyet, Anna Mae Walthall, Yvette Duvoisin, Herbert Sutch, Alphonse Dufort, Jean Dumercier, Jules Lemontier, Gaston Riviere, George Loyer, George Nicholls, Mrs. Gish, Mrs. Harron, Mary, Jessie, and Johnny Harron, Noel Coward.

The Great Love (Artcraft). D. W. Griffith (D), G. W. Bitzer (C), Capt. Victor Marier [Griffith and S. E. V. Taylor] (S). Robert Harron, Henry B. Walthall, Gloria Hope, Maxfield Stanley, George Fawcett, Rosemary Theby, George Siegmann, and as themselves, Lady Diana Manners, Elizabeth Asquith, Mrs. Buller, the Duchess of Beaufort, the Princess of Monaco, and Queen Alexandra.

Liberty Bond Short (Artcraft). D. W. Griffith (D), G. W. Bitzer (C). Kate Bruce, George Fawcett, Carol Dempster.

The Greatest Thing in Life (PAR–Artcraft). D. W. Griffith (D), G. W. Bitzer (C), Capt. Victor Marier [Griffith and S. E. V. Taylor] (S). Robert Harron, Adolphe Lestina, David Butler, Elmo Lincoln, Edward Peil, Kate Bruce, Peaches Jackson.

1919

A Romance of Happy Valley (PAR–Artcraft). D. W. Griffith (D), G. W. Bitzer (C), Capt. Victor Marier [Griffith] (S). Lydia Yeamans Titus, Robert Harron, Kate Bruce, George Fawcett, George Nicholls, Adolphe Lestina, Bertram Grassby, Porter Strong.

Broken Blossoms (Griffith–UA). D. W. Griffith (D, S), G. W. Bitzer and special effects by Hendrick Sartov (C), Louis F. Gottschalk and Griffith (M); based on "The Chink and the Child" by Thomas Burke in *Limehouse Nights*. Richard Barthelmess, Donald Crisp, Arthur Howard, Edward Peil, George Beranger, Norman Selby.

True Heart Susie (PAR–Artcraft). D. W. Griffith (D), G. W. Bitzer (C), Marion Fremont (S). Robert Harron, Wilbur Highby, Loyola O'Connor, George Fawcett, Clarine Seymour, Kate Bruce, Carol Dempster, Raymond Cannon.

The Greatest Question (Griffith–First National). D. W. Griffith (D), G. W. Bitzer (C), S. E. V. Taylor (S); story by William Hale. Robert Harron, Ralph Graves, Eugenie Besserer, George Fawcett, Tom Wilson, Josephine Crowell, George Nicholls.

1920

Way Down East (Griffith–UA). D. W. Griffith (D, P), G. W. Bitzer and Hendrick Sartov (C), Anthony Paul Kelly (S); elaborated by Griffith from the stage play by Lottie Blair Parker. Mrs. David Landau, Josephine Bernard, Mrs. Morgan Belmont, Patricia Fruen, Florence Short, Lowell Sherman, Burr McIntosh, Kate Bruce, Richard Barthelmess, Vivia Ogden, Porter Strong, George Neville, Edgar Nelson, Mary Hay, Creighton Hale, Emily Fitzroy.

1922

Orphans of the Storm (UA). D. W. Griffith (D, P), G. W. Bitzer, Hendrick Sartov,

Paul Allen (C); adapted from the Adolphe D'Ennery play *The Two Orphans.* Dorothy Gish, Joseph Schildkraut, Frank Losee, Catherine Emmett, Morgan Wallace, Lucille LaVerne, Sheldon Lewis, Frank Puglia, Creighton Hale, Leslie King, Monte Blue, Sidney Herbert, Leo Kolmer, Adolphe Lestina, Kate Bruce, Fay Marbe, Porter Strong, Louis Wolheim.

1923

The White Sister (Inspiration–Metro). Henry King (D), Roy Overbaugh (C); from the story by F. Marion Crawford. Ronald Colman, Gail Kane, J. Barney Sherry, Charles Lane, Juliette La Violette, Sig Serena, Alfredo Bertone, Ramon Ibanez, Alfredo Martinelli, Carloni Talli, Giovanni Viccola, Giacomo D'Attino, Michele Gualdi, Giuseppe Pavoni, Francesco Socinus, Sheik Mahomet, James Abbe, Duncan Mansfield.

1924

Romola (Inspiration–Metro Goldwyn). Henry King (D), Roy Overbaugh, William Schurr (C), Will M. Ritchey (S); based on the novel by George Eliot. Dorothy Gish, Ronald Colman, William H. Powell, Charles Lane, Herbert Grimwood, Bonaventura Ibanez, Frank Puglia, Amelia Summerville, Tina Ceccacci Renaldi, Eduilio Mucci, Angelo Scatigna, Alfredo Bertone, Ugo Uccellini, Alfredo Martinelli, Gino Borsi, Pietro Nistri, Alfredo Fossi, Attilio Deodati, Pietro Betti, Ferdinando Chianese, Toto Lo Bue, Carlo Duse, Giuseppe Zocchi, Eugenio Mattioli, Giuseppe Becattini, Rinaldo Rinaldi, Enrico Monti, Francesco Ciancamerla, Baron Serge Kopfe, Gastone Barnardi, Giovanni Salvini, Countess Tolomei, Marchese Imperiale, Princess Isabella Romanoff, Countess Tamburini, Princess Bianca Raffaello, Marchese Fabrizio Gonzaga, Prince Alexander Talone, Baron Alfredo del Judici, Baron Giuseppe Winspere.

1926

La Bohème (MGM). King Vidor (D), Hendrick Sartov (C), Fred de Gresac (S), Major Edward Bowes, David Mendoza, William Axt (M); suggested by Henry Murger's *Life in the Latin Quarter,* continuity by Ray Doyle and Harry Behn. John Gilbert, Renée Adorée, George Hassell, Roy D'Arcy, Edward Everett Horton, Karl Dane, Frank Currier, Matilde Comont, Gino Corrado, Gene Pouyet, David Mir, Catherine Vidor, Valentina Zimina.

The Scarlet Letter (MGM). Victor Seastrom (D), Hendrick Sartov (C), Frances Marion (S), Major Edward Bowes, David Mendoza, William Axt (M); based on the novel by Nathaniel Hawthorne. Lars Hanson, Henry B. Walthall, Karl Dane, William H. Tooker, Joyce Coad, Marceline Corday, Fred Herzog, Jules Cowles, Mary Hawkes, James A. Marcus.

1927

Annie Laurie (MGM). John S. Robertson (D), Oliver Marsh (C), Josephine Lovett (S). Norman Kerry, Creighton Hale, Joseph Striker, Hobart Bosworth, Patricia Avery, Russell Simpson, Brandon Hurst, David Torrence, Frank Currier.

1928

The Enemy (MGM). Fred Niblo (D), Oliver Marsh (C), Agnes Christine Johnston and Willis Goldbeck (S); based on a play by Channing Pollock, adapted by Willis Goldbeck, titles by John Colton. Ralph Forbes, Ralph Emerson, Frank Currier, George Fawcett, Fritzi Ridgeway, John S. Peters, Karl Dane, Polly Moran, Billy Kent Shaeffer.

The Wind (MGM). Victor Seastrom (D), John Arnold (C), Frances Marion (S); from the Dorothy Scarborough novel. Lars Hanson, Montagu Love, Dorothy Cummings, Edward Earle, William Orlamonde, Laon Ramon.

1930

One Romantic Night (UA). Paul I. Stein (D), Karl Struss (C), Melville Baker (S); based on *The Swan* by Ferenc Molnar. Conrad Nagel, Rod LaRocque, Marie Dressler, O. P. Heggie, Billie Bennett, Albert Conti, Edgar Norton, Philippe de Lacy, Byron Sage, Barbara Leonard.

1933

His Double Life (PAR). Arthur Hopkins and William C. DeMille (D), Arthur Edeson (C), Arthur Hopkins and Clara Beranger (S); based on the novel *Buried Alive* by Arnold Bennett. Roland Young, Montagu Love, Lucy Beaumont, Lumsden Hare, Charles Richman, Oliver Smith, Philip Tonge, Roland Hogue, Audrey Ridgewell.

1942

The Commandos Strike at Dawn (COL). John Farrow (D), William C. Mellor (C), Irwin Shaw (S); based on a story by C. S. Forester. Paul Muni, Anna Lee, Sir Cedric Hardwicke, Robert Coote, Ray Collins, Rod Cameron, Rosemary DeCamp, Alexander Knox, Elizabeth Fraser, Richard Derr, Erville Alderson, Barbara Everest, Louis Jean Heydt, George Macready, Arthur Margetson, Ann Carter, Elsa Janssen, Ferdinand Munier, John Arthur Stockton.

1943

Top Man (UNI). Charles Lamont (D), Hal Mohr (C), Zachary Gold (S); from a story by Ken Goldsmith. Donald O'Connor, Susanna Foster, Richard Dix, Peggy Ryan, Anne Gwynne, David Holt, Noah Berry, Jr., Marcia Mae Jones, Richard Love, Samuel S. Hinds, the Count Basie Orchestra, Borrah Minnevitch's Harmonica Rascals.

1945

Miss Susie Slagle's (PAR). John Berry (D), Charles Lang, Jr. (C), Anne Froelick and Hugo Butler (S); additional dialogue by Theodore Strauss, from a novel by Augusta Tucker. Veronica Lake, Sonny Tufts, Joan Caulfield, Ray Collins, Billy De Wolfe, Bill Edwards, Pat Phelan, Roman Bohnen, Morris Carnovsky, Renny McEvoy, Lloyd Bridges, Michael Sage, Dorothy Newton, E. J. Ballantine, Theodore Newton, J. Lewis Johnson, Ludwig Stossel, Charles Arnt.

1946

Duel in the Sun (Selznick International). King Vidor (D), David O. Selznick (P, S), Lee Garmes, Hall Rosson, Ray Rannahan (C), Dmitri Tiomkin (M); adapted by Oliver H. P. Garrett from the novel by Niven Busch; Technicolor. Jennifer Jones, Gregory Peck, Joseph Cotten, Lionel Barrymore, Herbert Marshall, Walter Huston, Charles Bickford, Tilly Losch, Joan Tetzel, Harry Carey, Otto Kruger, Scott McKay, Sidney Blackmer, Butterfly McQueen.

1948

Portrait of Jennie (Selznick–UA). William Dieterle (D), David O. Selznick (P), Joseph August (C), Paul Osborn and Peter Berneis (S); adapted by Leonardo Bercovici from the book by Robert Nathan; with a Technicolor sequence. Jennifer Jones, Joseph Cotten, Ethel Barrymore, Cecil Kellaway, David Wayne, Albert Sharpe, Henry Hull, Florence Bates, Felix Bressart, Clem Bevans, Maude Simmons, Esther Somers, John Farrell, Robert Dudley.

1955

The Cobweb (MGM). Vincente Minnelli (D), John Houseman (P), George Folsey (C), John Paxton (S); based on the novel by William Gibson; Cinemascope and Eastman Color. Richard Widmark, Lauren Bacall, Charles Boyer, Gloria Grahame, John Kerr, Susan Strasberg, Oscar Levant, Tommy Rettig, Paul Stewart, Jarma Lewis, Adele Jergens, Edgar Stehli, Sandra Descher, Bert Freed, Mabel Albertson, Fay Wray, Oliver Blake, Olive Carey, Eve McVeagh, Jan Arvan, Virginia Christine, Ruth Clifford, Myra Marsh, James Westerfield, Marjorie Bennett, Stuart Homes.

Night of the Hunter (UA). Charles Laughton (D), Paul Gregory (P), Stanley Cortez (C), James Agee (S); based on the novel by Davis Grubb. Robert Mitchum, Shelley Winters, Evelyn Varden, Peter Graves, Billy Chapin, Sally Jane Bruce, Don Beddoe, James Gleason, Gloria Castillo, Mary Ellen Clemons, Cheryl Gallaway.

1958

Orders to Kill (A Lynx Film released by United Motion Picture Organization). Anthony Asquith (D), Anthony Havelock-Allan (P), Desmond Dickinson (C), Paul Dehn (S); from a story by Donald C. Downes. Eddie Albert, Paul Massie, James Robertson Justice, Irene Worth, Leslie French, John Crawford, Lionel Jeffries, Sandra Dorne, Nicholas Phipps, Jacques Brunius, Anne Blake.

1960

The Unforgiven (UA). John Huston (D), James Hill (P), Franz Planer (C), Ben Maddow (S); from the novel by Alan LeMay; Technicolor. Burt Lancaster, Audrey Hepburn, Audie Murphy, John Saxon, Charles Bickford, Albert Salmi, Joseph Wiseman, June Walker, Kipp Hamilton, Arnold Merritt, Carlos Rivas, Doug McClure.

1966

Follow Me, Boys! (Buena Vista). Norman Tokar (D), Walt Disney (P), Winston Hibler (Co-P), Clifford Stine (C), Louis Pelletier (S); based on the book *God and My Country* by MacKinlay Kantor; Technicolor. Fred MacMurray, Vera Miles, Elliott Reid, Kurt Russell, Luana Patten, Ken Murray, Donald May, Sean McClory, Steve Franken, Parley Baer, William Reynolds, Lem's Boys, Craig Hill, Tol Avery, John Zaremba, Willis Bouchey, Madge Blake, Carl Reindel, Hank Brandt, Richard Bakalyan, Tim McIntire, Willie Soo Hoo, Tony Regan, Robert B. Williams, Jimmy Murphy, Adam Williams.

1967

Warning Shot (PAR). Buzz Kulik (D), Bob Banner (P), Joseph Biroc (C), Mann Rubin (S); Technicolor. David Janssen, Ed Begley, Keenan Wynn, Sam Wanamaker, Eleanor Parker, Stefanie Powers, George Grizzard, George Sanders, Steve Allen, Carroll O'Connor, Joan Collins, Donald Curtis, Walter Pidgeon, John Garfield, Jr.

The Comedians (MGM). Peter Glenville (D, P), Henri Decae (C), Graham Greene (S); from Greene's novel; Technicolor. Elizabeth Taylor, Richard Burton, Alec Guinness, Peter Ustinov, Paul Ford, Raymond St. Jacques, Zaeks Mokae, Roscoe Lee Browne, Douta Seck, Aliba Peters, Gloria Foster, Robin Langford, Georg Stanford Brown, James Earl Jones, Cicely Tyson.

GRETA GARBO

1921

How Not to Dress (PUB). Capt. Ragnar Ring (D).

1922

Our Daily Bread (PUB). Capt. Ragnar Ring (D).

1923

Luffar-Petter [Peter the Tramp] (Petschler). Erik A. Petschler (D, S). Erik A. Petschler, Helmer Larsson, Fredrik Olsson, Tyra Ryman, Gucken Cederborg.

1924

Gösta Berlings Saga (*The Saga of Gösta Berling*) (Svensk Filmindustri). Mauritz Stiller (D), Julius Jaenzon (C), Stiller and Ragnar Hyltén-Cavallius (S); from the novel by Selma Lagerlöf. Lars Hanson, Ellen Cederstrom, Mona Martenson, Jenny Hasselquist, Karin Swanstrom, Gerda Lundequist, Torsten Kammeren, Svend Tornbech, Otto Elg Lundberg, Sixten Malmerfelt.

1925

Die freudlose Gasse (*Joyless Street*) (Hirschel-Sofar). G. W. Pabst (D), Guido Seeber (C), Willy Haas (S); from the novel by Hugo Bettauer. Werner Krauss, Asta Nielsen, Jaro Furth, Agnes Esterhazy, Gregor Chmara, Valeska Gert, Einar Hanson, Loni Nest, Marlene Dietrich.

1926

The Torrent (MGM). Monta Bell (D), William Daniels (C), Dorothy Farnum (S); from the novel by Vicente Blasco-Ibañez. Ricardo Cortez, Gertrude Olmstead, Edward Connelly, Lucien Littlefield, Martha Mattox, Lucy Beaumont, Tully Marshall, Mack Swain, Arthur Edmund Carew, Lillian Leighton, Mario Carillo.

The Temptress (MGM). Fred Niblo and (uncredited) Mauritz Stiller (D), Tony Gaudio (C), Dorothy Farnum (S); from the novel by Vicente Blasco-Ibañez. Antonio Moreno, Marc MacDermott, Lionel Barrymore, Armand Kaliz, Roy D'Arcy, Alys Murrell, Steve Clemento, Roy Coulson, Robert Anderson, Francis McDonald, Hector A. Sarno, Virginia Brown Faire, Inez Gomez.

1927

Flesh and the Devil (MGM). Clarence Brown (D), William Daniels (C), Benjamin F. Glazer (S); from the novel *The Undying Past* by Hermann Sudermann. John Gilbert, Lars Hanson, Barbara Kent, William Orlamund, George Fawcett, Eugenie Besserer, Marc MacDermott, Marcelle Corday.

Love (MGM). Edmund Goulding (D), William Daniels (C), Frances Marion (S); from the novel *Anna Karenina* by Leo Tolstoy. John Gilbert, George Fawcett, Emily Fitzroy, Brandon Hurst, Philippe de Lacy.

1928

The Divine Woman (MGM). Victor Seastrom (D), Oliver Marsh (C), Dorothy Farnum (S); from the play *Starlight* by Gladys Unger. Lars Hanson, Lowell Sherman, Polly Moran, Dorothy Cumming, John Mack Brown, Cesare Gravina, Paulette Duval, Jean de Briac.

The Mysterious Lady (MGM). Fred Niblo (D), William Daniels (C), Bess Meredyth (S); from the novel *War in the Dark* by Ludwig Wolff. Conrad Nagel, Gustav von Seyffertitz, Edward Connelly, Albert Pollet, Richard Alexander.

1929

A Woman of Affairs (MGM). Clarence Brown (D), William Daniels (C), Bess Meredyth (S); from the novel *The Green Hat* by Michael Arlen. John Gilbert, Lewis Stone, John Mack Brown, Douglas Fairbanks, Jr., Hobart Bosworth, Dorothy Sebastian.

Wild Orchids (MGM). Sidney Franklin (D), William Daniels (C), Willis Goldbeck (S); from the story "Heat" by John Colton. Lewis Stone, Nils Asther.

A Man's Man (MGM). James Cruze (D), Forrest Halsey (S); based on a play by Patrick Kearney. William Haines, Josephine Dunn, Sam Hardy, Mae Busch, John Gilbert (Garbo plays herself in a cameo role).

The Single Standard (MGM). John S. Robertson (D), Oliver Marsh (C), Josephine Lovett (S); from the novel by Adela Rogers St. John. Nils Asther, John Mack

Brown, Dorothy Sebastian, Lane Chandler, Robert Castle, Mahlon Hamilton, Kathlyn Williams, Zeffie Tilbury.

The Kiss (MGM). Jacques Feyder (D), William Daniels (C), Hans Kraly (S); from a story by George M. Saville. Conrad Nagel, Anders Randolf, Holmes Herbert, Lew Ayres, George Davis.

1930

Anna Christie (MGM). Clarence Brown (D), William Daniels (C), Frances Marion (S); from the play by Eugene O'Neill. Charles Bickford, George F. Marion, Marie Dressler, James T. Mack, Lee Phelps.

Anna Christie (German-language version by MGM). Jacques Feyder (D); German translation by Walter Hasenclever. Hans Junkermann, Theo Shall, Salka Steuermann [Viertel].

Romance (MGM). Clarence Brown (D), William Daniels (C), Bess Meredyth and Edwin Justus Mayer (S); from the play by Edward Sheldon. Lewis Stone, Gavin Gordon, Elliott Nugent, Florence Lake, Clara Blandick, Henry Armetta, Mathilde Comont, Countess De Liguoro.

1931

Inspiration (MGM). Clarence Brown (D), William Daniels (C), Gene Markey (S); based on the novel *Sapho* by Alphonse Daudet. Robert Montgomery, Lewis Stone, Marjorie Rambeau, Judith Vosselli, Beryl Mercer, John Miljan, Edwin Maxwell, Oscar Apfel, Joan Marsh, Zelda Sears, Karen Morley, Gwen Lee, Paul McAllister, Arthur Hoyt, Richard Tucker.

Susan Lenox: Her Fall and Rise (MGM). Robert Z. Leonard (D), William Daniels (C), Wanda Tuchock, Zelda Sears, Edith Fitzgerald (S); from the novel by David Graham Phillips. Clark Gable, Jean Hersholt, John Miljan, Alan Hale, Hale Hamilton, Hilda Vaughn, Russell Simpson, Cecil Cunningham, Theodore von Eltz, Marjorie King, Helen Millard, Ian Keith.

1932

Mata Hari (MGM). George Fitzmaurice (D), William Daniels (C), Benjamin Glazer, Leo Birinski, Doris Anderson, Gilbert Emery (S). Ramon Novarro, Lionel Barrymore, Lewis Stone, C. Henry Gordon, Karen Morley, Alec B. Francis, Blanche Frederici, Edmund Breese, Helen Jerome Eddy, Frank Reicher.

Grand Hotel (MGM). Edmund Goulding (D), William Daniels (C), William A. Drake and (uncredited) Frances Marion (S); based on the novel and play by Vicki Baum. John Barrymore, Joan Crawford, Wallace Beery, Lionel Barrymore, Lewis Stone, Jean Hersholt, Robert McWade, Purnell B. Pratt, Ferdinand Gottschalk, Rafaela Ottiano, Morgan Wallace, Tully Marshall, Frank Conroy, Murray Kinnell, Edwin Maxwell.

As You Desire Me (MGM). George Fitzmaurice (D), William Daniels (C), Gene Markey (S); from the play by Luigi Pirandello. Melvyn Douglas, Erich von Stroheim, Owen Moore, Hedda Hopper, Rafaela Ottiano, Warburton Gamble, Albert Conti, William Ricciardi, Roland Varno.

1933

Queen Christina (MGM). Rouben Mamoulian (D), William Daniels (C), Salka Viertel, H. M. Harwood, S. N. Behrman (S), Herbert Stothart (M); based on a story by Viertel and Margaret F. Levin. John Gilbert, Ian Keith, Lewis Stone, Elizabeth Young, C. Aubrey Smith, Reginald Owen, Lawrence Grant, David Torrence, Gustav von Seyffertitz, Ferdinand Munier, Georges Renavent.

1934

The Painted Veil (MGM). Richard Boleslawski (D), Hunt Stromberg (P), William Daniels (C), John Meehan, Salka Viertel, Edith Fitzgerald (S), Herbert Stothart (M); from the novel by W. Somerset Maugham. Herbert Marshall, George Brent, Warner Oland, Jean Hersholt, Beulah Bondi, Katherine Alexander, Cecilia Parker, Soo Yong, Forrester Harvey.

1935

Anna Karenina (MGM). Clarence Brown (D), David O. Selznick (P), William Daniels (C), Clemence Dane, Salka Viertel, S. N. Behrman (S), Herbert Stothart (M); from the novel by Leo Tolstoy. Fredric March, Freddie Bartholomew, Maureen O'Sullivan, May Robson, Basil Rathbone, Reginald Owen, Reginald Denny, Phoebe Foster, Gyles Isham, Buster Phelps, Ella Ethridge, Joan Marsh, Sidney Bracey, Cora Sue Collins, Olaf Hytten, Joe E. Tozer, Guy D'Ennery, Harry Allen, Mary Forbes.

1937

Camille (MGM). George Cukor (D), William Daniels, Karl Freund (C), Zoë Akins, Frances Marion, James Hilton (S); Herbert Stothart (M); from the play and novel *La Dame aux camélias* by Alexandre Dumas. Robert Taylor, Lionel Barrymore, Elizabeth Allan, Jessie Ralph, Henry Daniell, Lenore Ulric, Laura Hope Crews, Rex O'Malley, Russell Hardie, E. E. Clive, Douglas Walton, Marion Ballou, Joan Brodel, June Wilkins, Fritz Leiber, Jr., Elsie Esmonds.

Conquest (MGM). Clarence Brown (D), Bernard H. Hyman (P), Karl Freund (C), Samuel Hoffenstein, Salka Viertel, S. N. Behrman (S), Herbert Stothart (M); based on the novel *Pani Walewska* by Waclaw Gasiorowski and a dramatization of it by Helen Jerome. Charles Boyer, Reginald Owen, Alan Marshall, Henry Stephenson, Leif Erickson, Dame May Whitty, C. Henry Gordon, Vladimir Sokoloff, Maria Ouspenskaya, Scotty Beckett.

1939

Ninotchka (MGM). Ernst Lubitsch (D, P), William Daniels (C), Charles Brackett, Billy Wilder, Walter Reisch (S), Werner R. Heymann (M); based on a story by Melchior Lengyel. Melvyn Douglas, Ina Claire, Bela Lugosi, Sig Rumann, Felix Bressart, Alexander Granach, Gregory Gaye, Rolfe Sedan, Edwin Maxwell, Richard Carle.

1941

Two-Faced Woman (MGM). George Cukor (D), Gottfried Reinhardt (P), Joseph

Ruttenberg (C), S. N. Behrman, Salka Viertel, George Oppenheimer (S), Bronislau Kaper (M); from the play by Ludwig Fulda. Melvyn Douglas, Constance Bennett, Roland Young, Robert Sterling, Ruth Gordon, Francis Carson.

BETTE DAVIS

1931

Bad Sister (UNI). Hobart Henley (D), Karl Freund (C), Raymond L. Schrock, Tom Reed, Edwin Knopf (S); based on the novel *The Flirt* by Booth Tarkington. Conrad Nagel, Sidney Fox, BD,* ZaSu Pitts, Slim Summerville, Charles Winninger, Emma Dunn, Humphrey Bogart, Bert Roach, David Durand.

Seed (UNI). John M. Stahl (D, P), Jackson Rose (C), Gladys Lehman (S); based on the novel of the same name by Charles G. Norris. John Boles, Genevieve Tobin, Lois Wilson, Raymond Hackett, BD, Frances Dade, ZaSu Pitts, Richard Tucker, Jack Willis, Don Cox, Dick Winslow, Kenneth Seling, Terry Cox, Helen Parrish, Dickie Moore.

Waterloo Bridge (UNI). James Whale (D), Arthur Edeson (C), Benn W. Levy, Tom Reed (S); based on the play of the same name by Robert E. Sherwood. Mae Clarke, Kent Douglas [Douglass Montgomery], Doris Lloyd, Ethel Griffies, Enid Bennett, Frederick Kerr, BD, Rita Carlisle.

1932

Way Back Home (RKO Radio). William A. Seiter (D), Pandro S. Berman (P), J. Roy Hunt (C), Jane Murfin (S), (unbilled) Max Steiner [M]; based on radio characters created by Phillips Lord. Phillips Lord, Effie Palmer, Mrs. Phillips Lord, Bennett Kilpack, Raymond Hunter, Frank Albertson, BD, Oscar Apfel, Stanley Fields, Dorothy Peterson, Frankie Darro.

The Menace (COL). Roy William Neill (D), Sam Nelson (P), L. William O'Connell (C), Dorothy Howell, Charles Logue, Roy Chanslor (S); based on *The Feathered Serpent,* a novel by Edgar Wallace. H. B. Warner, BD, Walter Byron, Natalie Moorehead, William B. Davidson, Crauford Kent, Halliwell Hobbes, Charles Gerrard, Murray Kinnell.

Hell's House (Capital Films Exchange). Howard Higgins (D), Benjamin F. Zeidman (P), Allen S. Siegel (C), Paul Gangelin, B. Harrison Orkow (S); based on a story by Howard Higgins. Junior Durkin, Pat O'Brien, BD, Junior Coughlan, Charley Grapewin, Emma Dunn, James Marcus, Morgan Wallace, Wallis Clark, Hooper Atchley.

The Man Who Played God (WB Vitaphone). John Adolfi (D), Darryl F. Zanuck (P), James Van Trees (C), Julien Josephson, Maude T. Howell (S); adapted from a short story by Gouverneur Morris and the play *The Silent Voice* by Jules Eckert Goodman. George Arliss, Violet Heming, Ivan Simpson, Louise Closser Hale, BD, Donald Cook, Paul Porcasi, Oscar Apfel, William Janney, Grace Durkin, Dorothy Libaire, Andre Luget, Charles Evans, Murray Kinnell, Wade Boteler, Alexander Ikonikoff, Raymond Milland, Hedda Hopper.

So Big (WB Vitaphone). William A. Wellman (D), Lucien Hubbard (Production

---

* *BD* indicates Davis's placement in the credits of films in which she did not receive top billing. The titles of films in which she did receive top billing are asterisked.

Supervisor), Sid Hickox (C), J. Grubb Alexander, Robert Lord (S); based on the novel of the same name by Edna Ferber. Barbara Stanwyck, George Brent, Dickie Moore, BD, Guy Kibbee, Mae Madison, Hardie Albright, Robert Warwick, Arthur Stone, Earle Foxe, Alan Hale, Dorothy Peterson, Dawn O'Day [Anne Shirley], Dick Winslow, Elizabeth Patterson, Rita LeRoy, Blanche Frederici, Lionel Bellmore.

The Rich Are Always with Us (First National–WB). Alfred E. Green (D), Ray Griffith (Production Supervisor), Ernest Haller (C), Austin Parker (S); based on the novel of the same name by E. Pettit. Ruth Chatterton, George Brent, Adrienne Dore, BD, John Miljan, Mae Madison, John Wray, Robert Warwick, Virginia Hammond, Walter Walker, Eula Gray, Edith Allen, Ethel Kenyon, Ruth Lee, Berton Churchill.

The Dark Horse (First National–WB). Alfred E. Green (D), Ray Griffith (Production Supervisor), Sol Polito (C), Joseph Jackson, Wilson Mizner (S); based on an original story by Melville Crossman. Warren William, BD, Guy Kibbee, Frank McHugh, Vivienne Osborne, Sam Hardy, Robert Warwick, Harry Holman, Charles Sellon, Robert Emmett O'Connor, Berton Churchill.

Cabin in the Cotton (First National–WB). Michael Curtiz (D), Hall Wallis (Production Supervisor), Barney McGill (C), Paul Green (S); based on the novel of the same name by Harry Harrison Kroll. Richard Barthelmess, BD, Dorothy Jordan, Henry B. Walthall, Berton Churchill, Walter Percival, William Le Maire, Hardie Albright, Edmund Breese, Tully Marshall, Clarence Muse, Russell Simpson, John Marston, Erville Anderson, Dorothy Peterson, Snow Flake, Harry Cording.

Three on a Match (First National–WB). Mervyn LeRoy (D), Ray Griffith (Production Supervisor), Sol Polito (C), Lucien Hubbard (S); based on an original story by Kubec Glasmon and John Bright. Joan Blondell, Warren William, Ann Dvorak, BD, Grant Mitchell, Lyle Talbot, Sheila Terry, Glenda Farrell, Clara Blandick, Buster Phelps, Humphrey Bogart, John Marston, Patricia Ellis, Hale Hamilton, Frankie Darro, Dawn O'Day [Anne Shirley], Virginia Davis, Dick Brandon, Allen Jenkins, Jack LaRue, Edward Arnold.

1933

Twenty Thousand Years in Sing Sing (First National–WB). Michael Curtiz (D), Ray Griffith (Production Supervisor), Barney McGill (C), Wilson Mizner, Brown Holmes, Courtenay Terrett, Robert Lord (S); based on the book of the same name by Warden Lewis E. Lawes. Spencer Tracy, BD, Lyle Talbot, Arthur Byron, Sheila Terry, Edward McNamara, Warren Hymer, Louis Calhern, Spencer Charters, Sam Godfrey, Grant Mitchell, Nella Walker, Harold Huber, William Le Maire, Arthur Hoyt, George Pat Collins.

Parachute Jumper (WB). Alfred E. Green (D), Ray Griffith (Production Supervisor), James Van Trees (C), John Francis Larkin (S); based on the story "Some Call It Love" by Rian James. Douglas Fairbanks, Jr., Leo Carrillo, BD, Frank McHugh, Claire Dodd, Sheila Terry, Harold Huber, Thomas E. Jackson, George Pat Collins, Pat O'Malley, Harold Healy, Ferdinand Munley, Walter Miller.

The Working Man (WB Vitaphone). John Adolfi (D), Lucien Hubbard (Production Supervisor), Sol Polito (C), Maude T. Howell, Charles Kenyon (S); based on the story "The Adopted Father" by Edgar Franklin. George Arliss, BD, Hardie Albright, Theodore Newton, Gordon Westcott, J. Farrell MacDonald, Charles Evans, Frederick Burton, Edward Van Sloan, Pat Wing, Claire McDowell, Harold Minjir, Douglas Dumbrille.

*_Ex-Lady_ (WB Vitaphone). Robert Florey (D), Lucien Hubbard (Production Supervisor), Tony Gaudio (C), David Boehm (S); based on an original story by Edith Fitzgerald and Robert Riskin. Gene Raymond, Frank McHugh, Monroe Owsley, Claire Dodd, Kay Strozzi, Ferdinand Gottschalk, Alphonse Ethier, Bodil Rosing.

*_Bureau of Missing Persons_ (First National–WB). Roy Del Ruth (D), Henry Blanke (Production Supervisor), Barney McGill (C), Robert Presnell (S); based on the book _Missing Men_ by Police Captain John H. Ayers and Carol Bird. Lewis Stone, Pat O'Brien, Glenda Farrell, Allen Jenkins, Ruth Donnelly, Hugh Herbert, Alan Dinehart, Marjorie Gateson, Tad Alexander, Noel Francis,. Wallis Clark, Adrian Morris, Clay Clement, Henry Kolker, Harry Beresford, George Chandler.

1934

Fashions of 1934 (First National–WB). William Dieterle (D), Henry Blanke (Production Supervisor), William Rees (C), F. Hugh Herbert, Gene Markey, Kathryn Scola, Carl Erickson (S), Sammy Fain, Irving Kahal (M), Busby Berkeley (Dances); based on the story "The Fashion Plate" by Harry Collins and Warren Duff. William Powell, BD, Frank McHugh, Verree Teasdale, Reginald Owen, Henry O'Neill, Philip Reed, Hugh Herbert, Gordon Westcott, Nella Walker, Dorothy Burgess, Etienne Girardot, William Burress, Spencer Charters, Jane Darwell, Arthur Treacher, Hobart Cavanaugh, Albert Conti.

The Big Shakedown (First National–WB). John Francis Dillon (D), Samuel Bischoff (Production Supervisor), Sid Hickox (C), Niven Busch, Rian James (S); based on the story "Cut Rate" by Samuel Engel. Charles Farrell, BD, Ricardo Cortez, Glenda Farrell, Allen Jenkins, Henry O'Neill, Philip Faversham, Robert Emmett O'Connor, John Wray, George Pat Collins, Adrian Morris, Dewey Robinson, Samuel S. Hinds, Matt Briggs, William B. Davidson, Earle Foxe, Frederick Burton.

Jimmy the Gent (WB Vitaphone). Michael Curtiz (D), Robert Lord (Production Supervisor), Ira Morgan (C), Bertram Milhauser (S); based on the story "The Heir Chaser" by Laird Doyle and Ray Nazarro. James Cagney, BD, Alice White, Allen Jenkins, Arthur Hohl, Alan Dinehart, Philip Reed, Hobart Cavanaugh, Mayo Methot, Ralf Harolde, Joseph Sawyer, Philip Faversham, Nora Lane, Howard Hickman, Jane Darwell, Joseph Crehan, Robert Warwick, Harold Entwhistle.

*_Fog over Frisco_ (WB Vitaphone). William Dieterle (D), Henry Blanke (Production Supervisor), Tony Gaudio (C), Robert N. Lee, Eugene Solow (S); based on an original story "The Five Fragments" by George Dyer. Donald Woods, Margaret Lindsay, Lyle Talbot, Arthur Byron, Hugh Herbert, Douglas Dumbrille, Robert Barrat, Henry O'Neill, Irving Pichel, Gordon Westcott, Charles C. Wilson, Alan Hale, William B. Davidson, Douglas Cosgrove, George Chandler, Harold Minjir, William Demarest.

Of Human Bondage (RKO Radio). John Cromwell (D), Pandro S. Berman (P), Henry W. Gerrard (C), Lester Cohen (S), (unbilled) Max Steiner (M); based on the novel of the same name by W. Somerset Maugham. Leslie Howard, BD, Frances Dee, Kay Johnson, Reginald Denny, Alan Hale, Reginald Owen, Reginald Sheffield, Desmond Roberts.

Housewife (WB Vitaphone). Alfred E. Green (D), Robert Lord (Production Supervisor), William Rees (C), Manuel Seff, Lillie Hayward (S); based on an original story by Robert Lord and Lillie Hayward. George Brent, BD, Ann Dvorak, John Halliday, Ruth Donnelly, Hobart Cavanaugh, Robert Barrat, Joseph Cawthorn, Phil Regan, Willard Robertson, Ronald Cosbey, Leila Bennett, William B. Davidson, John Hale.

1935

Bordertown (WB Vitaphone). Archie Mayo (D), Robert Lord (Production Supervisor), Tony Gaudio (C), Laird Doyle, Wallace Smith, Robert Lord (S); based on the novel of the same name by Carroll Graham. Paul Muni, BD, Margaret Lindsay, Gavin Gordon, Arthur Stone, Robert Barrat, Soledad Jiminez, Eugene Pallette, William B. Davidson, Hobart Cavanaugh, Henry O'Neill, Vivian Tobin, Nella Walker, Oscar Apfel, Samuel S. Hinds, Chris Pin Martin, Frank Puglia, Jack Norton.

*The Girl from Tenth Avenue (First National–WB). Alfred E. Green (D), Henry Blanke (Production Supervisor), James Van Trees (C), Charles Kenyon (S); based on a play by Hubert Henry Davies. Ian Hunter, Colin Clive, Alison Skipworth, John Eldredge, Philip Reed, Katherine Alexander, Helen Jerome Eddy, Gordon Elliott, Adrian Rosley, Andre Cheron, Edward McWade, Mary Treen, Heinie Conklin.

*Front Page Woman (WB Vitaphone). Michael Curtiz (D), Samuel Bischoff (Production Supervisor), Tony Gaudio (C), Roy Chanslor, Lillie Hayward, Laird Doyle (S); based on the story "Women Are Bum Newspapermen" by Richard Macaulay. George Brent, June Martel, Dorothy Dare, Joseph Crehan, Winifred Shaw, Roscoe Karns, Joseph King, J. Farrell MacDonald, J. Carroll Naish, Walter Walker, DeWitt Jennings, Huntley Gordon, Adrian Rosley, Georges Renavent, Grace Hale, Selmer Jackson, Gordon Westcott.

*Special Agent (Claridge–WB). William Keighley (D), Samuel Bischoff (P, in association with Martin Mooney), Sid Hickox (C), Laird Doyle, Abem Finkel (S); based on an idea by Martin Mooney. George Brent, Ricardo Cortez, Jack LaRue, Henry O'Neill, Robert Strange, Joseph Crehan, J. Carroll Naish, Joseph Sawyer, William B. Davidson, Robert Barrat, Paul Guilfoyle, Irving Pichel, Douglas Wood, James Flavin, Lee Phelps, Louis Natheaux, Herbert Skinner, John Alexander.

*Dangerous (WB Vitaphone). Alfred E. Green (D), Harry Joe Brown (Production Supervisor), Ernest Haller (C), Laird Doyle (S). Franchot Tone, Margaret Lindsay, Alison Skipworth, John Eldredge, Dick Foran, Walter Walker, Richard Carle, George Irving, Pierre Watkin, Douglas Wood, William B. Davidson, Frank O'Connor, Edward Keane.

1936

The Petrified Forest (WB Vitaphone). Archie Mayo (D), Henry Blanke (Production Supervisor), Sol Polito (C), Charles Kenyon, Delmer Daves (S); based on the play of the same name by Robert E. Sherwood. Leslie Howard, BD, Genevieve Tobin, Dick Foran, Humphrey Bogart, Joseph Sawyer, Porter Hall, Charley Grapewin, Paul Harvey, Eddie Acuff, Adrian Morris, Nina Campana, Slim Johnson, John Alexander.

*The Golden Arrow (First National–WB). Alfred E. Green (D), Samuel Bischoff (Production Supervisor), Arthur Edeson (C), Charles Kenyon (S); based on the play *Dream Princess* by Michael Arlen. George Brent, Eugene Pallette, Dick Foran, Carol Hughes, Catherine Doucet, Craig Reynolds, Ivan Lebedoff, G. P. Huntley, Jr., Hobart Cavanaugh, Henry O'Neill, Eddie Acuff, Earle Foxe, E. E. Clive, Rafael Storm, Sara Edwards, Bess Flowers, Mary Treen, Selmer Jackson.

*Satan Met a Lady (WB Vitaphone). William Dieterle (D), Henry Blanke (Production Supervisor), Arthur Edeson (C), Brown Holmes (S); based on the novel *The Maltese Falcon* by Dashiell Hammett. Warren William, Alison Skipworth,

Arthur Treacher, Winifred Shaw, Marie Wilson, Porter Hall, Maynard Holmes, Olin Howard, Charles Wilson, Joseph King, Barbara Blane, William B. Davidson.

1937

Marked Woman (WB First National). Lloyd Bacon (D), Hal Wallis (P, in association with Lou Edelman), George Barnes (C), Robert Rosson, Abem Finkel, Seton I. Miller (S). Humphrey Bogart, Eduardo Ciannelli, Jane Bryan, Lola Lane, Isabel Jewell, Rosalind Marquis, Mayo Methot, Ben Welden, Henry O'Neill, Allen Jenkins, John Litel, Damian O'Flynn, Robert Strange, Raymond Hatton, William B. Davidson, Frank Faylen, Jack Norton, Kenneth Harlan.

Kid Galahad (WB). Michael Curtiz (D), Hal B. Wallis (Executive Producer, in association with Samuel Bischoff), Tony Gaudio (C), Seton I. Miller (S); based on the novel of the same name by Francis Wallace. Edward G. Robinson, BD, Humphrey Bogart, Wayne Morris, William Haade, Jane Bryan, Harry Carey, Soledad Jiminez, Veda Ann Borg, Ben Welden, Joseph Crehan, Harlan Tucker, Frank Faylen, Joyce Compton, Horace MacMahon.

That Certain Woman (WB First National). Edmund Goulding (D), Hal B. Wallis (Executive Producer, in association with Robert Lord), Ernest Haller (C), Edmund Goulding (S), Max Steiner (M); based on Goulding's original screenplay *The Trespasser*. Henry Fonda, Ian Hunter, Anita Louise, Donald Crisp, Katherine Alexander, Mary Phillips, Minor Watson, Ben Welden, Sidney Toler, Charles Trowbridge, Norman Willis, Herbert Rawlinson, Rosalind Marquis, Frank Faylen, Willard Parker, Dwane Day, Hugh O'Connell.

It's Love I'm After (WB). Archie Mayo (D), Hal B. Wallis (Executive Producer, in association with Harry Joe Brown), James Van Trees (C), Casey Robinson (S); based on the story "Gentlemen After Midnight" by Maurice Hanline. Leslie Howard, BD, Olivia De Havilland, Patric Knowles, Eric Blore, George Barbier, Spring Byington, Bonita Granville, E. E. Clive, Veda Ann Borg, Valerie Bergere, Georgia Caine, Sarah Edwards, Lionel Bellmore, Irving Bacon.

1938

Jezebel (WB). William Wyler (D), Hal B. Wallis (Executive Producer, in association with Henry Blanke), Ernest Haller (C), Clements Ripley, Abem Finkel, John Huston, Robert Buckner (S), Max Steiner (M); based on the play of the same name by Owen Davis, Sr. Henry Fonda, George Brent, Donald Crisp, Fay Bainter, Margaret Lindsay, Henry O'Neill, John Litel, Gordon Oliver, Spring Byington, Margaret Early, Richard Cromwell, Theresa Harris, Janet Shaw, Irving Pichel, Eddie Anderson.

The Sisters (WB). Anatole Litvak (D), Hal B. Wallis (P, in association with David Lewis), Tony Gaudio (C), Milton Krims (S), Max Steiner (M); based on the novel of the same name by Myron Brinig. Errol Flynn, BD, Anita Louise, Ian Hunter, Donald Crisp, Beulah Bondi, Jane Bryan, Alan Hale, Dick Foran, Henry Travers, Patric Knowles, Lee Patrick, Laura Hope Crews, Janet Shaw, Harry Davenport, Ruth Garland, John Warburton, Paul Harvey, Mayo Methot, Irving Bacon, Arthur Hoyt.

1939

Dark Victory (WB First National). Edmund Goulding (D), Hal B. Wallis (P, in association with David Lewis), Ernest Haller (C), Casey Robinson (S), Max

Steiner (M); based on the play of the same name by George Emerson Brewer, Jr., and Bertram Block. George Brent, Geraldine Fitzgerald, Humphrey Bogart, Ronald Reagan, Henry Travers, Cora Witherspoon, Dorothy Peterson, Virginia Brissac, Charles Richman, Leonard Mudie, Fay Helm, Lottie Williams.

Juarez (WB). William Dieterle (D), Hal B. Wallis (P, in association with Henry Blanke), Tony Gaudio (C), John Huston, Aeneas MacKenzie, Wolfgang Reinhardt (S), Erich Wolfgang Korngold (M); based on the play *Juarez and Maximilian* by Franz Werfel and the book *The Phantom Crown* by Bertita Harding. Paul Muni, BD, Brian Aherne, Claude Rains, John Garfield, Donald Crisp, Joseph Calleia, Gale Sondergaard, Gilbert Roland, Henry O'Neill, Harry Davenport, Louis Calhern, Walter Kingsford, Georgia Caine, Montagu Love, John Miljan, Vladimir Sokoloff, Irving Pichel, Pedro De Cordoba, Gilbert Emory, Monte Blue, Manuel Diaz, Hugh Sothern, Mickey Kuhn.

The Old Maid (WB First National). Edmund Goulding (D), Hal B. Wallis (P, in association with Henry Blanke), Tony Gaudio (C), Casey Robinson (S), Max Steiner (M); based on the play Zoë Akins adapted from the novel of the same name by Edith Wharton. Miriam Hopkins, George Brent, Donald Crisp, Jane Bryan, Louise Fazenda, James Stephenson, Jerome Cowan, William Lundigan, Rand Brooks, Cecelia Loftus, Janet Shaw, DeWolf Hopper.

The Private Lives of Elizabeth and Essex (WB). Michael Curtiz (D), Hal B. Wallis (P, in association with Robert Lord), Sol Polito, H. Howard Greene (C), Norman Reilly Raine, Aeneas MacKenzie (S), Erich Wolfgang Korngold (M); based on the play *Elizabeth the Queen* by Maxwell Anderson; Technicolor. Errol Flynn, Olivia De Havilland, Donald Crisp, Vincent Price, Alan Hale, Henry Stephenson, Henry Daniell, James Stephenson, Leo G. Carroll, Nanette Fabares [Fabray], Rosella Towne, Maris Wrixon, Ralph Forbes, Robert Warwick, John Sutton, Guy Bellis, Doris Lloyd, Forrester Harvey.

1940

All This and Heaven Too (WB First National). Anatole Litvak (D), Jack L. Warner and Hal B. Wallis (P, in association with David Lewis), Ernest Haller (C), Casey Robinson (S), Max Steiner (M); based on the novel of the same name by Rachel Field. Charles Boyer, Jeffrey Lynn, Barbara O'Neil, Virginia Weidler, Helen Westley, Walter Hampden, Henry Daniell, Harry Davenport, George Coulouris, Montagu Love, Janet Beecher, June Lockhart, Ann Todd, Richard Nichols, Fritz Leiber, Ian Keith, Sibyl Harris, Mary Anderson, Edward Fielding, Ann Gillis, Peggy Stewart, Victor Kilian, Mrs. Gardner Crane.

The Letter (WB First National). William Wyler (D), Hal B. Wallis (P, in association with Robert Lord), Tony Gaudio (C), Howard Koch (S), Max Steiner (M); based on the play of the same name by W. Somerset Maugham. Herbert Marshall, James Stephenson, Frieda Inescort, Gale Sondergaard, Bruce Lester [David Bruce], Elizabeth Earl, Cecil Kellaway, Doris Lloyd, Sen Yung, Willie Fung, Tetsu Komai, Roland Got, Otto Hahn, Pete Kotehernaro, David Newell, Ottola Nesmith, Lillian Kemble-Cooper.

1941

The Great Lie (WB). Edmund Goulding (D), Hal B. Wallis (P, in association with Henry Blanke), Tony Gaudio (C), Lenore Coffee (S), Max Steiner (M); based on the novel *January Heights* by Polan Banks. George Brent, Mary Astor, Lucile

Watson, Hattie McDaniel, Grant Mitchell, Jerome Cowan, Sam McDaniel, Thurston Hall, Russell Hicks, Charles Trowbridge, Virginia Brissac, Olin Howland, J. Farrell MacDonald, Doris Lloyd, Addison Richards, Georgia Caine, Alphonse Martell.

The Bride Came C.O.D. (WB). William Keighley (D), Hal B. Wallis (P, in association with William Cagney), Ernest Haller (C), Julius J. and Philip G. Epstein (S), Max Steiner (M); based on a story by Kenneth Earl and M. M. Musselman. James Cagney, BD, Stuart Erwin, Jack Carson, George Tobias, Eugene Pallette, Harry Davenport, William Frawley, Edward Brophy, Harry Holman, Chick Chandler, Keith Douglas, Herbert Anderson, Creighton Hale, Frank Mayo, DeWolf Hopper, Jack Mower, William Newell.

°*The Little Foxes* (Samuel Goldwyn Production, released by RKO Radio). William Wyler (D), Samuel Goldwyn (P), Gregg Toland (C), Lillian Hellman (S); based on Hellman's stage play of the same name, with additional scenes and dialogue by Arthur Kober, Dorothy Parker, and Alan Campbell. Herbert Marshall, Teresa Wright, Richard Carlson, Patricia Collinge, Dan Duryea, Charles Dingle, Carl Benton Reid, Jessie Grayson, John Marriott, Russell Hicks, Lucien Littlefield, Virginia Brissac.

1942

°*The Man Who Came to Dinner* (WB). William Keighley (D), Hal B. Wallis (P, in association with Jerry Wald, Sam Harris, Jack Saper), Tony Gaudio (C), Julius J. and Philip G. Epstein (S); based on the play of the same name by George S. Kaufman and Moss Hart. Ann Sheridan, Monty Woolley, Richard Travis, Jimmy Durante, Reginald Gardiner, Billie Burke, Elizabeth Fraser, Grant Mitchell, George Barbier, Mary Wickes, Russell Arms, Ruth Vivian, Edwin Stanley, Charles Drake, Nanette Vallon, John Ridgely.

°*In This Our Life* (WB). John Huston (D), Hal B. Wallis (P, in association with David Lewis), Ernest Haller (C), Howard Koch (S), Max Steiner (M); based on the novel of the same name by Ellen Glasgow. Olivia De Havilland, George Brent, Dennis Morgan, Charles Coburn, Frank Craven, Billie Burke, Hattie McDaniel, Lee Patrick, Mary Servoss, Ernest Anderson, William B. Davidson, Edward Fielding, John Hamilton, William Forest, Lee Phelps.

°*Now, Voyager* (WB). Irving Rapper (D), Hal B. Wallis (P), Sol Polito (C), Casey Robinson (S), Max Steiner (M); based on the novel of the same name by Olive Higgins Prouty. Paul Henreid, Claude Rains, Gladys Cooper, Bonita Granville, Ilka Chase, John Loder, Lee Patrick, Franklin Pangborn, Katherine Alexander, James Rennie, Mary Wickes, Janis Wilson, Frank Puglia, Michael Ames, Charles Drake, David Clyde.

1943

°*Watch on the Rhine* (WB). Herman Shumlin (D), Hal B. Wallis (P), Merritt Gerstad, Hal Mohr (C), Dashiell Hammett (S, with additional scenes and dialogue by Lillian Hellman), Max Steiner (M); based on the Hellman play of the same name. Paul Lukas, Geraldine Fitzgerald, Lucile Watson, Beulah Bondi, George Coulouris, Donald Woods, Henry Daniell, Donald Buka, Eric Roberts, Janis Wilson, Mary Young, Kurt Katch, Erwin Kalser, Clyde Fillmore, Robert O. Davis, Frank Wilson, Clarence Muse, Anthony Caruso, Howard Hickman, Elvira Curci, Creighton Hale, Alan Hale, Jr.

Thank Your Lucky Stars (WB). David Butler (D), Mark Hellinger (P), Arthur Edeson (C), Norman Panama, Melvin Frank, James V. Kern (S), Arthur Schwartz and Frank Loesser (Music and Lyrics), LeRoy Prinz (Dances); based on a story by Everett Freeman and Arthur Schwartz. Dennis Morgan, Joan Leslie, Edward Everett Horton, S. Z. Sakall, Richard Lane, Ruth Donnelly, Don Wilson, Henry Armetta, Joyce Reynolds; guest stars Humphrey Bogart, Eddie Cantor, Bette Davis, Olivia De Havilland, Errol Flynn, John Garfield, Ida Lupino, Ann Sheridan, Dinah Shore, Alexis Smith, Jack Carson, Alan Hale, George Tobias, Hattie McDaniel, Willie Best, Spike Jones and His City Slickers.

Old Acquaintance (WB). Vincent Sherman (D), Henry Blanke (P), Sol Polito (C), John Van Druten, Lenore Coffee (S), Franz Waxman (M); based on the play of the same name by John Van Druten. Miriam Hopkins, Gig Young, John Loder, Dolores Moran, Philip Reed, Roscoe Karns, Anne Revere, Esther Dale, Ann Codee, Joseph Crehan, Pierre Watkin, Marjorie Hoshelle, George Lessey, Ann Doran, Leona Maricle, Francine Rufo.

1944

Mr. Skeffington (WB). Vincent Sherman (D), Julius J. and Philip G. Epstein (P, S), Ernest Haller (C), Franz Waxman (M); based on the novel of the same name by "Elizabeth." Claude Rains, Walter Abel, Richard Waring, George Coulouris, Marjorie Riordan, Robert Shayne, John Alexander, Jerome Cowan, Johnny Mitchell, Dorothy Peterson, Peter Whitney, Bill Kennedy, Tom Stevenson, Halliwell Hobbes, Bunny Sunshine, Gigi Perreau, Dolores Gray, Walter Kingsford, Molly Lamont.

Hollywood Canteen (WB). Delmer Daves (D, S), Alex Gottlieb (P), Bert Glennon (C). Joan Leslie, Robert Hutton, Janis Paige, Dane Clark, Richard Erdman, James Flavin, Joan Winfield, Jonathan Hale, Rudolph Friml, Jr., Bill Manning, Larry Thompson, Mell Schubert, Walden Boyle, Steve Richards; guest stars the Andrews Sisters, Jack Benny, Joe E. Brown, Eddie Cantor, Kitty Carlisle, Jack Carson, Joan Crawford, Helmut Dantine, Bette Davis, Faye Emerson, Victor Francen, John Garfield, Sydney Greenstreet, Alan Hale, Paul Henreid, Andrea King, Peter Lorre, Ida Lupino, Irene Manning, Nora Martin, Joan McCracken, Dolores Moran, Dennis Morgan, Eleanor Parker, William Prince, Joyce Reynolds, John Ridgely, Roy Rogers and Trigger, S. Z. Sakall, Alexis Smith, Zachary Scott, Barbara Stanwyck, Craig Stevens, Joseph Szigeti, Donald Woods, Jane Wyman, Jimmy Dorsey and His Band, Carmen Cavallaro and His Orchestra, Rosario and Antonio, Sons of the Pioneers, Virginia Patton, Lynne Baggett, Betty Alexander, Julie Bishop, Robert Shayne, Johnny Mitchell, John Sheridan, Colleen Townsend, Angela Green, Paul Brooke, Marianne O'Brien, Dorothy Malone, Bill Kennedy.

1945

The Corn Is Green (WB). Irving Rapper (D), Jack Chertok (P), Sol Polito (C), Casey Robinson, Frank Cavett (S), Max Steiner (M); based on the play of the same name by Emlyn Williams. John Dall, Joan Lorring, Nigel Bruce, Rhys Williams, Rosalind Ivan, Mildred Dunnock, Gwenyth Hughes, Billy Roy, Thomas Louden, Arthur Shields, Leslie Vincent, Robert Regent, Tony Ellis, Elliot Dare, Robert Cherry, Gene Ross.

1946

* *A Stolen Life* (WB). Curtis Bernhardt (D), Bette Davis (P), Sol Polito, Ernest Haller (C), Catherine Turney (S), Max Steiner (M); adapted by Margaret Buell Wilder, based on the novel *Uloupeny Zivot* by Karel J. Benes. Glenn Ford, Dane Clark, Walter Brennan, Charles Ruggles, Bruce Bennett, Peggy Knudsen, Esther Dale, Clara Blandick, Joan Winfield.

* *Deception* (WB). Irving Rapper (D), Henry Blanke (P), Ernest Haller (C), John Collier, Joseph Than (S), Erich Wolfgang Korngold (M); based on a play variously titled *Monsieur Lamberthier, Satan,* and *Jealousy* by Louis Verneuil. Paul Henreid, Claude Rains, John Abbott, Benson Fong, Richard Walsh, Suzi Crandall, Richard Erdman, Ross Ford, Russell Arms, Bess Flowers, Gino Cerrado, Clifton Young, Cyril Delevanti, Jane Harker.

1948

* *Winter Meeting* (WB). Bretaigne Windust (D), Henry Blanke (P), Ernest Haller (C), Catherine Turney (S), Max Steiner (M); based on the novel of the same name by Ethel Vance. Janis Paige, James Davis, John Hoyt, Florence Bates, Walter Baldwin, Ransom Sherman.

* *June Bride* (WB). Bretaigne Windust (D), Henry Blanke (P), Ted McCord (C), Ranald MacDougall (S), David Buttolph (M); based on the play *Feature for June* by Eileen Tighe and Graeme Lorimer. Robert Montgomery, Fay Bainter, Betty Lynn, Tom Tully, Barbara Bates, Jerome Cowan, Mary Wickes, James Burke, Raymond Roe, Marjorie Bennett, Ray Montgomery, George O'Hanlon, Sandra Gould, Esther Howard, Jessie Adams, Raymond Bond, Alice Kelley, Patricia Northrop, Debbie Reynolds.

1949

* *Beyond the Forest* (WB). King Vidor (D), Henry Blanke (P), Robert Burks (C), Lenore Coffee (S), Max Steiner (M); based on the novel of the same name by Stuart Engstrand. Joseph Cotten, David Brian, Ruth Roman, Minor Watson, Dona Drake, Regis Toomey, Sarah Selby, Mary Servoss, Frances Charles, Harry Tyler, Ralph Littlefield, Creighton Hale, Joel Allen, Ann Doran.

1950

* *All About Eve* (20TH). Joseph L. Mankiewicz (D, S), Darryl F. Zanuck (P), Milton Krasner (C), Alfred Newman (M); based on the story "The Wisdom of Eve" by Mary Orr. Anne Baxter, George Sanders, Celeste Holm, Gary Merrill, Hugh Marlowe, Thelma Ritter, Marilyn Monroe, Gregory Ratoff, Barbara Bates, Walter Hampden, Randy Stuart, Craig Hill, Leland Harris, Claude Stroud, Eugene Borden, Steve Geray, Bess Flowers, Stanley Orr, Eddie Fisher.

1951

* *Payment on Demand* (RKO Radio). Curtis Bernhardt (D), Jack H. Skirball, Bruce Manning (P), Leo Tover (C), Bruce Manning and Curtis Bernhardt (S); based on original story by Manning and Bernhardt "The Story of a Divorce." Barry Sullivan, Jane Cowl, Kent Taylor, Betty Lynn, John Sutton, Frances Dee, Peggie

Castle, Otto Kruger, Walter Sande, Brett King, Richard Anderson, Natalie Schafer, Katherine Emery, Lisa Golm, Moroni Olsen.

1952

Another Man's Poison (Eros–UA). Irving Rapper (D), Douglas Fairbanks, Jr., Daniel M. Angel (P), Robert Krasker (C), Val Guest (S), Paul Sawtell (M); based on the play *Deadlock* by Leslie Sands. Gary Merrill, Emlyn Williams, Anthony Steel, Barbara Murray, Reginald Beckwith, Edna Morris.

Phone Call from a Stranger (20TH). Jean Negulesco (D), Nunnally Johnson (P, S), Milton Krasner (C), Franz Waxman (M); based on a story by Ida Alexa Ross Wylie. Shelley Winters, Gary Merrill, Michael Rennie, Keenan Wynn, Evelyn Varden, Warren Stevens, Beatrice Straight, Ted Donaldson, Craig Stevens, Helen Westcott, BD.

1953

The Star (Bert E. Friedlob–20TH). Stuart Heisler (D), Bert E. Friedlob (P), Ernest Laszlo (C), Katherine Albert, Dale Eunson (S); original story by Albert and Eunson. Sterling Hayden, Natalie Wood, Warner Anderson, Minor Watson, June Travis, Katherine Warren, Kay Riehl, Barbara Woodel, Fay Baker, Barbara Lawrence, David Alpert, Paul Frees.

1955

The Virgin Queen (20TH). Henry Koster (D), Charles Brackett (P), Charles G. Clarke (C), Harry Brown, Mindred Lord (S), Franz Waxman (M); original story "Sir Walter Raleigh" by Brown and Lord. Richard Todd, Joan Collins, Jay Robinson, Herbert Marshall, Dan O'Herlihy, Robert Douglas, Romney Brent, Marjorie Hellen, Lisa Daniels, Lisa Davis, Barry Bernard, Robert Adler, Noel Drayton, Ian Murray, Margery Weston, Rod Taylor, Davis Thursby, Arthur Gould-Porter.

1956

The Catered Affair (MGM). Richard Brooks (D), Sam Zimbalist (P), John Alton (C), Gore Vidal (S), Andre Previn (M); based on the teleplay of the same name by Paddy Chayefsky. Debbie Reynolds, Ernest Borgnine, Barry Fitzgerald, Rod Taylor, Robert Simon, Madge Kennedy, Dorothy Stickney, Carol Veazie, Joan Camden, Ray Stricklyn, Jay Adler, Dan Tobin, Paul Denton, Augusta Merighi, Sammy Shack, Jack Kenny, Robert Stephenson, Mae Clarke.

Storm Center (Phoenix–COL). Daniel Taradash (D), Julian Blaustein (P), Burnett Guffey (C), Daniel Taradash, Elick Moll (S), George Dunning (M). Brian Keith, Kim Hunter, Paul Kelly, Kevin Coughlin, Joe Mantell, Sallie Brophy, Howard Wierum, Curtis Cooksey, Michael Raffetto, Edward Platt, Kathryn Grant, Howard Wendell, Burt Mustin, Edith Evanson.

1959

John Paul Jones (Samuel Bronston–WB). John Farrow (D), Samuel Bronston (P), Michel Kelber (C), John Farrow, Jesse Lasky, Jr. (S), Max Steiner (M); from the story "Nor'wester" by Clements Ripley. Robert Stack, Marisa Pavan, Charles Coburn, Erin O'Brien, Tom Brannum, Bruce Cabot, Basil Sydney, Archie Duncan, Thomas Gomez, Judson Laure, Bob Cunningham, John Charles Farrow, Eric Pohlmann, Pepe Nieto, John Crawford, Patrick Villiers, Frank Latimore, Ford Rainey, Bruce Seaton—MacDonald Carey, Jean Pierre Aumont, David Farrar, Peter Cushing, Susana Canales, Jorge Riviere, BD.

The Scapegoat (du Maurier–Guinness–MGM). Robert Hamer (D), Michael Balcon (P), Paul Beeson (C), Gore Vidal, Robert Hamer (S), Bronislau Caper (M); based on the novel of the same name by Daphne du Maurier. Alec Guinness, BD, Nicole Maurey, Irene Worth, Pamela Brown, Annabel Bartlett, Geoffrey Keen, Noel Howlett, Peter Bull, Leslie French, Alan Webb, Maria Britneva, Eddie Byrne, Alexander Archdale, Peter Sallis.

1961

Pocketful of Miracles (Franton–UA). Frank Capra (D), and (P), in association with Glenn Ford and Joseph Sistrom), Robert Bronner (C), Hal Kanter, Harry Tugend (S), Walter Scharf (M); based on Robert Riskin's screenplay *Lady for a Day* from the story "Madame la Gimp" by Damon Runyon. Glenn Ford, BD, Hope Lange, Arthur O'Connell, Peter Falk, Thomas Mitchell, Edward Everett Horton, Mickey Shaughnessy, David Brian, Sheldon Leonard, Ann-Margret, Peter Mann, Barton MacLane, John Litel, Jerome Cowan, Jay Novello, Frank Ferguson, Willis Bouchey, Fritz Feld, Ellen Corby, Gavin Gordon, Benny Rubin, Jack Elam, Mike Mazurki, Hayden Rorke, Doodles Weaver, Paul E. Burns, George E. Stone, Snub Pollard.

1962

What Ever Happened to Baby Jane? (7A and Aldrich–WB). Robert Aldrich (D), Kenneth Hyman (Executive Producer), Ernest Haller (C), Lukas Heller (S), Frank DeVol (M); based on the novel of the same name by Henry Farrell. Joan Crawford, Victor Buono, Marjorie Bennett, Maidie Norman, Anna Lee, Barbara Merrill, Julie Allred, Gina Gillespie, Dave Willock, Ann Barton.

1964

Dead Ringer (WB). Paul Henreid (D), William H. Wright (P), Ernest Haller (C), Albert Beich, Oscar Millard (S), Andre Previn (M); based on the story "La Otra" or "Dead Pigeon" by Rian James. Karl Malden, Peter Lawford, Philip Carey, Jean Hagen, George Macready, Estelle Winwood, George Chandler, Mario Alcade, Cyril Delevanti, Monika Henreid, Bert Remsen, Charles Watts, Ken Lynch.

The Empty Canvas (Joseph E. Levine–Carlo Ponti–Embassy). Damiano Damiani (D), Carlo Ponti (P), Roberto Gerardi (C), Tonino Guerra, Ugo Liberatore, Damiano Damiani (S); based on the novel *La Noia* by Alberto Moravia. Horst Buchholz, Catherine Spaak, Daniela Rocca, Lea Padovani, Isa Miranda, Leonida Repaci, George Wilson, Marcella Rovena, Daniela Calvino, Renato Moretti, Edoardo Nevola, Jole Mauro, Mario Lanfranchi.

Where Love Has Gone (Joseph E. Levine–PAR). Edward Dmytryk (D), Joseph E. Levine (P), Joseph MacDonald (C), John Michael Hayes (S); based on the novel of the same name by Harold Robbins. Susan Hayward, BD, Michael Connors, Joey Heatherton, Jane Greer, DeForest Kelley, George Macready, Anne Seymour, Willis Bouchey, Walter Reed, Ann Doran, Bartlett Robinson, Whit Bissell, Anthony Caruso, Jack Greening, Olga Sutcliffe, Howard Wendell, Colin Kenny.

Hush . . . Hush, Sweet Charlotte (Associates and Aldrich–20TH). Robert Aldrich

(D, P), Joseph Biroc (C), Henry Farrell and Lukas Heller (S), Frank DeVol (M); based on Henry Farrell's story "Whatever Happened to Cousin Charlotte?" Olivia De Havilland, Joseph Cotten, Agnes Moorehead, Cecil Kellaway, Victor Buono, Mary Astor, William Campbell, Wesley Addy, Bruce Dern, George Kennedy, Dave Willock, John Megna, Ellen Corby, Helen Kleeb, Marianne Stewart, Frank Ferguson, Mary Henderson, Lillian Randolph, Geraldine West, William Walker, Idell James, Teddy Buckner and His All-Stars.

1965

*The Nanny (7A–Hammer–20TH). Seth Holt (D), Jimmy Sangster (P, S), Harry Waxman (C); based on the novel of the same name by Evelyn Piper. Wendy Craig, Jill Bennett, James Villiers, William Dix, Pamela Franklin, Jack Watling, Maurice Denham, Alfred Burke, Nora Gordon, Sandra Power, Harry Fowler.

1968

*The Anniversary (7A–Hammer–20TH). Roy Ward Baker (D), Jimmy Sangster (P, S), Harry Waxman (C); based on the play of the same name by Bill MacIlwraith. Sheila Hancock, Jack Hedley, James Cossins, Christian Roberts, Elaine Taylor, Timothy Bateson, Arnold Diamond.

1969

*Connecting Rooms (L.S.D.–Hemdale). Franklin Gollings (D, S), Harry Field, Arthur Cooper (P); based on the play of the same name by Marion Hart. Michael Redgrave, Alexis Kanner, Kay Walsh, Gabrielle Drake, Olga Georges-Picot, Leo Genn, Richard Wyler.

1971

*Bunny O'Hare (American International Pictures). Gerd Oswald (D, P), James H. Nicholson, Samuel Z. Arkoff (Executive Producers), Loyal Griggs, John Stephens, Michael Dugan (C), Stanley Z. Cherry, Coslough Johnson (S); based on the story "Bunny and Billy" by Stanley Z. Cherry. Ernest Borgnine, Jack Cassidy, Joan Delaney, Jay Robinson, John Astin, Reva Rose.

1972

*Madame Sin (2 X). David Greene (D), Julian Wintle, Lou Morheim (P), Tony Richmond (C), Barry Oringer, David Greene (S); from an original concept by Lou Morheim and Barry Shear. Robert Wagner, Denholm Elliott, Gordon Jackson, Dudley Sutton, Catherine Schell, Paul Maxwell, Piksen Lim.
*The Judge and Jake Wyler (UNI TV). David Lowell Rich (D), Richard Levinson, William Link (P), William Margulies (C), David Shaw, Richard Levinson, William Link (Teleplay). Doug McClure, Eric Braeden, Joan Van Ark, Gary Conway, Lou Jacobi, James McEachin, Lisabeth Hush, Kent Smith, Barbara Rhoades.
Lo Scopone Scientifico (C.I.C. Production). Luigi Comencini (D), Dino de Laurentis (P), Giuseppe Ruzzolini (C), Rodolfo Sonego (S). Alberto Sordi, Silvana Mangano, Joseph Cotten, BD, Domenico Modugno, Mario Carotenuto.

1973

Scream, Pretty Peggy (UNI TV). Gordon Hessler (D), Lou Morheim (P), Lennie South (C), Jimmy Sangster, Arthur Hoffe, (Teleplay). Ted Bessell, Sian Barbara Allen, Charles Drake.

1976

Burnt Offerings (UA-PEA). Dan Curtis (D, P), Jacques Marquette, Stevan Larner (C), William F. Nolan, Dan Curtis (S), Robert Cobert (M); based on the novel by Robert Marasco. Karen Black, Oliver Reed, Burgess Meredith, Eileen Heckart, Lee Montgomery, Dub Taylor, BD, Anthony James, Orin Cannon, James T. Myers, Todd Turquand, Joseph Riley.

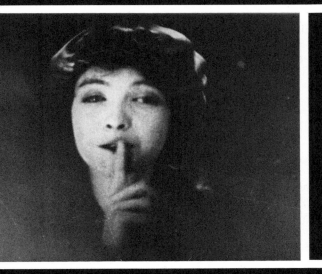

Selected Bibliography

ASTOR, MARY. *A Life on Film.* New York: Delacorte Press, 1971.

BAINBRIDGE, JOHN. *Garbo.* New York: Doubleday, 1955. Reprint 1971.

BARTHES, ROLAND. *Mythologies.* Selected and translated from the French by Annette Lavers. New York: Hill & Wang, 1972.

BAZIN, ANDRÉ. *Qu'est-ce que le cinéma?,* Vols. 1–4. Paris: Éditions du Cerf, 1958–62.

BEHLMER, RUDY, ed. *Memo from David O. Selznick.* New York: Viking, 1972.

BILLQUIST, FRITIOF. *Garbo.* New York: G. P. Putnam's Sons, 1960.

BRAUDY, LEO. *The World in a Frame, What We See in Films.* Garden City, N.Y.: Anchor Press/Doubleday, 1976.

BROOKS, LOUISE. "Gish and Garbo." *Sight and Sound,* Winter 1958–59, pp. 13–17.

CAREY, GARY. *Cukor & Co.* New York: The Museum of Modern Art, 1971.

————. "The Lady and the Director: Bette Davis and William Wyler." *Film Comment,* Fall 1970, pp. 18–24.

CAVELL, STANLEY. *The World Viewed, Reflections on the Ontology of Film.* New York: Viking, 1971.

CONWAY, MICHAEL; MCGREGOR, DION; and RICCI, MARK. *The Films of Greta Garbo.* New York: Citadel, 1963.

COOKE, ALISTAIR, ed. *Garbo and the Night Watchmen.* London: Jonathan Cape, 1937.

CORLISS, RICHARD. *Greta Garbo.* New York: Pyramid Publications, 1974.

CROWTHER, BOSLEY. *The Lion's Share.* New York: E. P. Dutton & Co., 1957.

DAVIS, BETTE. *The Lonely Life.* New York: G. P. Putnam's Sons, 1962.

————. "What Is a Star?" *Films and Filming,* September 1965, pp. 5–7.

DURGNAT, RAYMOND. *Eros in the Cinema.* London: Calder and Boyars, 1966.

————. *Films and Feelings.* Cambridge, Mass.: The M. I. T. Press, 1967.

————, and KOBAL, JOHN. *Greta Garbo.* New York: E. P. Dutton & Co., 1965.

FARBER, MANNY. *Negative Space.* New York: Praeger Publishers, 1971.

FERGUSON, OTIS. *The Film Criticism of Otis Ferguson.* Edited and with a preface by Robert Wilson, foreword by Andrew Sarris. Philadelphia: Temple University Press, 1971.

FUNKE, LEWIS and BOOTH, JOHN E., eds. *Actors Talk About Acting.* New York: Random House, 1961.

GISH, LILLIAN. "Conversation with Lillian Gish," *Sight and Sound,* Winter 1957–58, pp. 128–130.

————. *Dorothy and Lillian Gish.* New York: Charles Scribner's Sons, 1973.

———— with PINCHOT, ANN. *The Movies, Mr. Griffith and Me.* Englewood Cliffs, N.J.: Prentice-Hall, 1969.

GRIFFITH, RICHARD. *The Movie Stars.* Garden City, N.Y.: Doubleday, 1970.

————, and MAYER, ARTHUR. *The Movies.* New York: Simon and Schuster, 1957.

HASKELL, MOLLY. *From Reverence to Rape.* New York: Holt, Rinehart and Winston, 1974.

HENDERSON, ROBERT M. *D. W. Griffith, His Life and Work.* New York: Oxford University Press, 1972.

HIGHAM, CHARLES. *Hollywood Cameramen: Sources of Light.* Bloomington, Ind.: Indiana University Press, 1970.

————, and GREENBERG, JOEL. *The Celluloid Muse.* Chicago: Henry Regnery Co., 1969.

KYROU, ADO. *L'Amour-érotisme au cinéma.* Paris: Le Terrain Vague, 1957.

LAMBERT, GAVIN. *On Cukor.* New York: G. P. Putnam's Sons, 1972.

————. "Portrait of an Actress: Bette Davis." *Sight and Sound,* August-September 1951, pp. 12–19.

MADSEN, AXEL. *William Wyler.* New York: Thomas Crowell Co., 1973.

MANKIEWICZ, JOSEPH L. *More About All About Eve.* A colloquy by Gary Carey with

Joseph L. Mankiewicz together with his screenplay, *All About Eve*. New York: Random House, 1972.

MILNE, TOM. *Rouben Mamoulian*. Bloomington, Ind.: Indiana University Press, 1970.

MORIN, EDGAR. *Les Stars*. Paris: Éditions du Seuil, 1972.

PAYNE, ROBERT. *The Great Garbo*. New York: Praeger Publishers, 1976.

PENSEL, HANS. *Seastrom and Stiller in Hollywood*. New York: Vantage Press, 1969.

PUDOVKIN, V. I. *Film Technique (1929), and Film Acting (1933)*. New York: Vision Press, 1954.

RINGGOLD, GENE. *The Films of Bette Davis*. New York: Citadel, 1966.

ROSEN, MARJORIE. *Popcorn Venus: Women, Movies and the American Dream*. New York: Coward, McCann and Geoghegan, 1973.

SARRIS, ANDREW. *The American Cinema*. New York: Dutton Paperbacks, 1968.

SCHICKEL, RICHARD. *The Stars*. New York: Dial Press, 1962.

SENNETT, TED. *Warner Brothers Presents*. New York: Castle Books, 1971.

SHIPMAN, DAVID. *The Great Movie Stars, The Golden Years*. New York: Bonanza Books, 1970.

SJÖLANDER, TURE. *Garbo*. New York: Harper & Row, 1971.

STINE, WHITNEY. *Mother Goddam, The Story of the Career of Bette Davis, with a running commentary by Bette Davis*. New York: Hawthorn Books, 1974.

TYLER, PARKER. *Sex Psyche Etcetera in the Film*. Baltimore: Pelican, 1971.

TYNAN, KENNETH. "Garbo," *Sight and Sound*, April-June 1954, pp. 187–190, 220.

VERMILYE, JERRY. *Bette Davis*. New York: Pyramid Publications, 1973.

VIDOR, KING. *A Tree Is a Tree*. New York: Harcourt Brace, 1953.

———. *King Vidor on Filmmaking*. New York: David McKay Co., Inc., 1972.

WALKER, ALEXANDER. *The Celluloid Sacrifice*. New York: Hawthorn Books, 1967.

———. *Stardom, The Hollywood Phenomenon*. New York: Stein and Day, 1970.

ZIEROLD, NORMAN. *Garbo*. New York: Stein and Day, 1969.

Index

Page numbers set in **boldface** type indicate illustrations.